T0385728

THE TWO MORALITIES

CONSERVATIVES, LIBERALS, AND THE ROOTS OF OUR POLITICAL DIVIDE

• • •

RONNIE JANOFF-BULMAN

Yale

UNIVERSITY PRESS

New Haven and London

Published with assistance from the Mary Cady Tew Memorial Fund.

Copyright © 2023 by Ronnie Janoff-Bulman. All rights reserved. This book may not be reproduced, in whole or in part, including illustrations, in any form (beyond that copying permitted by Sections 107 and 108 of the U.S. Copyright Law and except by reviewers for the public press), without written permission from the publishers.

Yale University Press books may be purchased in quantity for educational, business, or promotional use. For information, please e-mail sales.press@yale.edu (U.S. office) or sales@yaleup.co.uk (U.K. office).

Set in Adobe Garamond type by Integrated Publishing Solutions. Printed in the United States of America.

ISBN 978-0-300-24408-3 (hardcover : alk. paper)
Library of Congress Control Number: 2022940409
A catalogue record for this book is available from the British Library.

This paper meets the requirements of ANSI/NISO Z39.48-1992 (Permanence of Paper).

10 9 8 7 6 5 4 3 2 1

For Mike
and
Sam, Clara, Isaac, and Eli

Contents

Introduction

In the summer of 1789, during the early days of the French Revolution, the National Assembly of France met to write a new constitution. A particularly contentious issue was the question of the king's power. Should he have an absolute veto over acts of the assembly? The supporters of the king, who believed he should have such a veto, sat to the right of the assembly's president, and the antiroyalists, who thought he should not, sat to the left. Those on the right supported tradition and the status quo. Those on the left sought reform and change. The French newspapers used the seating divisions to describe the assembly's activities, and the left-right distinction took hold. This physical representation remains a powerful metaphor for the two sides of the political spectrum—liberals and conservatives. Yet today a fitting image in the United States would include not only seats on the left and the right but also a wide, seemingly unbridgeable chasm between them.

We no longer have conversations but instead hurl accusations across this divide. We do not discuss our differences; we demean each other's motives. Liberals and conservatives dwell in mirror-image worlds of their own perceived virtue and the other's debasement. Left and right seem to inhabit different moral universes.

I am a social psychologist, and my research in recent years has focused on morality, particularly the moral motives that underlie our everyday behavior. In the course of this work I became interested in uncovering the moral motives associated with the political ideologies of the left and right. Morality, informed by moral psychology, provides an invaluable lens for perceiving the roots of political differences in the United States. Relying on a basic distinction in psychology, I argue that there are two natural forms of morality, and these respectively underlie political liberalism and conservatism. I believe that the currently dominant model linking morality and politics, described by Jonathan Haidt in *The Righteous Mind: Why Good People Are Divided by Politics* (2012), misrepresents the moral bases of political differences. A new perspective is warranted and is the substance of this book.

I am asking you to take a step back and consider the possibility, amid our current poisonous politics, that the underlying motives of both liberalism and conservatism are moral and reflect genuine concern for our country. The left and right will always have strong policy disagreements, but constructive debate and negotiation are not possible when each side demonizes the other. We can either break as a nation or find a way to detoxify our politics. In writing this book I am putting my faith in the latter course—or at least I'm not willing to give up yet.

In claiming moral bases for political ideologies, I am *not* arguing that those who wield them—politicians or parties—are necessarily moral. Donald Trump and the Republicans who push his Big Lie certainly tell us otherwise. Ideologies can be weaponized for self-serving ends. Despite Trump's heated populist rhetoric, however, his signature accomplishments as president were traditional conservative fare: a tax cut that primarily benefited the wealthy, and the appointment of conservative judges to the courts.

Why do certain positions resonate strongly on one side of the political spectrum? Why, for example, is the conservative agenda anti-abortion and in favor of the unfettered free market, whereas liberals favor a woman's right to choose and economic regulation? Do distinct moralities address different societal challenges? What are the psychological differences between liberals and conservatives, and how do they reflect the moralities of the left and right? Most generally, what moral psychologies underpin liberalism and conservatism? This book is an attempt to answer these questions. It is not a recipe for repairing the nation. Instead, my goal is to provide a new explanatory framework for understanding our political differences.

The book is divided roughly in half and moves from a focus on moral psychology to a focus on politics and policy differences. In part 1, "Morality and Collective Concerns," I ask you to consider broad differences between liberals and conservatives through the lens of moral psychology. The primary focus is on the moral orientations that underlie the politics of left and right. I discuss their distinct moralities, the societal challenges they address, and personality differences between liberals and conservatives, as well as how perceptions of their own group versus outsiders inform charitable giving, immigration attitudes, and the rural-urban political landscape. These first five chapters are largely divorced from party politics, which I turn to in the second half of the book.

In part 2, "Politics, Parties, and Policies," I focus on the potent disagreements that divide liberals and conservatives. I use the two moralities to unpack the policies of left and right and discuss why certain issues and positions are embraced on each side of the political spectrum, including guns, same-sex marriage, abortion, Obamacare, entitlements, and climate change. I also address two major threats to the nation—inequality and authoritarianism—and their relation to party politics and the two moralities.

The country has always had left and right political divisions, but these days our polarization is particularly threatening. We need to lower the temperature rather than throw more fuel on the fire. From the beginning my intent in writing this book was to be nonadversarial. This was relatively easy in the early chapters, with their focus on moral psychology. It was more difficult when discussing specific policy positions. I have tried to support my claims with empirical findings from social psychology, political science, and other academic fields. I should also note that I found it impossible to be nonadversarial when discussing Trump and his Republican abettors in the late chapter on authoritarianism and anti-democratic forces, but I suspect that my judgment and credibility would have been seriously questioned had I pretended to be neutral on that subject.

Today our extreme polarization is evident in Washington, in the media, and even in our tendency to self-sort in deciding where to live. With our increasing distance, both physical and psychological, we seem more interested in justifying our contempt and anger than in finding common ground or understanding. This book may therefore seem like an exercise in wishful thinking. I prefer to think of it as a demonstration of trust in our shared commitment, if not to each other as political rivals, then to the nation and its ideals. We need to move past our rancor and enmity and consider our ideological differences in a less combative way. Recognizing the moral bases and collective concerns of both the left and the right can be a start.

PART ONE
Morality and Collective Concerns

• • •

1

Two Faces of Morality

What comes to mind when you think of a moral person? Someone who cares for a sick friend? A person who forfeits an advantage by choosing not to cheat? We are likely to agree that both are instances of morality. In our everyday interactions we share an understanding of morality. Yet when it comes to politics, this shared understanding breaks down. Instead, each side of the political divide views the other as malevolent and irredeemable, as they embrace disparate policies that reflect distinct moralities. What are these moralities, and why do they diverge specifically in the realm of politics? Why do particular issues resonate so differently on different sides of the political spectrum? To answer these questions we need to examine the nature and demonstrations of morality in our everyday moral appraisals. Caring for a sick friend and refraining from cheating are both moral, but they reflect distinct forms of morality that not only inform but underlie our political differences.

The Fundamental Motivational Distinction

Let us begin with the most fundamental distinction in human motivation: approach and avoidance. Whether we're meeting close friends or staying away from disagreeable co-workers, enjoying tasty meals or rejecting rotten food, listening to music by favorite composers or skipping pieces we find grating, we navigate our daily existence through approach and avoidance. Approach motivation moves us toward desirable ends, and avoidance motivation moves us away from undesirable outcomes.

This distinction has deep roots in psychology. In *Principles of Psychology*, published in 1890, William James described pleasure as a "tremendous reinforcer" of behavior and pain as a "tremendous inhibitor," and these differences were echoed in learning theories based on rewards and punishments as well as drive theories based on aversions and appetites.[1] The central appraisal in approach and avoidance motivation is whether a potential outcome is positive or negative. Are we trying to attain something desirable, pleasurable, or beneficial? Or are we trying to avoid something undesirable, painful, or harmful?

Typically these differences in positive-negative valence are readily apparent—as in unexpectedly encountering a good friend versus a large snake. Here the valence is recognizable in the object itself. Sometimes it is a function of a person's perceptions. Consider two different reactions to online dating. Sue looks forward to interacting with new people and is eager to engage with online dating sites. Ellen, in contrast, fears rejection and assiduously avoids these sites. In fact, psychologists have distinguished between a desire for affiliation and a fear of rejection, with the former emphasizing positive outcomes associated with social interactions and the latter emphasizing negative outcomes. A similar distinction has been made in the domain of academics, where some students have an achievement orientation, focused on success, and others are motivated by a fear of failure.[2] In consumer behavior, buycotts versus boycotts also exemplify approach-avoidance differences. Buycotts are efforts to purchase (approach) a company's products to reward its good behavior, whereas boycotts are efforts to refrain from (avoid) buying a company's goods as a form of protest.

Work in neuroscience has supported approach-avoidance differ-

ences in the brain. Researchers have found lateralization of the prefrontal cortex based on this basic motivational distinction. Approach
is associated with greater activity in the left prefrontal cortex, and
avoidance is associated with greater activity in the right prefrontal
cortex.[3] The prefrontal cortex is located at the front of the brain and
is generally related to executive functions such as planning, problem
solving, and decision making.

We all rely on approach and avoidance every day, as we try to
avoid unpleasant or dangerous outcomes and bring about pleasant
and beneficial ones. These two motivations are essential for successful
adaptation to our environment. As comparative psychologists have
noted, all animals have approach and avoidance mechanisms, although
they vary from rigid and simple to flexible and complex. At the most
basic, universal level, the approach mechanisms facilitate mating and
getting food and shelter, whereas the withdrawal mechanisms facilitate huddling, defense, and flight to avoid danger.[4] Both sets of behaviors are essential for survival.

Two Natural Forms of Morality

Approach and avoidance can also inform our understanding of morality. In my research I have differentiated between two natural forms
of morality that reflect these motivational differences and labeled
them *proscriptive* and *prescriptive*.[5] Proscriptive morality is avoidance-
based and involves avoiding negative outcomes, specifically harm to
others. It inhibits "bad" behaviors. Prescriptive morality is approach-
based. It is focused on positive outcomes and activates "good" behaviors.

The two types of morality are evident in the college student who
refrains from cheating on a take-home exam (proscriptive) and one
who shares personal class notes with a sick friend (prescriptive), or in

parents' efforts to teach their toddlers not to take other children's toys (proscriptive) and to share their toys with playmates (prescriptive). These are different behaviors: children can refrain from taking others' toys while still refusing to share their own. Proscriptive morality is about not harming, and prescriptive morality is about helping. They are not two sides of the same coin—not harming is different from helping.

Proscriptive and prescriptive moralities require very different efforts from us. Proscriptive morality begins with a temptation to behave immorally—perhaps to cheat, steal, or lie. To be moral is to *refrain* from these behaviors, to not do what we *should not* do. Prescriptive morality, in contrast, does not involve restraint of a negative motivation (a temptation) but instead requires initiating a positive motivation to engage in a moral behavior—to do what we *should* do. It requires activation, rather than inhibition, in an attempt to approach "the good." Whereas temptation and desire are enemies of proscriptive moral regulation, the enemies of prescriptive morality are inertia and apathy.

The General Confession of the Book of Common Prayer, dating to 1662, recognizes the two types of morality: "We have left undone those things which we ought to have done; And we have done those things which we ought not to have done." The differences between shoulds and should nots typically manifest themselves in acts versus omissions. Yet we should recognize that the restraint that characterizes proscriptive morality can sometimes be evident in acts rather than their absence. Behaviors themselves can be constraining. Take speed limits, for example ("obey the speed limit"), where the primary purpose is not to "activate" our foot on the gas pedal but rather to constrain our temptation to speed. Similarly, the major motivation behind school uniform requirements is constraint, despite manifesting in behavior (donning clothes). In both cases, speed limits and school uniforms, the goal is to place strict limits on the expression of personal behavior. Inaction is not possible—the car on the highway must move and the student in the school must wear clothes. Proscriptive morality is fundamentally constraining, whereas prescriptive morality requires the activation of a positive motivation and is fundamentally enabling.

Research with very young children has shown that these two types of self-regulation—activation and inhibition—do not develop in parallel. Grazyna Kochanska and colleagues studied young children's willingness to comply with their mothers' requests in a laboratory setting. There were two types of request. Each mother asked her child to pick up toys and return them to baskets and, in a second room, to refrain from playing with attractive toys that were easily accessible. In other words, there was a *should* request (toy cleanup) that required activation and a *should not* request (toy prohibition) that required inhibition. The children, studied from the ages of fourteen months to forty-five months, complied far more with the *should not* request than with the *should* request, and compliance with one type of request did not predict compliance with the other. The activation task posed a greater regulatory challenge to young children. Kochanska and her colleagues concluded that their data provide "impressive evidence of substantial differences" between the two types of self-regulation.[6]

Suppress Selfishness and Activate Altruism

Diverse areas of psychology, from research with very young infants to studies of people's evaluation of others, strongly support the centrality and significance of morality in human interactions. Using both natural and experimentally created groups, social psychologists have found that morality is the most important attribute in our judgments of other people and our evaluations of groups.[7]

In spite of popular mantras touting individualism, we are deeply social animals. There are survival advantages to living in groups, and by smoothing our interactions, morality plays a crucial role in facilitating group living.[8] If you wanted to devise a set of principles to help ensure that group members get along, you would likely come up with some version of these two tenets: don't over-benefit yourself, which directly or indirectly harms others, and do be concerned about the welfare of other group members. In other words, don't lie, cheat, or hurt others to get ahead at their expense, and do your best to help other members of your group. In essence, these are the two forms of morality—proscriptive and prescriptive. One suppresses selfishness, and the other activates altruism.

In recent years, our perception of human morality has changed from recognizing only selfishness and hyper-egoism to a more positive perception that acknowledges altruism as a fundamental side of human nature.[9] For years, psychology accepted evolutionary psychologists' reductionist view of humans competing for individual survival with little inherent morality. Economists' self-interested actor, *Homo economicus,* is also consistent with this perspective. Early evolutionary accounts of altruism focused on kin selection, whereby individuals will incur a cost to themselves only to help others who share their genes. Hence altruism was selfishness in disguise.

This evolutionary explanation could not account for altruism toward non-kin, leading theorists to the idea of reciprocal altruism, whereby we help others because we expect they will help us in the future. This might work in small groups with direct interactions among members, but reciprocal altruism cannot account for altruistic behavior in large groups, in which people don't directly interact. So yet another theory was proposed—indirect reciprocity, or signaling theory, which emphasizes reputation. Here the good reputation that would follow from altruistic behavior would presumably produce in-kind behavior from others.[10]

This was not sufficient either. As Ernst Fehr and Simon Gachter write, "Unlike other creatures, people frequently cooperate with genetically unrelated strangers, often in large groups, with people they will never meet again, and when reproductive gains are small or absent. These patterns of cooperation cannot be explained with the evolutionary theory of kin selection and the selfish motives associated with signaling theory or the theory of reciprocal altruism."[11]

A number of scientists, including E. O. Wilson, have turned to group selection to solve the "puzzle" of human altruism. From this perspective, we are the evolutionary products of multilevel selection, with selfishness shaped by individual selection based in within-group competition and altruism shaped by competition between groups.[12] Whether or not group selection accounts for our altruism, it is nevertheless the case that we are not only self-interested but altruistic as well, sometimes putting others' interests above our own at a personal cost of time, effort, or resources. We have the makings of both saints and sinners. Frans de Waal calls us "bipolar apes" because of our capacity for great kindness and great cruelty.[13] Culture works to reinforce the former and minimize the latter. We are motivated to act selfishly for our own benefit, but also altruistically, for the benefit of others, and the rules and norms of group living encourage us to constrain our selfishness and activate our better angels.

Recent work with infants demonstrates our very early sensitivity to helping and harming, suggesting that some rudimentary moral understanding may be innate. Researchers have studied infant reactions to helping and harming using a paradigm with three puppets—a protagonist, a helper, and a hinderer. The protagonist puppet tries but fails to reach a goal such as opening a box, climbing a hill, or retrieving a ball. The helper puppet facilitates the protagonist's goal, and the hinderer puppet prevents it. In the hill-climbing case, for example, Kiley Hamlin, Karen Wynn, and Paul Bloom presented six-month-old infants with scenes involving three googly-eyed geometric shapes. The googly-eyed circle tries to go up a hill but can't make it on its own. Soon a googly-eyed "helping" triangle comes from below and appears to push the circle to the top. In a second sequence the circle once again tries and fails to get to the top of the hill. This time, a "hindering" googly-eyed square comes from the top of the hill and appears to push the circle down to the bottom. The infants in the study watched these two sequences several times and were then shown a tray with two toys that resembled the googly-eyed triangle and the googly-eyed square. Which did they reach for? Without exception the six-month-old infants chose the triangle. Before they could walk or talk, they showed a clear preference for the helper.[14]

We are apparently born with an elementary sensitivity to helping and not harming others. From birth, infants react to other babies crying, and at one year they try to calm distressed others by touching them or giving them a toy. Children readily engage in spontaneous pro-social behaviors. As Michael Tomasello and Amrisha Vaish conclude, "Findings on infants' and toddlers' instrumental helping, informative pointing, concern, comforting, and selective helping of harmed and/or cooperative others demonstrate that from early on, children are tuned to others' needs and emotional states and are motivated to act pro-socially toward them. Moreover, this research shows that children's early pro-sociality is the real thing in that it is intrinsically motivated, based in concern for others."[15] Prescriptive morality *provides* benefits to others by engaging our altruism and concern for others. Proscriptive morality *protects* others by restricting our selfishness and self-advantaging behaviors. Again, not harming is not the same as helping; avoiding the bad is distinct from approaching the good. Together, proscriptive and prescriptive moral regulation facilitate group living and maximize the well-being of human societies.

Different Attributes for Different Moralities

There appear to be times when the same behaviors can be framed as both proscriptions and prescriptions, but a closer look suggests otherwise. For example, "do not lie" and "tell the truth" seem identical, but they differ. A requirement to tell the truth is not the same as the requirement to not lie, because not lying includes not saying anything. This is evident in a court of law, where defendants are legally barred from lying but have the right to remain silent rather than provide truthful (presumably incriminating) information. In our research, my students and I have found that prescriptive and proscriptive morality differ in a number of ways beyond their distinct motivational origins.[16]

Proscriptive morality is more mandatory and stricter than prescriptive morality. This may in part reflect the greater psychological impact of "bad" over "good." More specifically, psychologists have found that negatively valenced events generally affect us more strongly than similar positively valenced events. Amos Tversky and Daniel Kahneman's work on loss aversion, for example, shows that objectively equal outcomes are not subjectively equal, because losses loom larger to people than gains. From the perspective of approach and avoidance, ignoring a harmful outcome is potentially more dangerous than ignoring a positive outcome, and harmful consequences are usually more difficult to reverse.[17]

When presented with a list of "good" and "bad" behaviors, for example, our research participants rated the extent to which we *should* do the former and *should not* do the latter. The "good" included: be generous, stand up for others, be kind, donate to charity, be honest, help others in need, be trustworthy, admit mistakes. The "bad" included: be selfish, lie, harm others intentionally, be manipulative, cheat, be mean, steal, be wasteful. Participants indicated we *should* engage in the good behaviors to the same extent that they indicated we *should not* engage in the bad ones, suggesting that proscriptive and prescriptive morality carried the same moral weight. But when we phrased the question differently and asked what it was mandatory to do or not do, participants more often said it was mandatory to avoid the bad behaviors. The good behaviors were seen as more discretionary.[18]

Perhaps not surprisingly, eight of the ten commandments of Judeo-Christian religions are proscriptive, including commands not to steal, murder, commit adultery, or lie ("bear false witness"). Only two are prescriptive: remember the Sabbath and honor your parents. More discretion is involved in complying with these two commandments, which presumably can be satisfied in multiple ways.

The more mandatory nature of proscriptive morality and greater discretion afforded prescriptive morality suggest natural associations with the ethical theories of deontology and consequentialism. Deontology, which emphasizes duties, is a strict morality by which one has an obligation to behave in particular (moral) ways. Behaviors in themselves are right or wrong. Consequentialism, as the name suggests, bases moral judgments on the consequences of behavior. A quick way to grasp the distinction is to ask whether it's okay to steal a loaf of bread to feed a starving child: deontology says no, consequentialism says yes. From the perspective of these two theories, the greater discretion associated with *shoulds* may follow from the nature of prescriptive morality itself, for although it is moral to help others, it is impossible to help all those in need. But it is usually possible to refrain from harming all others (by not, for instance, killing, cheating, or stealing). Not harming—proscriptive morality—can be applied universally, whereas helping, prescriptive morality, cannot. You can be a deontologist about not harming, in other words, but you almost always have to be a consequentialist about helping. The latter requires making choices, and potential consequences become a critical part of determining the moral potency of right and wrong.

These differences are consistent with how philosophers think about duty and desire in moral motivation. For Immanuel Kant, morality is based in duty and does not involve inclinations. Actions must be taken "from duty" rather than "in accord" with duty; the will must be involved, but it must exclude any influence of "inclination."[19] We don't get moral credit if we actually *want* to engage in the behavior.

Yet it seems that this might apply only to proscriptive morality, where we must resist a temptation to advantage ourselves. If a student doesn't want to cheat because he or she likes the class and respects the professor, the student is unlikely to be regarded as particularly moral for not cheating. But in the domain of prescriptive morality, inclination or desire does not discount moral appraisals. Helping because you want to, rather than out of a sense of duty, seems worthy of moral credit. In our research, we found precisely that: in the case of proscriptive morality, moral credit is given when the person acts from a sense of duty. In the case of prescriptive morality, moral credit follows from action based in either duty or desire; when we act from inclination, we are perceived as moral. And although we can get moral credit and blame in both domains, our research also showed that we get more credit for helping than not harming and more blame for harming than not helping. Proscriptive morality is condemnatory, and prescriptive morality is commendatory.[20]

The mandatory, duty-based nature of proscriptive morality provides insights into a set of findings that have intrigued researchers studying morality. Joshua Knobe has demonstrated that negative side effects in moral dilemmas are seen as more intentional than positive side effects. Consider the following two scenarios:

> The vice president of a company went to the chairman of the board and said, "We are thinking of starting a new program. It will help us increase profits, but it will also harm the environment." The chairman of the board answered, "I don't care at all about harming the environment. I just want to make as much profit as I can. Let's start the new program." They started the new program. Sure enough, the environment was harmed.

> The vice president of a company went to the chairman of the board and said, "We are thinking of starting a new program. It will help us increase profits, but it will also help the environment." The chairman of the board answered, "I don't care at all about helping the environment. I just want to make as much profit as I can. Let's start the new program." They started the new program. Sure enough, the environment was helped.

The only difference between the two scenarios is the program's effect on the environment. Yet Knobe found that people reacted to them very differently. They blamed the chairman who knowingly caused the harmful side effect, and they believed that his actions were intentional, but they did not praise the chairman whose program knowingly led to helpful side effects, and they did not view his actions as intentional. This is a robust result that has been found across ages (in children as young as four) and across cultures. Although a third of Knobe's respondents in the help condition believed that the chairman intentionally helped the environment, in the harm condition more than 80 percent of respondents thought that the chairman intentionally harmed the environment. In both cases the impact on the environment was a side effect of the program, but a negative side effect is seen as far more intentional than a positive one. This has become known as the Knobe effect, and Knobe concluded that people determine intentionality based on their determination of the action as morally good or bad.[21] Why?

The stricter, more mandatory nature of a morality that protects against harm can inform an explanation. In both scenarios, the impact on the environment was foreseeable. The chairman doesn't care about the outcome in either case, so we might expect minimal attribution of intentionality in both cases. We essentially get the expected result in the positive condition. The chairman should have cared; he receives little praise, and the benefits are not regarded as intentional on his part. But with the negative side effect, he gets considerable blame because the effect is perceived as intentional. The mandatory nature of avoiding harm (proscriptive morality) tells us that we are obligated to act to prevent foreseeable negative outcomes. We are required to intervene. The chairman, once he knew of the likely consequences, had an obligation to prevent them, but he didn't care. He is therefore blamed for his failure to act.

Proscriptive morality is harsher than prescriptive morality. It is mandatory, duty-based, and condemnatory. In research we conducted on shame and guilt, two key moral emotions, we also found that shame, the harsher of the two, is more strongly associated with proscriptive morality, and guilt with prescriptive morality. In the case of shame, we recognize that we acted immorally by doing the wrong thing—by cheating, stealing, or lying. In the case of guilt, we recognize that we didn't act morally by doing the right thing: we failed to approach the "good" by not acting like a caring friend, honest person, or loving partner.[22]

Guilt highlights positive possibilities and pushes us forward toward righting the wrong and toward future moral outcomes. It activates positive behaviors to improve the situation. Shame highlights negative past behaviors, what we shouldn't have done, and leaves us confronting our own immorality. It motivates us to withdraw. Guilt is associated with efforts to amend, whereas shame is associated with efforts to hide. The two emotions thus echo the activation-inhibition differences of prescriptive and proscriptive morality.

The stricter nature of proscriptive morality also implies a greater threat of error in this moral realm. This calls for greater specificity—we need to know precisely what we should not do—and this is reflected in linguistic differences between the two types of morality. Proscriptive morality is generally represented in relatively concrete terms and particularly in verbs specifying discrete behaviors: I should not . . . *lie, hurt others, steal,* and *cheat.* Prescriptive morality is represented in more abstract language, including verbs such as *help* and *respect others* that describe general categories of behavior, as well as the adjectives we apply to people. It is worth noting that in work on approach and avoidance motivation, these same linguistic differences emerge. Approach motivation is represented in relatively abstract language.[23] Whereas greater specificity is advantageous for avoiding harm, the more discretionary nature of prescriptive morality is better served by a disposition to advance the good. People with that disposition, represented by adjectives such as *kind* and *considerate,* are most apt to make moral choices that benefit others.

Kant's duty-based morality focuses primarily on specific moral acts, which linguistically are best represented by concrete verbs. Here the moral focus is on whether a person did or did not engage in a particular behavior. Aristotle, in contrast, emphasizes that virtues are the font of right action.[24] Virtues are reflected in moral character or traits, which are more like adjectives than verbs, particularly adjectives that describe people's character (such as *benevolent* or *kind*). The Kantian view of morality is proscriptive, and Aristotle's virtue perspective seems particularly relevant to prescriptive morality. Yet there are both prescriptive and proscriptive virtues, just as there are both prescriptive and proscriptive vices. Whereas virtues reflect moral "goodness," vices reflect immorality or "badness." Virtues such as generosity and courage enable good deeds (prescriptive), while virtues such as self-discipline and humility inhibit bad behaviors (proscriptive). Similarly, there are prescriptive and proscriptive vices: apathy and sloth are associated with not doing the right thing (prescriptive immorality), whereas greed and malice are associated with doing the wrong thing (proscriptive immorality).

The linguistic differences associated with the two forms of morality—greater specificity for avoiding the bad, and greater abstraction for advancing the good—bring to mind legal scholars' distinction between *rules* and *standards*. Features of rules include certainty and uniformity, whereas standards allow for flexibility and openness to the situation. Rules are precise and so constrain a decision maker; standards allow for greater discretion. Thus rules, like proscriptive morality, have the benefit of precision but the disadvantage of rigidity.[25]

At the societal level, proscriptive morality is generally regulated through laws—mandatory rules backed up by the threat of punishment. Prescriptive morality is more often regulated through social norms, or societal standards, which are themselves more discretionary. To make these norms more obligatory, we tie them to specific social roles. Parents must care for their children, firefighters must help and fight fires, and teachers must tend to the children in their classroom.[26] In these roles the discretion of the parent, firefighter, and teacher has narrowed considerably, for they now have a duty to care.

The Ambiguity of Prescriptive Immorality

In 1980, a car turned over in Joliet, Illinois. It caught fire and the people in the car died. A policeman arrived on the scene, directed traffic, and didn't try to determine whether anyone was in the car. The city was sued for damages for failing to save the occupants of the car. Damages were denied; apparently there was no obligation to help. The judge in the case, Richard Posner, noted that the United States Constitution "is a charter of negative rather than positive liberties. . . . The men who wrote the Bill of Rights were not concerned that Government might do too little for the people but that it might do too much to them."[27]

In discussing proscriptive and prescriptive morality, we are attending to the moral or immoral actor. When discussing negative and positive rights, however, our attention shifts to the potential recipient of harm or help. A person's negative rights obligate non-action, that is non-interference, by another, whereas an individual's positive rights obligate action. Negative rights therefore engage proscriptive morality, and positive rights engage prescriptive morality. The federal Constitution guarantees negative rights, including, for example, the right to be free of government interference in our speech or religion, but it is stingy with positive rights. It does not, for example, recognize a right to housing, education, or employment, benefits that would reflect prescriptive morality.

Although the law might not require an intervention to save the occupants of a burning car, we might nevertheless question the morality of inaction. Proscriptive immorality is quite clear when we have harmed another, cheated, lied, and the like, but there is considerably more ambiguity about prescriptive immorality. When is it immoral not to help? We are moral when we offer aid and help others, but at what point does failing to do so cross the line into immorality: when we don't help a neighbor who is ill? when we don't help a starving child across the ocean? What amount of suffering, and by whom, and what level of effort not made is required for a judgment of immorality when we fail to act?

The philosophers Peter Singer and Peter Unger have recently asked us to consider these questions seriously.[28] They offer scenarios to get us to question our complacency. Here is an example paraphrased from Unger's *Living High and Letting Die:*

> Bob has most of his retirement savings invested in a rare and valuable car, a Bugatti. He is confronted with the choice of throwing a switch to redirect a railway trolley away from a child, thereby saving it, but toward his Bugatti, which has accidentally been placed on the side spur of the line. He can pull the switch and save the child, or he can leave the switch as it stands so that his Bugatti remains in mint condition, which will result in the child's death. Bob chooses to save his car and doesn't pull the switch.

Presumably your response, like mine, is to strongly condemn Bob. We believe he clearly made the wrong choice. How could he choose a car over a child? Peter Singer presents a parallel situation:

> Imagine you're walking to work. You see a child drowning in a lake. You're about to jump in and save her when you realize you're wearing your best suit, and the rescue will end up costing hundreds in dry cleaning bills. Should you still save the child?

"Yes, of course," we respond. Yet, Singer tells us, in our own lives we choose otherwise. The two scenarios are analogous to our own situation. We are in a position to save starving children, and yet we fail to do so. We could readily sacrifice some of our own money—money that would otherwise go to things and experiences beyond what is needed to live a comfortable life.

Singer and Unger argue that most of us have money we could give away without any serious hardship. They conclude that we therefore have an obligation to save children's lives by donating this money to organizations that fight global poverty (such as Oxfam or UNICEF). The scenarios are a means of forcing us to confront our own inconsistency and self-satisfaction in the face of transgressive failures to act. Singer and Unger are raising critical questions about the nature of right and wrong in the face of inaction—that is, questions about prescriptive immorality.

There is no comparable ambiguity about proscriptive immorality, which involves doing harm. Overall, proscriptive morality is mandatory and duty-based, strict and condemnatory, whereas prescriptive morality is more discretionary, less strict, and condemnatory, and based in duty or desire. We are moral when we refrain from cheating, and we are moral when we help a sick friend. Proscriptive morality *protects* others, and prescriptive morality *provides* for others. These two types of morality together comprise our full moral repertoire; both are essential for us to be regarded as moral. To understand what this has to do with the politics of the left and right, we need to make a fuller map of the moral domain.

2

Mapping Morality

In creating a moral map, my goal was not to chart a course but to define the landscape. The Model of Moral Motives, or MMM, is my map of the moral domain, and it incorporates the two forms of morality, proscriptive and prescriptive—to protect and provide—as its key features.[1] In this model, protect and provide motives are applied to three contexts typically distinguished by social psychologists: the personal (self), interpersonal (other), and collective (group). In the model these contexts are the targets of our moral behavior. The top row of the model focuses on protection from harm—harm to the self, another, and the group. The bottom row focuses on providing benefits to improve well-being—for the self, another, and the group. I will discuss all six cells of the map, but the moral bedrock of our political differences lies with the group context.

Personal Morality

Although the six cells of the moral map are psychologically generic, and uniform in their social function, cultures elaborate on them to create unique societies.[2] Let's start with the Personal column. Given morality's essential role in facilitating group living and group survival, you might wonder why the moral map contains any focus on the self at all. Yet how we act toward ourselves—in the absence of any interaction with others—has important implications for the larger

	Personal (Self)	Interpersonal (Other)	Collective (Group)
Protect (proscriptive morality)			
Provide (prescriptive morality)			

The six-celled Model of Moral Motives (MMM)

group and its members. So let's begin with the two Personal cells, Moderation and Industriousness.

Moderation (Protect-Self)

Major philosophies of the East and West through the ages have recognized the importance of moderation and self-restraint for a moral life. The personal strength that serves to "protect against excess" is considered a core virtue in Confucianism, Taoism, Buddhism, Hinduism, Christianity, Judaism, Islam, and ancient Greek philosophy. In the *Analects,* Confucius advocated self-control in avoiding extravagances, and in *Fusul al-Madani,* Abu Nasr al-Farabi wrote of the importance of moderation.[3] Moderation is one of the three jewels of Taoist thought, and Aristotle considered the golden mean the virtuous middle path between excess and deficiency. In ancient Greece, the Temple of Apollo at Delphi bore the inscription "meden agan": nothing in excess.

Moderation with regard to the self frequently applies to how we

	Personal (Self)	Interpersonal (Other)	Collective (Group)
Protect (proscriptive morality)	**Moderation** Self-Discipline		
Provide (prescriptive morality)	**Industriousness** Hard Work		

The Personal cells of MMM

treat our bodies—not overindulging in food, drink, drugs, and the like. The practice of self-discipline has implications for our own health and welfare, but it also has important implications for the group. Apart from signaling that the person is a moral, worthy group member, self-discipline ultimately serves to protect the group's resources and counter wastefulness. A community's resources are not squandered if community members refrain from excess consumption. The current prejudice against obesity likely reflects a morality based on moderation. Although obesity is frequently attributable to illness, medication, physical problems, and factors beyond individual control, there is nevertheless considerable disapproval of people who are fat. All too often it seems an acceptable prejudice in contemporary society.

Industriousness (Provide-Self)

The Provide-Self cell of the moral map is Industriousness, which captures the significance of hard work and diligence. Aesop's fable about the grasshopper and the ant illustrates this moral motive. While the ant works to store up food for the winter, the grasshopper spends the summer singing. With the arrival of winter, the ant will survive and the improvident grasshopper will go hungry. Industriousness is a matter of pulling one's own weight and valuing self-reliance. There is considerable disapproval of laziness.[4]

Diligence is one of Catholicism's seven heavenly virtues, and diligence and hard work are also important aspects of Buddhist teaching.[5] The Buddha's final words were "Strive on with diligence." Hinduism, too, values industriousness; as written in the Bhagavad Gita, "Who so performeth—diligent, content—the work allotted him, whatever it be, lays hold of perfectness!" (18.45). Islam similarly prizes hard work; as the fifty-third sura of the Koran tells us, "Man will not get anything unless he works hard." Hard work is also an essential characteristic of an ideal Confucian.

Max Weber introduced the phrase "Protestant work ethic" in his book *The Protestant Ethic and the Spirit of Capitalism* (1905) to describe the Protestant value of industriousness. He traced its origins to the Reformation but noted that even in the Middle Ages there was respect for everyday labor. More recent research, too, has found that the description "hard-working" is a highly valued attribute in the determination of a person's integrity.[6]

Industriousness provides for the self in both material and intangible ways—it is a key element of self-respect—but it also has value for the group. Like moderation, it signals to others that the person is a moral member of the community. More important, hard-working individuals reduce the burden on the group and contribute to the community's shared knowledge and skills. Sloth and indolence are liabilities for the community; industriousness not only minimizes these encumbrances but increases the competencies of the group as a whole.

	Personal (Self)	Interpersonal (Other)	Collective (Group)
Protect (proscriptive morality)	Moderation Self-Discipline	**Not Harming** Not Cheating	
Provide (prescriptive morality)	Industriousness Hard Work	**Helping** Fairness	

Adding the Interpersonal cells of MMM

The Personal column of the moral map addresses morality focused on the self, but this belies the behaviors' ultimate impact on the larger community. In addition, we should recognize that for the moral person, the two self-focused moralities do not operate in isolation but exist alongside the other cells of the map. A moral person is not only industrious but helps others and avoids self-advantaging behaviors.

Interpersonal Morality

When we think about morality, the rules and standards that typically come to mind are those in the middle column, which refers to our direct treatment of others. This column represents our default morality. Here the targets of our actions or inactions are other people—one person or a small number of specifiable others. The most salient moral behaviors are at play in our interactions with other people; these are guides for how we should treat one another as we live together as social animals. Helping and not harming, treating others fairly and not cheating, inform others of our own morality. More important, they involve actions or inactions that have a direct impact on the safety and well-being of others.

Not Harming (Protect-Other)

Proscriptive morality gives us a basic rule for group living—do not harm. The proscription against physically harming another is likely the most fundamental moral rule across societies, the very minimum requirement of successful collective existence. Its power is evident in responses to the well-known trolley scenarios. Consider the following dilemma:

> A trolley is heading toward five people on the track who will be killed if the trolley stays on its present course. You are standing on a footbridge between the trolley and the five people, and next to you is a very large man. If you push this man off the footbridge and onto the tracks below, you can save the five people. Is it morally acceptable to push the man to his death to save the five?

Most people all over the world strongly believe that it is not morally acceptable to push the man. Now consider this dilemma:

> A trolley is heading toward five people on the track who will be killed if the trolley stays on its present course. You can save the five people by pulling a switch that will turn the trolley onto a side track. There is a single person on the side track who will be killed if you pull the switch. Is it morally acceptable to pull the switch to save the five?

The reaction here is quite different. Throughout the world, people agree that it is morally acceptable to pull the switch. Both scenarios pit the death of a single person against the death of five. We might think that people would choose maximizing the number of lives saved in both cases, but they don't. Given that the consequences are the same, what explains the dramatic difference in responses?

Research by Joshua Greene and others has shown that the pushing scenario triggers far stronger emotions than the switch scenario, an explanation supported by neuroscience findings showing differences in activation of the emotion centers of the brain, particularly the ventromedial prefrontal cortex. We have a strong negative gut reaction to direct physical harm that is absent when reacting to more impersonal dilemmas. Unlike the automatic emotional response to the footbridge scenario, our reaction to the switch dilemma is based largely on "thinking," a more controlled response. This is evident in the activation of the dorsolateral prefrontal cortex, which makes use of decision rules.[7]

When the footbridge scenario involves pulling a switch to drop the large man onto the tracks, the majority of people now find it morally acceptable. Removing the personal effort of pushing, what Greene calls "force of muscle," minimizes our emotional response. When the scenario is again changed, so that people are asked to envision using a pole to push the man off the footbridge, we get the same response as the original footbridge problem—strong resistance. Once again there is physical harm based on "force of muscle."[8]

We are disturbed by imagining the physical act of pushing, and this response is uncontrolled and immediate. It speaks to the power of the proscription "do not harm" regarding physical force. Pushing, hitting, punching, and other forms of violence set off an automatic distress signal that serves the group well. We have an aversion to physically harming another group member.[9] The most basic rule against doing harm not surprisingly involves physically hurting another.

Yet the proscription against harm extends beyond the physical to behaviors that benefit the self at the expense of other group members—as in cheating, lying, or stealing. The overriding proscriptive moral motivation is to protect others, and refraining from these behaviors serves this purpose. Some evolutionary psychologists have argued that the avoidance of cheating is so essential for social living that human cognition has evolved to include a cheater-detection module.[10] Whether or not such a specific module exists, we seem to be attuned cognitively and socially to cheating by group members, a vigilance that ultimately serves to protect the collective.

Helping (Provide-Other)

Just as good parenting involves both protective responses that shield the child from danger and nurturing responses that enable the child to thrive, so our moral interactions demand that we strive both to protect others from harm and provide for their well-being. The prescriptive interpersonal cell of the Model of Moral Motives provides for others through helping and fairness. Helping entails providing aid to another in need. Related to helping is fairness, which involves providing another with his or her due. Interestingly, the human penchant for reciprocity incorporates rudimentary elements of both helping and fairness. Returning favors or resources involves providing not only benefits to another but also benefits that are generally proportional to the inputs received from the other. When we provide help to others, we are responding to their needs and demonstrating care. When we provide for others based on fairness, we recognize their contributions and attempt to match their inputs with outcomes.

Fairness is different from simply not cheating. In restraining cheating we act so as not to advantage ourselves at others' expense. Fairness is about giving others their due whether or not we are also recipients of the benefits involved. Fairness is focused, not on inhibiting one's own behavior to protect others, but instead on matching others' inputs with their outcomes. When a teacher grades students on an exam, for example, the grades should reflect each student's performance and not the teacher's biases.

In caring for others, we exhibit behaviors that partly reflect an inheritance from our evolutionary ancestors. Primatologists have noted numerous examples of compassionate concern in primates, including concern for others beyond immediate kin. A poignant example is that of Joni, a young chimpanzee raised by the comparative psychologist Ladygina Kohts. Joni liked to spend time on the roof of the house, and it was difficult to get the chimp to come down. Kohts discovered that if she acted distressed and pretended to cry, Joni would immediately rush to comfort her, gently touching Kohts's face and looking around for an offender.[11]

In lab experiments, Felix Warneken and Michael Tomasello have found that chimpanzees help other chimps and humans without any expectation of reward. They spontaneously retrieved out-of-reach objects for experimenters, overcame obstacles to help, and engaged in behaviors that produced food for another chimp and not themselves.[12]

Our ability to feel empathy for others suggests a built-in preparedness to help. We typically have little control over its activation, but empathy is related to increased helping and pro-social behaviors. It is a natural catalyst for caring and altruism. It is not, however, the sole basis for helping, which is probably a good thing, given that we are most likely to empathize with people most similar to us.[13] The moral rules and norms of any society include providing help to other group members. Every major religion has some version of the golden rule: do unto others as you would have them do unto you.[14] We often decide to help because we know it is the right thing to do.

Collective Morality

All of morality is in the service of successful group living, although as we have seen, the behaviors don't necessarily focus directly on the group. We ourselves are the proximal targets of Moderation and Industriousness, and other individuals are the targets of Not Harming and Helping. The third column of the moral map shifts the focus to the group as a whole. Here the target is the collective, be it a local community or society at large—but the shift involves more than a change of target. As Michael Tomasello and Amrisha Vaish note, the evolution of morality is a two-step process: "The first step is mutualistic collaboration and pro-socially motivated interactions with specific individuals, and the second step is the more abstract, agent-neutral, norm-based morality of individuals who live in more large-scale cultural worlds."[15]

The movement from the Personal (Self) and Interpersonal (Other) columns to the Collective column represents an important shift from self-regulation to social regulation, from a concern with how we should regulate our behavior to be moral members of society to a concern with how the group as a whole should be regulated to create a "moral" society. The Personal and Interpersonal cells—Moderation, Industriousness, Not Harming, and Helping—are about our own moral conduct. The Collective cells implicate our own behavior but are more centrally focused on the norms, laws, and policies that regulate and bind the group as a whole. The question of what makes a society moral is an inquiry into social regulation and what motivates it.

In the model there are two Collective moralities, reflecting the distinct protect-provide motives for the group. Social Order, a pro-

	Personal (Self)	Interpersonal (Other)	Collective (Group)
Protect (proscriptive morality)	Moderation Self-Discipline	Not Harming Not Cheating	**Social Order**
Provide (prescriptive morality)	Industriousness Hard Work	Helping Fairness	**Social Justice**
	SELF REGULATION		SOCIAL REGULATION

Adding the Collective cells of MMM: the new focus on social regulation

scriptive morality, is about avoiding the "bad"—protecting the group from threats to its safety and stability. Social Justice, a prescriptive morality, is about approaching the "good"—providing benefits for the group and improving its welfare.

Social Order (Protect-Group)

The goal of Social Order morality is the safety and security of the group. This involves not only defending against attacks from outside but also countering chaos and unrest within the group. The focus on protection produces an emphasis on strength and power, in the interests of defense, and on stability and order, in the interests of security. A preference for strong leaders and respect for authority are key features of this collective morality, as is support for agents of enforcement within the group.

Social Order morality also finds expression in members' adherence to strict group norms, social hierarchy, and clearly defined social roles, which are deemed natural and adaptive features of a stable society. Custom and tradition are regarded as valuable guides that have stood the test of time. The collective is viewed as a bulwark against self-interest, self-expression, and personal gratification that could threaten the group. Conformity signals allegiance and loyalty to the group and contributes to communal solidarity.

In *Patterns of Culture* (1934), the anthropologist Ruth Benedict distinguished between two types of human cultures: Apollonian cultures that emphasize order and restraint, and Dionysian cultures that emphasize abandon. She chose the names of Zeus's two sons because in ancient Greece the worshipers of Apollo, god of the sun and rational thinking, valued order and restraint, whereas the worshipers of Dionysus, the god of wine, valued excess and abandon.[16] This Apollonian-Dionysian typology was used earlier by Friedrich Nietzsche in *The Birth of Tragedy* (1872), but his interest was in applying the descriptors to the dramatic arts. He argued that their successful fusion produced great tragedies such as those of Aeschylus and Sophocles. Benedict was interested in describing human cultures. She claimed that the Pueblo Native Americans of the Southwest were Apollonian, whereas the Great Plains Native Americans were Dionysian. A Social Order morality is Apollonian.

One aspect of this restraint is conformity and adherence to strict group standards of behavior. In her far-reaching research, Michele Gelfand distinguishes between tight and loose cultures. In tight cultures there are strong norms for how to behave and strong disapproval and punishment for those who don't follow the norms; in loose cultures people are less likely to follow norms and less likely to be punished for deviance. In the tight, highly ordered country of Singapore, for example, hefty fines are doled out for such seemingly minor offenses as forgetting to flush a toilet in a public stall (up to $1,000), alcohol is banned from public places between 10:30 p.m. and 7:00 a.m., and one can be imprisoned for homosexual acts, online dissent, or making too much noise in public. In New Zealand, an open, loose country, discrimination against gays and lesbians is illegal, prostitution is legal, and people can drive with open bottles of alcohol as long as they don't exceed the legal blood alcohol limit. In her study of thirty-three countries, Gelfand found that tight nations were more likely to be religious and autocratic and to confer fewer political rights on its citizens.[17]

Tightness is a feature of Social Order morality. Apollonian rather than Dionysian, it regards "permissiveness" as anathema and evokes the restrictiveness of proscriptive morality. Traditional social roles and behaviors are deemed essential for social stability.

Strict adherence to group norms suggests the duty-based requirements of deontology, which is also associated with proscriptive morality. Social Order morality largely relies on negative incentives— the threat of punishment—to motivate group members to conform to group norms and social roles.[18] This includes informal mechanisms involving social stigma as well as ostracism that contaminate the identities of those who break the rules. A negative incentive system also includes more formal mechanisms such as criminal justice systems that exist in well-functioning societies, and a Social Order morality is associated with support for harsh sentences within these systems. Conformity, authority, and strict enforcement of social behaviors and social roles all prevent chaos and minimize disorder.

Social Justice (Provide-Group)

Social Justice, the other collective morality, has goals that are very different from those of Social Order and are not advanced by the invocation of conformity and strength. The overriding aim is providing for the group—improving group welfare and creating greater equality. Group bonds are strengthened through a sense of shared communal responsibility. Equal worth and equal treatment are hallmarks of the collective Social Justice morality, which focuses on the distribution of resources within a group. Social Justice emphasizes narrowing the gap, both socially and economically, between the haves and have nots in a group. The emphasis is on promoting the positive rather than preventing the negative.

Respect is a form of recognition that acknowledges that we are participants in a common ethical world.[19] In its focus on providing for group members, Social Justice morality is concerned with the distribution of public goods across the collective. How we distribute these resources is a reflection of the respect we have for group members— a "costly" form that goes beyond words to action. A primary focus of Social Justice morality is therefore greater economic equality, minimizing the wealth inequalities in a group. From this perspective it is interesting to consider Martin Luther King's speech to the striking Black sanitation workers in Memphis a month before he was assassinated: "Now our struggle is for genuine equality, which means economic equality. For we know that it isn't enough to integrate lunch counters. What does it profit a man to be able to eat at an integrated lunch counter if he doesn't have enough money to buy a hamburger?"[20] Or as the journalist Nikole Hannah-Jones notes:

> Wealth is "what enables you to buy homes in safer neighborhoods with better amenities and better-funded schools. It is what enables you to send your children to college without saddling them with tens of thousands of dollars of debt and what provides you money to put a down payment on a house. It is what prevents family emergencies or unexpected

job losses from turning into catastrophes that leave you homeless and destitute. It is what ensures what every parent wants—
that your children will have fewer struggles than you did. . . .
It's not incidental that wealthier people are healthier and live
longer."[21]

Economic inequality is evident in people's everyday quality of
life. Social Justice morality is concerned with the distribution of social goods, including food, shelter, education, and health care, because
people's quality of life is its ultimate goal. The Universal Declaration
of Human Rights, adopted by the United Nations General Assembly
in December 1948, recognizes all humans as "born free and equal in
dignity and rights." Among the many rights specified in its thirty articles are not only the right to work and to education but the right to
a standard of living that is "adequate" for the health and well-being
of individuals and their families, including "food, clothing, housing
and medical care and necessary social services."[22]

Social regulation by punishment is generally absent here. Although
the goals of Social Justice morality are clear, the means are more discretionary, as we might expect for a prescriptive morality. Long-term
advocacy of particular Social Justice efforts, such as social safety nets,
would presumably be based on their outcomes and efficacy, given
prescriptive morality's affinity for consequentialism.[23]

Social Justice morality is committed to providing these public
goods as the minimum necessary for a caring community. Fulfilling
its egalitarian objectives means not only providing for the most vulnerable in society but demanding more from those at the top. The
Social Justice goal is to decrease the gap that separates those at the top
and bottom rungs of the economic ladder, based on a commitment
to the greater equality and shared responsibility believed to be essential for a healthy, moral society.

Politics and the Group Moralities

The moral bases of the political left and right reside in the collective moralities, Social Justice and Social Order, and it is no doubt readily apparent how these line up. Social Order is the moral underpinning of political conservatism, and Social Justice is the moral underpinning of political liberalism.[24]

Conservatism has been called a "philosophy of imperfection," focused on a negative, pessimistic view of humanity.[25] Strict group norms and defined social roles are viewed as safeguards against the destabilizing effects of selfish human nature, and strength, authority, and tradition serve to protect the group from both internal and external threats. Political liberalism, by contrast, emphasizes the more optimistic side of human nature—altruism rather than selfishness—and promotes positive efforts to benefit the well-being of the community. There is an emphasis on resource allocation and communal sharing.

Liberalism focuses on providing for the group, and its prescriptive morality is evident in the objective of making things better—*approaching the good* and moving forward to improve current circumstances. Conservatism is focused on protecting the group, and therefore on keeping things from getting worse—that is, *avoiding the bad*. Here is the inhibition of proscriptive morality, because inherent in protecting the group is protecting its structure by maintaining current social arrangements. The left-right tension between embracing progress, which necessitates change, and maintaining the status quo, which is of course anti-change, is intrinsic to the conflict between Social Justice and Social Order.

Proscriptive and prescriptive morality characterize the two cells within each context of the moral map—Personal, Interpersonal, and Collective—but it is only in the Collective cells that we find political differences. Liberal-conservative differences do not show up in the first four cells of the model: Moderation, Industriousness, Not Harming, and Helping. Absent the influence of political orientation, the prescriptive and proscriptive cells within the Personal and Interpersonal columns are seen as necessary and mutually supporting.[26] People who are high on one type of morality are generally high on the other. The people most likely to avoid self-indulgence are also most apt to work hard, and those who are most likely to help and treat others fairly are also least likely to harm.

All moral members of a group believe in helping others, although as we'll see, there are differences in whom we choose to help. Nevertheless the conviction that we should help characterizes all moral people, as does the conviction that we should not harm. A person who helps one friend yet steals from another would likely not be considered moral, just as a person who evidences moderation with regard to food, drinking, and drugs would likely not be considered moral if she or he chooses not to work and lives off of friends. Self-discipline is not the sole provenance of one group; exercise regimens and responsible drinking, for example, are found among both liberals and conservatives, and people work hard across all walks of life and political identification.

In the domain of self-regulation we embrace both prescriptive and proscriptive forms of morality. Together, the protect and provide moralities afford us maximal flexibility in our behavioral repertoire and prepare us to meet a broad array of moral challenges. Yet when we move to the group level, the two forms of morality diverge. Social Justice and Social Order are negatively correlated.[27] Why?

Only here, in the domain of social regulation, does morality relate directly to the policies and philosophies governing collectives, including political communities. The Collective cells are about how we should act with regard to the group as a whole, but importantly, they are about how the collective should be run. Self-regulation and social regulation involve different levels of analysis; for self-regulation it is the individual, whereas for social regulation the level of analysis is the group.

Just as prescriptive and proscriptive morality both operate within the individual, allowing for appropriate responses to different moral challenges, prescriptive and proscriptive morality are also distributed across group members. Some parts of the population espouse one group-based morality and other parts espouse the other. In this way a society can rely on both Social Order and Social Justice, which may give it adaptability in facing the tasks and challenges confronting it, some of which call for providing for group members and others for protecting the group. A person who relied entirely on one type of morality would be poorly equipped for successful self-regulation. Similarly, a society relying entirely on one type of morality would be poorly equipped for successful social regulation.

This relative balance across a group's population is the bane of political partisans. The left always believes that its candidates are far more qualified and better for the nation, and those on the right believe the same about theirs. In the United States, sometimes the two parties' presidential nominees don't even seem close in qualifications or appeal, with one candidate's corruption or lack of qualifications seeming all too obvious to the opposing side. Yet in virtually all presidential elections, the results are far closer than a partisan would ever choose or predict.

In recent years, this has had much to do with party affiliation, and political party has become a salient identity for Americans. Political parties have become strongly associated with liberal or conservative ideologies and policies—and these, in turn, are grounded in distinct moralities.[28] Political parties can distort these moralities to appeal to particular voters or to win at all costs, but the fundamental distinction between protecting and providing remains. For decades the American public has regularly been asked to choose between a more conservative Social Order candidate and a more liberal Social Justice candidate. As the ideological identities of the parties have become clearer with each successive election, the voting population has grown more predictably divided. In later chapters I address the specific ideologies of the left and right and why particular policies and positions resonate on each side of the political spectrum. But first, let's examine the best-known theory regarding politics and morality—and why I think it is flawed.

3

What the Reigning Theory Gets Wrong

If you spend any time looking into the relation between morality and politics, you will undoubtedly encounter Jonathan Haidt's Moral Foundations Theory, or MFT. This very popular model of morality appears not only in academic journals in many disciplines but also on the opinion pages of major newspapers. Haidt's recent work on the dangers of social media is important.[1] Earlier he reignited psychologists' interest in morality and made a major contribution by broadening our understanding of the moral domain. He and his colleagues posited five moral foundations generally referred to as Care, Fairness, Loyalty, Authority, and Sanctity.[2] Care involves concerns for the suffering of others; Fairness refers to concerns about unfair treatment and rights; Loyalty is the opposite of betrayal and concerns our obligations as group members; Authority refers to our obligations in hierarchical relationships (including obedience); and Sanctity involves our concerns about contagion, both physical and spiritual.

Haidt's model was initially based on a reading of three books, a chapter, and a journal article; he and a graduate student, Craig Joseph, concluded that there are four "intuitive ethics," which they first described in a paper in *Daedalus* in 2004.[3] These four were suffering, hierarchy, reciprocity, and purity. In a footnote the authors suggested a fifth module related to loyalty, and in subsequent papers they posited the five that are now recognized as the foundations of Moral Foundations Theory.

Haidt and Jesse Graham developed a questionnaire to assess people's endorsement of each of the five moral foundations.[4] The popularity of Moral Foundations Theory in psychology is attributable not only to the authors' creative contribution to our theoretical understanding of morality but also, I believe, to the ready availability of a questionnaire to measure the foundations. Once researchers had an easily administered tool to use in their research, they produced a steady flow of empirical papers on morality, employing this theory in particular.

Another reason for the appeal of Haidt's model, particularly in op-ed pieces, lies in the empirical links the authors made to liberalism and conservatism. These links were highlighted in Haidt's bestselling book, *The Righteous Mind* (2012), which has a chapter titled "The Conservative Advantage." The theory enabled conservatives to feel moral superiority. Unfortunately, however, the boom in empirical work on Moral Foundations Theory took off without sufficient examination of the theory itself. We now have conclusions that have been popularized but are based on an incomplete model.

In Haidt's theory, Care and Fairness are labeled "individualizing" foundations because they focus on the rights and welfare of individuals. Loyalty, Authority, and Sanctity are "binding" foundations, where the locus of moral concern is the group rather than the individual. The interpersonal-collective distinction of the Model of Moral Motives parallels the individuated-binding distinction of Moral Foundations Theory. According to Haidt and colleagues, liberals value the individualizing foundations—Harm and Fairness—and rely on these two moral foundations. Conservatives value these as well, but they also value the binding foundations, Loyalty, Authority, and Sanctity. They thus rely on all five foundations.[5] Consequently, Haidt and his colleagues claim, not only do conservatives understand liberals better than liberals understand conservatives, but only conservatives have a morality that serves to bind the group, a primary function of morality—thus the "conservative advantage." Unlike conservatives, Haidt argues, liberals pursue policies that "promote *pluribus* at the expense of *unum*."[6]

What's Missing

The obvious provocative implication of these conclusions is that liberals are not group oriented and do not have a morality that serves to bind the group. The problem, however, is not that liberals lack a binding, group-based morality but rather that Haidt and his colleagues failed to include it in their Moral Foundations Theory.

Consider the three binding moralities in their theory: Loyalty, Authority, and Sanctity. All three are proscriptive moralities—they reflect a concern for Social Order. My colleagues and I have found that the three binding moralities in Moral Foundations Theory are positively associated with the Model of Moral Motives' Social Order and not at all associated with the model's Social Justice.[7] Each of these foundations promotes order in a collective. Strong leadership, allegiance to the group, and intolerance of anything "unwholesome" or "deviant" are ways to strengthen groups through conformity and strict norms. Thus MFT's three binding moralities are all subsumed by MMM's Social Order, a proscriptive group morality.

Where is a prescriptive group morality in Moral Foundations Theory? Where is Social Justice, or any path to Social Justice? The theory has no such moral foundation, no semblance of a group morality focused on communal responsibility and providing for the group rather than protecting it.[8] Thus the theory tells us that liberals lack a binding morality because the theory itself lacks such a foundation.

Haidt's individualizing foundations—Care and Fairness—reflect both prescriptive and proscriptive morality and parallel the Interper-

	Personal (Self)	Interpersonal (Other)	Collective (Group)
Protect (proscriptive morality)	?	Individualizing	Binding
Provide (prescriptive morality)	?		?

Comparing the Model of Moral Motives and Moral Foundations Theory

sonal (Other) column of my moral map, where other individuals are the targets of moral actions and inactions.[9] Here there is close correspondence between the two moral maps. Interestingly, Haidt does not include foundations reflecting Personal (Self) morality in his theory, despite his goal of creating a comprehensive map of the moral domain. But for our purpose of understanding the moral bases of the left and right, this is not a problem; the self-based moralities are not directly associated with political ideology.

It is the binding group moralities that matter, and here Moral Foundations Theory is incomplete: it fails to include a foundation akin to Social Justice. Both liberals and conservatives have binding moralities—Social Order for conservatives and Social Justice for liberals. It is not liberals who lack a group-based morality; it is the theory that lacks the binding morality liberals endorse.

Interestingly, some of Haidt's and his colleagues' own research findings should have raised a red flag for them. For instance, they found that men score higher than women on two of the three binding foundations, Loyalty and Authority.[10] The obvious conclusion is that men are more concerned about binding the collective and are more group oriented than women. Yet a well-acknowledged difference in the large psychological literature on gender is that women tend to be more communal than men, and men more agentic than women.[11] These may well be socialized differences that are likely to change over time, but they nevertheless reflect empirical findings. Given women's greater communal orientation, it seems odd that Haidt found men to be more group oriented. Similarly, Graham has suggested that Social Justice is subsumed by the Care foundation.[12] Yet we know that both Helping in the Model of Moral Motives and Care in Moral Foundations Theory are embraced by both liberals and conservatives. Social Justice, however, is championed by liberals. These inconsistencies point to a serious omission in Haidt's theory: a prescriptive binding foundation is absent from the model.

A fan of Moral Foundations Theory might respond by pointing out that Fairness is a foundation in the theory, and Fairness includes Social Justice. Fairness is an individualizing (Interpersonal in my model) foundation that both liberals and conservatives espouse. Yet we know that only liberals embrace Social Justice, suggesting that the two moral constructs are distinct. Haidt nevertheless confounds the two in his theory's Fairness foundation, defining it as "Concerns about unfair treatment, cheating, and more abstract notions of justice and rights."[13] And the six-item scale of Haidt's questionnaire that assesses the Fairness foundation mixes questions about Fairness and Social Justice. For example, respondents are to indicate the extent of their agreement with the following two items: "When the government makes laws, the number one principle should be ensuring that everyone is treated fairly," and "Justice is the most important requirement for a society."[14] Fairness and Social Justice are both included in the individualizing Fairness foundation, and in the absence of a group-based prescriptive morality, Haidt concludes that only conservatives have a binding morality.

Interpersonal or Collective Morality?

The failure of Moral Foundations Theory to distinguish between Social Justice and Fairness suggests that we should closely examine these two moral motives to see how they differ. An exploration of Fairness and Social Justice can inform the important role of context—interpersonal (other) versus collective (group) or, in the theory's parlance, individualizing or binding—in assessing morality. As we'll see in later chapters, these differences have important implications for policy positions on the left and right.

You may have been surprised to see that Fairness and Social Justice are different moral motives in my moral map. They are distinct, and *where* they are represented is key to understanding their differences. Fairness is in the interpersonal column, and Social Justice in the collective column. Both are moral distributional principles, but they reflect different conceptions of deservingness that are directly tied to the interpersonal versus group contexts. The same action or outcome can be seen as either moral or immoral, depending on whether we use an interpersonal interaction or the larger group to interpret the situation.

This is the case for both prescriptive and proscriptive moralities. Fairness and Social Justice are prescriptive moralities focused on providing for others, yet they can result in very different judgments of right and wrong. Distinct interpretative contexts—interpersonal or group—underlie the differences between Fairness and Social Justice, and as we'll see, between Not Harming and Social Order as well. In the Model of Moral Motives, Fairness involves deservingness based on inputs, and outcomes proportional to these inputs. To assess it, you need information about the contributions or attributes of specific targets in an interaction. In contrast, the model's Social Justice involves deservingness based in common group membership, with outcomes relatively equal across group members. An inclusive group identity, rather than an individual's inputs or qualities, determines the outcome.[15] The lens shifts from a local interaction to a larger frame, that of the collective.

The difference between Fairness and Social Justice can be illustrated by an increase in wages. A Fairness-based increase would account for workers' specific performance or extra hours (such as overtime), whereas an increase in the minimum wage for all Americans would reflect Social Justice.

My choice of labels—*Fairness* and *Social Justice*—seems to correspond to people's natural understanding of the concepts and their differences. In describing instances of Fairness, our research participants most often talked about individuals engaged in discrete interpersonal events involving reciprocity or outcomes that were proportional to inputs. Instances of Social Justice usually involved a person or collective described in terms of membership in a group such as a social category, and outcomes were focused on equality.[16]

A fundamental difference between Fairness and Social Justice is thus the individual versus group-based interpretation of deservingness or entitlement. This parallels the distinction between personal identity and social identity posited by social psychologists; the former is based in our specific attributes, the latter on the groups by which we define ourselves. When we think about the characteristics that define us as unique individuals—such as our height, helpfulness, athleticism, musical ability, or sense of humor—we are considering our personal identity. Yet we can also think of ourselves in terms of the groups we belong to, including our religious group, social class, occupational group, gender, or racial group.[17] Even when we are thinking about our own identities, different contexts produce different perceptions, by which the same behavior can lead to very different moral judgments. This applies to both the proscriptive and prescriptive domains of morality.

Shifting Contexts and PTSD

Before discussing the important role of context for evaluations of Fairness and Social Justice, I want to use the example of post-traumatic stress disorder, or PTSD, to illustrate the powerful impact of shifting contexts in the case of proscriptive morality, based in the motive to protect. Different interpretive contexts can help us better understand post-traumatic stress in veterans returning from recent wars.

My interest in war-related trauma grew out of my early research on trauma and victimization, which culminated in my book *Shattered Assumptions* (1992). My trauma theory posits that we have fundamental assumptions at the core of our inner world that give us a sense of relative invulnerability. We believe that our world (though not necessarily the world at large) is benevolent and meaningful, and we are worthy individuals. Extreme events that shatter these assumptions induce trauma. The most common response I heard in my many years of research with survivors was, "I never thought it could happen to me." When the world is no longer seen as benevolent or meaningful, and negative outcomes seem random and unpredictable, survivors are left with a sense of terror at their fragility. Their inner worlds are disintegrated.

There is a strong positive relation between exposure to combat and post-traumatic stress; soldiers who are victims or who witness combat-related injuries or atrocities confront their own mortality and recognize human fragility. In recent wars, however, there has been a key additional element that accounts for trauma: the shattering of assumptions about the self, arising from perceptions of one's own immorality. Warfare has changed: where it once involved states with comparable armies, it is now almost always "war among people," with ill-defined battlefields. It is hard to distinguish between civilians and combatants, and every civilian is a potential enemy.[18] When the boundary between civilians and combatants is blurred, the killing and maiming of innocent civilians becomes increasingly common. I believe that in the context of the war zone, such atrocities are readily interpreted in terms of *group* protection—actions that protect not only the buddies in one's unit but American interests. The soldier is fighting in the name of America, presumably to protect its values, and this group-based Social Order morality enables the soldier to justify civilian deaths. The "moral self" remains intact, justified by the very difficult circumstances of modern warfare.

When the soldier returns home, however, the context for interpreting his or her acts shifts dramatically. Removed from the war zone and one's combat unit, the group context disappears and the default *interpersonal* morality—"do not harm"—instead produces a powerful self-indictment. The harms perpetrated on enemy civilians are now perceived as immoral, shattering assumptions about the moral self. The morality of protecting "America" and the group in combat, the essence of war-related training, presents intense difficulties for those who come home and judge themselves in a "normal" context. Soldiers shift from a proscriptive group morality to a proscriptive interpersonal morality—from protecting the group to protecting individuals, and specifically from protecting America and its values to "do not harm." The result is post-traumatic stress, based on shattered assumptions about the self. The very same behaviors produce different moral judgments, depending on the interpretive lens used. In the case of war-related PTSD, the context shifts—from war zone to home—and with it the morality used to evaluate one's own actions.

Shifting Contexts: Fairness and Social Justice

More often, shifting contexts do not involve actual changes in circumstances but instead differences in perspective. In our evolutionary history, successful small group (tribal) living was likely dependent on both Fairness, based in individual attributes, and Social Justice, based in a common group identity. Survival was likely based in part on rewarding the efforts and competence of individuals (Fairness), who thus had an incentive to be, for example, better hunters. Yet survival likely also depended on building group interdependence and keeping the group together through communal sharing of resources. Social Justice would have balanced the gross inequalities and dissatisfaction that might otherwise have resulted from applying the Fairness principle alone. Together the two moralities minimized the likelihood of dissolution and contributed to the group's survival.

Social Justice and Fairness are different, but both are moral principles, and a person can endorse both. As independent principles, however, they can also conflict. Consider an increasingly common occurrence in affluent communities throughout the United States: wealthy parents contributing large amounts of money to their local public schools. At first glance, few of us might find anything amiss about parents' desire to support local public education. These parents have a lot of money and choose to use some of it to advance their and their neighbors' children's opportunities. Contributing to local public schools seems desirable and moral, even admirable. But if we expand our perspective to include the larger community or society, we begin to realize that such private giving widens the gap between rich and poor. Parents with fewer financial resources are unable to help fund their children's schools, and thus private donations confer an advantage on the already fortunate. Schools with wealthier children grow wealthier while the poorer schools grow poorer by comparison. From the perspective of the larger society, we may reach a different moral conclusion regarding the parents' contributions: they make inequality worse.

These different lenses reflect two distinct moral principles. Fairness focuses us locally on the parents' behavior, and Social Justice focuses us on the larger collective consequence. Ultimately our opinion depends on which lens we use to interpret the situation.

Unpaid internships for students are also high on Fairness and low on Social Justice. In contemporary America, these internships have become sought-after opportunities for high school students in pursuit of selective colleges and for college students in their pursuit of high-quality jobs or acceptance into elite graduate schools. They provide valuable experience and contacts, but the interns are not paid for their work. Although no doubt many of these internships are obtained through personal contacts, there is also an assumption that students with the strongest academic credentials and experiences are most apt to be chosen. In other words, the best students deserve these plum positions. When considering the individual applicants, this certainly seems fair; the students' own efforts and attributes determine the outcome.

Yet once again, if you broaden your frame of reference and consider unpaid internships from the perspective of the larger group or society, they look quite different. The positions are unpaid, so only the privileged can afford them. What about the many excellent students who have to support themselves or work to save for college or living expenses after college? They cannot afford an unpaid internship and so have to pass up opportunities that might give them a leg up in their future academic or occupational pursuits. Again we have a situation that favors the privileged and exacerbates societal inequalities—one that may be Fair but Socially Unjust.[19]

Actions or outcomes can be moral when understood in individual terms but immoral when interpreted in terms of the broader collective or of society at large. The opposite may also happen—there are situations that may be considered Socially Just but not Fair, as we'll see when we explore disagreements between the political left and right. In a series of studies, my colleagues and I looked specifically at liberals' and conservatives' endorsement of Fairness and Social Justice. Fairness was represented by such items as: "The effort a person puts into something ought to be reflected in the size of the reward he or she receives," and "Members of a team ought to receive different rewards depending on the amount each person contributed."[20] These reflect proportionality—that outcomes should be dependent on inputs. Social Justice was represented by such items as: "In the healthiest societies, those at the top should feel responsible for improving the well-being of those at the bottom," and "Increased economic equality is ultimately beneficial to everyone in society."

We found that Social Justice was positively associated with liberalism but Fairness was not correlated with political ideology; in other words, it was endorsed by both liberals and conservatives. Importantly, Fairness and Social Justice were uncorrelated; a strong sense of Fairness did not allow us to predict that a person would have a high or low sense of Social Justice, and vice versa. Each moral motive operates independently.

There was no difference between liberals and conservatives in the strength of their endorsement of Fairness—both believe strongly in proportional outcomes. The differences between the left and right reside in the collective domain; liberals are high on Social Justice morality and conservatives are low. Conservatives are far less likely to interpret the above situations—parental school donations and student internships—in terms of the larger group context.

With the differences between Fairness and Social Justice in mind, it is illuminating to consider John Rawls's view, in *Theory of Justice* (1971), that a "veil of ignorance" is the optimal means of determining a just society. According to Rawls, if we met to decide on the principles to govern our society and we didn't know anything about ourselves— not our gender, health, education, family background, race, religion, specific attributes, competencies, advantages, or disadvantages—we would choose a society with equal basic liberties and equal opportunities to reach positions of status. In addition, and importantly, distributions in the society would benefit those who are least well off, a rule Rawls referred to as the difference principle. Generated wealth should be used to help those who are not at the top. From the perspective of the Model of Moral Motives, the cleverness of Rawls's thought experiment lies in his elimination of Fairness as an operative principle, because the veil of ignorance eradicates any reliance on individual attributes or inputs to determine outcomes.[21] We have no idea where we would find ourselves or how we would fare in Rawls's imaginary society. We instead recognize that we are all members of that society, entitled to the shared resources of the group.

Fairness and Social Justice are both prescriptive moral principles, but they represent distinct preferences for allocating resources and providing benefits to others. One focuses on individual attributes of recipients and the other on group membership, and so they are located in the Interpersonal and Collective columns, respectively, of my model. The Fairness and Social Justice judgments discussed above do not involve actual differences in context but different interpretations of the same behaviors and outcomes. As we begin to unpack the relation between morality and political ideology, we will want to keep in mind the distinction between Fairness and Social Justice. Failing to do so can lead one to erroneous conclusions regarding the morality of the left and right.

Returning to Haidt

This is the error made by Haidt and his colleagues. In failing to distinguish between Fairness and Social Justice, they omit a liberal collective morality and conclude that only conservatives have a binding group-based morality. In fact, the left and right each have a binding morality, with liberals focused on providing for the group and conservatives focused on protecting it.

When Haidt wrote his book, in 2012, he seems to have realized that there might be a problem with his Fairness foundation. At the end of the chapter titled "The Conservative Advantage," after discussing liberals' reliance on the individualizing foundations and conservatives' reliance on both the individualizing and binding foundations, he writes that there might be a need to modify the Fairness foundation "to make it focus more strongly on proportionality."[22] This revision would align his theory's Fairness foundation with my model's Fairness, which is based on proportional outcomes. Unfortunately, however, in proposing to restrict his Fairness foundation, Haidt did not carve out Social Justice to create a separate prescriptive binding morality. There remains in his theory no Social Justice morality focused on providing for the group. Despite Haidt's claim of a "conservative advantage," both liberals and conservatives have a group morality that binds *pluribus* into *unum.*

The left, concerned about Social Justice, and the right, concerned about Social Order, both care about the group, but in distinct ways. Interestingly, however, there is a group that does not rely on a group-based morality—not liberals but libertarians.[23] Not that libertarians are not moral—but in their dealings with other people and the larger group, their morality is wholly based in individualizing, interpersonal morality—on Not Harming and Helping, Not Cheating and Fairness. They have a self-focused morality, too, based in both Moderation and Industriousness. But they are motivated by neither Social Justice nor Social Order concerns. They lack any binding morality. Libertarians' morality is based, not in providing for or protecting the group, but solely in providing for and protecting the individual. They are not interested in binding the group because they believe that group living is best served by individual liberty. Unlike libertarians, both liberals and conservatives recognize that we are social animals who have always lived in groups and are well served by collective moralities that bind group members.

4

Threat and Coordination
Versus Hope and Cooperation

During the U.S. presidential campaign of 2008, the journalist Fareed Zakaria wrote this about the two major candidates' foreign policy views: "[John] McCain is a pessimist about the world, seeing it as a dark, dangerous place where, without the constant and vigorous application of American force, evil will triumph. [Barack] Obama sees a world that is in many ways going our way. As nations develop, they become more modern and enmeshed in the international economic and political system. . . . America's job is to push these progressive forces forward, using soft power rather than hard."[1] This was an oversimplification. The Democratic nominee, Obama, was certainly aware of hard-power threats to American interests, and the Republican nominee, McCain, no doubt understood America's appeal as (in Ronald Reagan's words) a "city on a hill." But Zakaria was making an important point about each candidate's message to his voters.

The link between conservatism and protect motives, and between liberalism and provide motives, is apparent in presidential candidates' divergent campaign strategies to bolster their chances of electoral success—not just Obama's and McCain's strategies but those of every pair of Republican and Democratic candidates going back at least to Lyndon Johnson and Barry Goldwater in 1964. The right emphasizes fear and the left emphasizes hope. Recognizing and creating threats increases the popularity of candidates on the right. President George W. Bush's State of the Union address in 2002, with its doomsday scenario, the axis of evil, and the war on terror, became the basis of his reelection campaign speeches, which focused the public on fear and danger. President Trump's fear-mongering, with its focus on rapists, thugs, foreign hordes, and carnage, could not be more different from Hillary Clinton's campaign slogan, "Better Together," or President Obama's optimistic mantra, "Yes, we can," reflected in his first inaugural address: "On this day, we gather because we have chosen hope over fear, unity of purpose over conflict and discord." Conservatives use provocative images that produce fear: criminals, terrorists, foreign invaders. Liberals rely on images that create concern for people's welfare, based in the promise of a more caring nation—a hungry child, a shuttered school, a sick person without health care. Implicit in each side's messaging is the inducement of a distinct moral motivation— to protect or provide.

Liberals increase their attractiveness by fostering hope and the possibility of a better society. In contrast, as the perception of threat rises, the desire for protection rises with it, and so does the appeal of conservativism. Charles Black, a top McCain campaign adviser in 2008, recognized this in noting that another terrorist attack on U.S. soil would have been a big help to McCain in the presidential race.[2]

This danger-conservatism link was apparent in political attitudes following the attacks of September 11 on the World Trade Center. Individuals who lived near the World Trade Center at the time of the attacks became more conservative in the eighteen months following the attack. And experimental studies have shown that even imagining threatening or comforting stimuli can affect our political views. Thinking about death increased support for conservative political candidates. In a separate study, when conservatives imagined being physically safe, they moved toward more liberal positions.[3]

The emphasis on danger versus hope is reflected in the pessimism of the right and the optimism of the left. These differences are apparent in the results of a poll of American voters conducted in February 2021 by the *Economist* magazine, which asked which of the following comes closest to their own view: "It's a big, beautiful world, mostly full of good people, and we must find a way to embrace each other and not allow ourselves to become isolated," or "Our lives are threatened by terrorists, criminals, and illegal immigrants, and our priority should be to protect ourselves." Fully 77 percent of Biden voters endorsed the big, beautiful world choice, whereas two-thirds of Trump voters endorsed the threatening world view.

Coordination Versus Cooperation

Protecting against threats to the group helps maintain what we have and who we are; it reinforces the status quo. Providing for improved welfare and group well-being moves us forward and involves change. The tension between stasis and change is inherent in the differences between Social Order and Social Justice, as the two moralities respond to distinct challenges confronting collectives. Both defense and resource distribution promote group survival and thriving. From primates to hunter-gatherers to modern societies, the most basic tasks for groups involve defense and food (resource) finding and sharing.

The moralities, then, offer solutions to particular group problems. Intrinsic to each morality is a characteristic strategy for solving the challenge, be it protecting the group or providing for it. What are these strategies?

Threat and Coordination

A society or nation that optimizes protection would not only emphasize power and strength but also be vigilant for threats, from within or outside, and able to respond quickly and efficiently when dangers arise. It would maximize coordination. Deference to strong leaders, strict norm adherence, and punishment for non-compliance all enhance coordination—and not surprisingly are features of Social Order morality.

A particularly interesting finding from Michele Gelfand's research on tight and loose cultures is the strong link she found between tightness and threat.[4] Again, tightness is akin to conformity and describes societies that have strong norms about how to behave and strong enforcement of compliance. Gelfand and colleagues found that tight nations had experienced considerable threat. It might come from any number of sources, including natural disasters, disease, famine, resource scarcity, or aggressive neighboring countries. These ecological and historical threats could readily produce chaos, and these nations relied on strict adherence to social norms and punishment for deviance in order to prevent societal breakdown. Nations with a history of minimal threats could afford to be more permissive.

Economic games are a way to study distinct strategies for dealing with challenges to a group. There is a category of economic games, called coordination games, that provide interesting analogs of Social Order objectives. In these games, there is no conflict of interest between players; the goal for a social actor is to match the other players' actions. The challenge is epistemological—that is, it requires common knowledge of the correct actions to perform.[5]

The prototype of coordination games is choosing which side of the road to drive on. Most simply, imagine two drivers meeting on a narrow road; both have to swerve to avoid a head-on collision. If they both make the same swerving maneuver (for example, both swerve to their right), they will successfully pass each other, but if they choose different swerving maneuvers, they will collide. To avoid danger, they need to know which way to move. The optimal outcome in a coordination game requires information—that is, knowing how to act and conforming to minimize danger. Leadership plays the important role of providing the necessary information for coordinated responses. In coordination games, clear rules and norms, as additional features of the game or provided by an authority, maximize the likelihood that players will act on shared knowledge and avoid harm. Simple rules like "follow the leader" or "do what others do" provide easy solutions in coordination games and suggest the importance of strong leadership and authority as well as conformity, key features of Social Order morality.[6] The strict norms, or tightness, of this collective morality guide behavior and reflect the group conformity that facilitates coordination.

Coordination is an advantage when the group faces threats, and the speed and synchrony of individual responses may be vital to survival. When responding to a natural disaster or a terrorist attack, power and authority reside at the top, and there is deference to strong leaders who can direct the coordinated effort. Well-defined norms and social roles also make it clear to people how to act and minimize social ambiguity.

The literature on organizational behavior and management shows a positive link between coordination and the hierarchy endorsed by conservatives. Drawing on this work, Joe Magee and Adam Galinsky conclude that hierarchy is an antidote to chaos and increases group performance by facilitating coordination. "As a mechanism of coordination, hierarchy provides clear lines of direction and deference that maximize the coordination of action for many kinds of tasks. . . . When roles and hierarchical relations are not clear, work tends to become confusing, inefficient, and frustrating, and, thus, coordination suffers."[7]

Shared knowledge and defined roles and positions enable efficient action. Strong leaders, conformity, hierarchy, and strict norm adherence facilitate coordination, a strategy particularly suited to dealing with threats and protecting the group. The obvious example is the military, where discipline is enforced by severe punishments. Conformity, hierarchy, and strict norms are also features of the Social Order morality that underlies conservatism, which focuses on dealing with threats and protecting the group.

Interdependence and Cooperation

Social Justice, a prescriptive morality, addresses the crucial tasks of communal living by providing for the group and allocates communal resources for the benefit of all. Unlike Social Order, which focuses on avoiding negative outcomes and relies on coordination, Social Justice focuses on attaining positive outcomes and relies on cooperation. A second major category of economic games, called cooperation games, largely maps onto the type of problem addressed by Social Justice morality. Here the core challenge is motivational: the actors need to know something about the intentions of others in the game. All players benefit when there is cooperation, but getting to an optimal solution involves recognizing and accepting the players' interdependence.

The prototype of cooperation games is the prisoner's dilemma, in which two people are accused of a crime. Imagine that John and Josh are in separate rooms with no means of communicating. They have been accused of robbing a bank and have been picked up by the police for questioning. Each has a choice: to remain silent or confess to the robbery. Each is told that if he confesses and his partner remains silent, he will get a very light sentence and his partner will get serious time. Confession betrays one's partner and is regarded as defection in the game; silence is regarded as cooperation. If John confesses and Josh doesn't, John will get a one-year sentence and Josh will get eight years—and vice versa if Josh confesses and John doesn't. If both con-

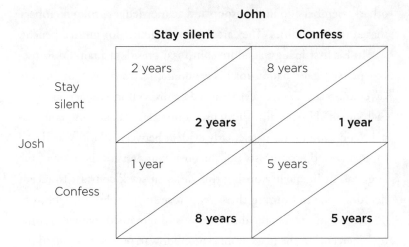

Payouts in the prisoner's dilemma

fess, they will each get five years, but if both remain silent they will both get two years, the best mutual outcome. For each partner, confessing draws the lesser sentence, no matter what his partner does— five years versus eight years if the partner confesses, one year versus two years if the partner stays silent. But if both confess, they'll both spend considerably more time in jail than if both had remained silent. The problem to be solved in the prisoner's dilemma, as in the Social Justice task of providing, is how to get people to cooperate for their mutual benefit.[8]

Cooperation is promoted by a recognition of interdependence and a pro-social orientation in which there is concern for others' outcomes and not just one's own.[9] Unlike Social Order morality, which focuses on the negative, selfish side of human nature, Social Justice morality focuses on the more altruistic side. This promotes not only increased trust but an embrace of mutual reliance, which helps solve the problem of cooperation. Social Justice ascribes particular value to others' membership in the group and acknowledges group members' shared responsibilities. They are to work together for mutual benefit.

In his first inaugural address, in 1933, President Franklin Roosevelt prepared the nation for his economic recovery plan by stating, "We now realize, as we never realized before, our interdependence on each other." Historically, this sense of interdependence and communal responsibility was particularly evident between World War II and 1970, a period economists call the great compression because of the large fall in inequality during this time. In stark contrast to recent decades, incomes during these years rose for people in the bottom 90 percent of the income distribution and remained stagnant for the top 1 percent. In the mass mobilization for war, people recognized the interdependence of our nation's members and valued their common group membership as Americans. In these years of greater Social Justice there was a relatively low level of inequality, attributable to relatively high wages for the working class and public support for government policies that leveled income—including high marginal taxes on the wealthy, which contributed to greater economic equality.[10]

The role of interdependence in fostering Social Justice and liberalism has also been demonstrated in the laboratory. Jojanneke van der Toorn, Jamie L. Napier, and John F. Dovidio found that support for liberal policies increased when research participants perceived the interdependence of groups within society. The more a participant believed that different groups are needed for society to work, the more liberal the person was. The more an individual identified with their own group within society and valued conformity, the more conservative the person was.[11]

The left, with its provide orientation, values cooperation as a problem-solving strategy. This is evident in liberals' orientation to global problems, not only domestic ones. When asked about solving global problems such as climate change and the pandemic, for example, most liberals believe that "international cooperation is the only way we can make progress"; a minority of conservatives believed this. Conservatives instead prefer self-sufficiency and independence, emphasizing nationalism in addressing global problems.[12] Liberals view these problems through the lens of interdependence, whereas conservatives emphasize national interests, reflecting fundamental differences in approach and avoidance orientations—approaching the good (progress via international cooperation) versus avoiding the bad (national harm from other countries' ill will). The left seeks opportunities for positive outcomes while the right is attentive to threats.

Psychological Differences

Given that Social Order is the collective morality of the right and Social Justice is the collective morality of the left, it should not be surprising that the psychological attributes of each group's members fit with these moral motives. The focus on protecting versus providing is evident in conservatives' and liberals' individual psychologies. Research on the psychological traits of liberals and conservatives reveals a distinct cluster of features associated with each political orientation, features that both reflect and reinforce the moral underpinnings of their politics.

In discussing differences in the psychological attributes of liberals and conservatives, we should bear in mind that when psychologists talk about group differences, they mean average differences between the groups. There is lots of variability within each group. Consider a physical difference that is quite large—the height of men and women. The average man is definitely larger than the average woman, but clearly there are women who are taller than most men and men who are shorter than most women. On average, though, men are taller than women. Similarly, when dealing with psychological differences between liberals and conservatives, we are not making claims about all individuals on one or the other side of the political spectrum; rather, we are talking about average differences: psychological attributes more likely to be found in one group than the other.

The psychology of conservatives reflects an attunement to threats, whereas the psychology of liberals does not. Such vigilance is important if group protection is critical. Compared with liberals, conservatives are high on threat sensitivity. They are more attentive to negative stimuli and are more likely than liberals to react physiologically to threatening stimuli. For example, when looking freely at collages including both positive images (such as sunsets and cute animals) and negative images (such as burning houses and dangerous animals), eye-tracking techniques found that conservatives spent more time than liberals looking at the negative images and were also quicker to fixate on these images. In other research, conservatives turned more quickly to and spent more time engaged with images of aversive stimuli (maggots, a spider on a man's face, or a crowd fighting with a man) than with positive images (a happy child, a cute rabbit, or a bowl of fruit), whereas liberals oriented to and spent more time engaged with the happy stimuli. When researchers presented ambiguous stimuli, conservatives were more likely to interpret them negatively. When male and female actors, for instance, portrayed ambiguous facial expressions, conservative respondents were more likely than liberals to interpret the faces as threatening and dominant. Conservatives also show higher physiological reactivity (such as greater blink amplitude and greater electrodermal activity) to sudden, unpleasant noises and threatening visual images.[13]

Research on message framing has found similar differences. Manipulating gain-loss framing around a neutral topic (such as voting behavior), researchers found that conservatives viewed messages framed in terms of losses ("Voting prevents your values from being undermined") as both more persuasive and more valid. Liberals were more persuaded by gain framing ("Voting allows one to be heard").[14]

A simple experiment with a computer game, conducted by Natalie Shook and Russell Fazio, illustrates these different orientations. Participants in the computer game BeanFest accumulated points by making accurate decisions about which beans to accept (approach) or reject (avoid). The beans differed by shape and markings, and some beans earned the participant points while others lost them points. There was a monetary incentive, and participants' goal was to learn which beans were associated with which outcome, so as to increase their points. Shook and Fazio found that conservative participants followed a more cautious strategy than liberals. Overall they approached fewer beans; liberals saw a new bean and checked it out, whereas conservatives were more likely to avoid it. More important, learning by conservatives was more asymmetrical than that of liberals: they learned negative stimuli (which beans to avoid) better than positive stimuli (which beans to approach).[15]

Interestingly, conservative study participants were more likely both to correctly identify negative beans and to miscategorize positive beans as negative. In the end they overestimated the number of negative beans in the game. Outside the laboratory, conservatives are also more attuned to negative stimuli, which signal threat, so it is therefore not surprising that conservatives score higher than liberals on a scale measuring "perception of a dangerous world."[16] Of course, a danger when people look for threats is that they may perceive them when they are not there. Liberals are concerned that conservatives overestimate threats and danger; conservatives are concerned that liberals underestimate them.

The tendency to feel disgust ("disgust sensitivity") has also been found to be associated with political conservatism. Disgust is strongly linked to avoidance. No doubt originally this involved avoidance of pathogens and disease that threatened survival. It is a physio-emotional response that protects us by compelling movement away from things that might otherwise infect or contaminate us. Higher disgust sensitivity is associated with more conservative political views, especially regarding such social issues as abortion and immigration, and compared with liberals, conservatives are more sensitive to disgust.[17]

From attention to negative stimuli and greater reactivity to threat to greater sensitivity to disgust, the psychology of the right reflects a vigilance and bias toward negative stimuli we might expect if the aim is to protect the group from dangers. In his uncertainty-threat model of conservatism, John Jost argues that the management of threat and uncertainty is a central motive for conservatives, and this seems to be reflected in their cluster of psychological features. Conservatism and threat are central to understanding the politics of the right. For Jost and colleagues, political conservatism is a way to manage individual anxiety and uncertainty.[18] In other words, it serves an individual need. From my group-based morality perspective, the individual's attunement to threat serves to protect collective goals; threat sensitivity supports a Social Order morality. These views are mutually reinforcing: individual needs and how one perceives the group's goals are likely to mirror each other.

Liberals, unlike conservatives, are not threat sensitive, but are they characterized by the presence rather than the absence of particular psychological traits? The core aim of Social Justice morality is to provide benefits to the group, with an emphasis on greater equality in the allocation of resources. Rather than an avoidance orientation, liberals' prescriptive group morality is based in approach. This requires seeking opportunities to advance the group's well-being, which means moving forward and embracing change. Consistent with these goals, liberals score high on the psychological trait of openness.[19] They engage in exploratory behaviors, have a high tolerance for uncertainty, and focus on gains rather than losses. The psychological traits of liberals and conservatives take us back to the most fundamental difference between their collective moralities—approach and avoidance. Threat sensitivity serves avoidance, and openness serves approach.

Liberals' comfort with novelty and the unexplored is evident in their willingness to approach new stimuli, as in the BeanFest computer game. It is also apparent in their openness to unknown others. It is this openness that paves the way to the perceived interdependence and shared outcomes of Social Justice morality. Cooperation in a nation requires acceptance of shared membership across all group members, and psychological openness facilitates this perception of commonality. Relatedly, research on moral dilemmas has shown that compared with conservatives, liberals are more accepting of norm violations if they serve the greater good; conservatives are more strictly deontological.[20]

Liberals' comfort with novelty encourages exploration of the new and different. Conservatives are comfortable with the known; safety, whether physical or psychological, lies in the familiar and in structure and stability that thwart potential danger and disorder. These differences between liberals and conservatives are evident in their preferences, with liberals more open to the unfamiliar and less structured. Thus conservatives prefer more familiar foods than liberals and even have a stronger preference for poetry that rhymes, rather than open verse. Liberals prefer abstract paintings, whereas conservatives prefer representational paintings. We can even infer the psychological differences between liberals and conservatives from a quick scan of their bedrooms and offices. Conservatives have more organizational and cleaning items, such as calendars and ironing boards, as well as sports paraphernalia. Liberals tend to favor travel memorabilia, art supplies, and books on varied topics.[21]

Distinct clusters of psychological traits characterize the left and right, and some political scientists have argued that political liberalism and conservatism are part of our genetic inheritance. That is, there is a strong degree of heritability in our political positions, with genetics accounting for between 40 and 60 percent of the variance in political ideology.[22] It is unlikely that genetics directly accounts for our specific policy positions. Nevertheless, our psychological inheritance could push us toward one or the other side of the political spectrum. For example, early temperament differences in adaptability and fearfulness, which are associated with approach and openness versus avoidance and threat sensitivity, could contribute to a liberal or conservative political orientation.

In their twenty-year longitudinal study of personality, Jack Block and Jeanne Block found that twenty-three-year-old conservatives were likely to have been described, two decades earlier, as "feeling easily victimized, easily offended, indecisive, fearful, rigid, inhibited, and relatively over-controlled and vulnerable." Twenty-three-year-old liberals were more likely to have been described as "developing close relationships, self-reliant, energetic, somewhat dominating, relatively under-controlled, and resilient." In a separate long-term study, R. Chris Fraley and colleagues found that fearfulness in childhood (at fifty-four months) was associated with conservatism at age eighteen, whereas high activity levels in childhood, often associated with exploration, were associated with liberalism at age eighteen.[23]

We shouldn't overestimate the role of temperament and psychological traits. Surely political orientation is the result of multiple factors as well as life experiences. Parental socialization is likely to be one of these factors. George Lakoff proposed parenting metaphors for political orientation—the Strict Father for conservatism and the Nurturant Parent for liberalism—and research by Matthew Feinberg and colleagues has shown that political attitudes are in fact associated with these differences in family experiences.[24]

More generally, research on parenting and politics has shown different parenting styles associated with the two sides of the political spectrum. Fraley and colleagues have found that parents' attitudes when the children were one month old predicted the children's political orientation eighteen years later. When the child was one month old, parents completed an inventory that assessed two distinct parenting styles. *Traditional parenting attitudes* included such items as "Children should always obey their parent" and "Children will be bad unless they are taught what is right." *Progressive parenting* included such items as "Children should be allowed to disagree with their parents if they feel their own ideas are better" and "A child's ideas should be seriously considered in making family decisions." Fraley and colleagues found that traditional parenting attitudes predicted the child's conservatism at age eighteen and progressive parenting attitudes predicted the child's liberalism at age eighteen.[25]

In our own research with parents and their college-aged children, we also found a positive association between political conservatism and parenting that emphasized parental authority and obedience. Clearly not all conservatives had strict parents as children, but when parents were strict, their offspring were more likely to be conservative than liberal. Other psychologists, using a very different methodology, have explored liberals' and conservatives' life narratives. In describing their lives, conservatives emphasized the role of authority figures who strictly enforced moral rules, whereas liberals emphasized lessons about empathy and openness.[26] Distinct parenting styles may strongly influence children's openness and threat sensitivity, which in turn are likely to orient us toward the divergent approach-avoidance moralities underlying political liberalism and conservatism.

Children tend to have the same political orientation as their parents. This is likely due in part to parenting style, but it may also be a matter of simply embracing parents' positions in much the way that children typically adopt their parents' religion. A large review of political socialization has found that political ideology is transmitted from parents to children, particularly when the family is close. Peer groups, too, have a strong influence on political beliefs, especially in late adolescence and early adulthood.[27] From this perspective, political orientation is a matter of accepted identity, and with it comes the group-based morality of Social Order or Social Justice.

Pandemic Politics and Masks

These two collective moralities have distinct features and functions. Social Order focuses on protecting the group, and conservatives remain sensitive to threats as they value strength and authority, conformity and loyalty. These features facilitate the coordination associated with effective response to group threats. Social Justice focuses on providing for the group, and liberals, in their openness, value interdependence, trust, and shared benefits as they seek cooperation to create a more humane and equal society.

Before moving to the politics of the left and right more generally, I feel compelled to address what may seem like a ready refutation of my contention that conservatism is based in protecting the group from harm: the conservative response to Covid-19, especially the role of masks from the start of the pandemic.[28] There is no denying that in dealing with a pandemic, the wisest course is to follow science, not politics. Yet in the United States, how people responded to Covid-19 has largely depended on where they stand politically. The left has followed the public health guidelines, practicing social distancing, getting vaccinated, and wearing masks. The right has largely ignored them, in particular remaining maskless from the beginning, when Donald Trump was in the White House.[29] But aren't masks a means of protection? Shouldn't the right therefore have been especially supportive of masks as a response to the Covid threat, especially given that the first vaccine was not approved until December 2020, at the end of Trump's term? Wouldn't we expect a coordinated response, reflecting a Social Order morality, focused on strict norms for how to best manage the virus? Why is it that in this instance it was liberals who engaged in this protective behavior? Not surprisingly, I believe there is no real inconsistency, and the response of the right confirms rather than refutes their Social Order morality.

A deadly virus is an atypical enemy. It does not respond to strength and power, prime currencies of Social Order morality. Strength and power are advantages when confronting more traditional enemies; they deter open conflict and are critical for overcoming adversaries. As such they are highly valued in Social Order morality, with its focus on protection. But whereas power can often defeat invaders, it has no effect on this one. And the invisibility of Covid-19 as well as its absence of intent makes it a difficult foe to rally one's forces against.

Certainly a coordinated federal response, led by Trump, would have helped minimize the Covid-19 deaths and hospitalizations that ravaged the country. We know, from taped conversations with Bob Woodward, that President Trump knew that Covid-19 was deadly and dangerous as early as March 2020. Yet publicly, he chose to describe the disease as no worse than the flu, something affecting the very old and infirm that would miraculously go away.[30] Covid-19 might be immune to displays of strength, but Trump himself wasn't. He opted to appear strong and tough by showing that he was unfazed. If you can't use strength to defeat the enemy, simply minimize its threat, even at the expense of citizens' health. And so we had Trump's public pronouncements that Covid-19 was no big deal and that dire health warnings were a hoax. Masks became a sign that you were fearful rather than powerful—a symbol of weakness.[31]

Although the refusal to wear masks could be interpreted (and was promoted) as radical individualism, conformity seems the better explanation. Had Trump, with his cultlike following, chosen to wear a mask, MAGA (Make America Great Again) masks would have no doubt proliferated, worn by his followers as signs of allegiance.[32] Instead, it was not wearing a mask that signaled loyalty. That Trump was defying scientists' public health directives seemed to add to his followers' perception of his toughness.

In a rural Virginia town with strong support for Trump, a sixty-eight-year-old attorney was one of the few community members who wore a mask. His description of his experience being teased in a local hardware store is telling: "I felt like a sissy. I go in there and was treated like one, too. 'You want us to carry that nail out for you?'" A social media posting by another resident read: "The people I see being the biggest advocates of this [mask-wearing] are women and effeminate men."[33] The "sissy factor" was a powerful deterrent on the right. Given their reverence of strength and power, these signs of weakness were soon perceived as attacks on their personal freedom. The enemy the country needed protection against was not a disease "no worse than the flu," but a liberal bureaucracy intent on weakening and feminizing the once strong American people. Refusal to wear a mask became a sign of resistance.

Trump put down Biden as weak and insecure for wearing a mask, and the right put down the weak-kneed, overreacting left for doing the same. Maskless crowds gathered in churches and at Trump rallies, and the virus increasingly took its toll. One noteworthy early superspreader event was the ten-day Sturgis Motorcycle Rally in August 2020. More than 460,000 bikers gathered in a small town in South Dakota, with fewer masks in evidence than T-shirts saying, "Screw Covid-19." An attendee from Colorado, echoing Trump's words about the virus, said, "I'm not convinced it's real. I think it's nothing more than the flu. If I die from the virus, it was just meant to be."[34]

A team of researchers investigated the impact of the Sturgis Motorcycle Rally by using anonymous cellphone location data to look at case counts of the virus, and specifically Covid-19 trends in the parts of the country with the most attendees. Within weeks, the health consequences of the biker rally were apparent. The researchers reported that 266,796 cases of the virus could be linked to the Sturgis rally. The public health costs associated with the increased caseload were estimated at $12.2 billion, enough to have paid each of the 462,182 attendees $26,553.64 to stay home.[35]

When Trump, during his reelection campaign, himself came down with the virus and was sick enough to be taken to Walter Reed National Military Medical Center, he committed himself to a show of strength. While in the hospital he took a brief ride in his armored SUV to wave to supporters and signal to the public that he was doing well. This was pure political theater, but it endangered the two Secret Service agents who rode with him in the hermetically sealed vehicle. Doctors and Secret Service agents alike were appalled by the stunt.[36] Once Trump had Covid, did he use it as a teaching moment? Did he urge people to take measures to avoid the virus? No. Instead he once again played the strongman. He insisted on leaving the hospital after only a few days, returned to the White House, and made a prominent display of removing his mask while facing the public on the Truman Balcony.

Wearing masks to protect against the disease thus became a symbol of weakness on the right, and going without a mask became a sign of strength—it meant that you were tough enough not to buy in to the liberal overreaction. Importantly, it also identified you as a loyal follower of Trump. Wearing a mask would risk ostracism by his acolytes. It would bring shame: one would be forced to view oneself as weak, gullible, and disloyal. Recall that shame, as opposed to guilt, follows proscriptive transgressions.

It was the left that wore masks but saw them as a sign of neither strength nor weakness. Those are currencies of Social Order morality, not Social Justice morality. When it comes to ensuring the health and welfare of the population, strength and power are inconsequential. Obviously, regardless of one's political views, people should follow the recommendations of public health experts when responding to a pandemic, and liberals chose to wear masks when the scientific consensus supported doing so. But there is another reason compliance with science was so successful on the left. Masks became a symbol of cooperation—of providing benefit to others and not simply oneself. On the left, masks became an expression of concern for your neighbors. People covered their faces with the sense of pride that comes from generosity and altruistic motives. Failure to wear a mask was seen as a sign of selfishness, not strength. A person who did not do so would feel guilty for having failed in the obligation to help others. Guilt is a prescriptive self-indictment, just as Social Justice is a prescriptive morality.

A Return to Political Messaging

In the fall of 2020, with almost fourteen million people unemployed and more than two hundred thousand already dead from the virus he mismanaged, Trump turned to "law and order" to fuel his reelection campaign. These are words that directly cater to conservatives' Social Order concerns. Recognizing the powerful role of fear in appealing to conservatives, he used graphic images of street clashes and Black-on-white assaults, melding racism and violence. When nationwide Black Lives Matter protests against police misconduct led to incidents of violence, he was quick to retweet videos of his supporters "defensively" attacking protesters. As was often the case for Trump, his tactics, though more overt and weaponized than those of his political predecessors, nevertheless drew from a playbook that had been written decades earlier, coupling fear of disorder with racism.

The Republican Party's southern strategy was an electoral ploy created to increase the support of white southern voters.[37] The dismantling of Jim Crow laws and the momentum of the civil rights movement in the 1960s deepened white grievance and racial tensions in the South. Republican politicians used these grievances to claim to white southerners that they, not the Democrats, had become the party that best represented conservative white interests. The southern strategy worked: it brought about the political realignment of the South. As the *New York Times* columnist Bob Herbert wrote, "There was very little that was subconscious about the G.O.P.'s relentless appeal to racist whites. Tired of losing elections, it saw an opportunity to renew itself by opening its arms wide to white voters who could never forgive the Democratic Party for its support of civil rights and voting rights for blacks."[38]

Research on political messaging has shown that messaging that links Blacks to crime, or welfare, benefits conservative candidates and hurts liberal candidates.[39] Trump's coupling of racism with the fear of violence recalls Richard Nixon's coded language of "law and order" as shorthand for stopping Black "aggressors" and civil rights marches and protests. When George H. W. Bush ran against the Democrat Michael Dukakis in 1988, his infamous Willie Horton ad specifically played on fears of Black criminals. (Willie Horton was a Black convict who had committed a murder after being given a weekend furlough from a Massachusetts prison while Dukakis was the state's governor.) Trump's turn to fear and racism in the final months of his reelection campaign was thus hardly a novel appeal to voters on the right. The Republican Party by then had a tradition of taking a legitimate motive, that of protecting the group, and twisting it to get votes. Conservative voters were susceptible to these tactics because of their threat-sensitive reactions to "dissimilar others."

Reactions to Outsiders: Immigration
and the Rural-Urban Divide

In recent years, some popularized work has suggested that conservatives are more charitable than liberals. The initial source of this
belief was Arthur C. Brooks's book *Who Really Cares: The Surprising
Truth About Compassionate Conservatism* (2006). Brooks found that
a smaller percentage of income had been donated to charity in states
that voted for the Democratic presidential nominee John Kerry in
2004 compared with states that voted for the Republican nominee
George W. Bush, and twenty-four of the twenty-five states where
charitable giving was above average also went for Bush. Conservative
pundits ran with it, particularly because it seemed to counter the
stereotype of the generous, compassionate liberal. The conservative
columnist George Will titled his op-ed "Bleeding Hearts but Tight
Fists."[1] In 2012, the *Chronicle of Philanthropy* released "How America
Gives," a report that included a section on "America's Giving Divide." Based on Internal Revenue Service data, the report presented
giving patterns across the United States, and one of the key findings
was again that Republican states gave more to charity than Democratic states. The eight states with the most generous residents went
for McCain in 2008, and the seven states with the least generous residents went for Obama.

In a more recent paper, however, the political scientists Michele F.

Margolis and Michael Sances reached a different conclusion. Reanalyzing the data, they found no relation between charitable donations and Republican presidential vote share.[2] Importantly, however, they found that there were large differences in *where* liberals and conservatives gave their money, with Republican donations largely going to their own churches. The researchers noted that "conservatives give more to religious organizations, especially their own church, and liberals give more to secular charities."[3] States that voted for George W. Bush and John Kerry in 2004 differed, not in how much they gave, but rather in where they donated their money.

We see a similar pattern when we compare charitable donations reported by the Republican nominee Mitt Romney and the Democratic nominee Barack Obama during the 2012 presidential campaign. Romney donated a larger percentage of his income (29.4 percent versus 21.8 percent), but fully 80 percent of Romney's contributions were to the Mormon Church, and another large share went to a family foundation that also directed money to the church. The Obamas' charitable contributions included no church donations and went to a variety of secular and humanitarian organizations.[4]

When giving to their own churches, conservatives are in essence benefiting the people most like themselves—and indirectly, benefiting themselves. Certainly many churches engage in social welfare efforts, although research suggests the percentage of donations going toward such efforts is relatively small, typically between 10 percent and 25 percent, with 75 percent of donations going to local church operations.[5] Regardless, it is telling that conservatives choose to give more to their churches than to more distant humanitarian charities. Liberals are more likely to give to groups that do not directly benefit themselves or those most like themselves.

Liberals cast a wider net of collective responsibility, which we would expect if Social Justice and greater equality characterize their binding morality. This wider net was captured in a recent series of studies that again found that liberals and conservatives donate similar amounts to charities, but liberals give to a greater number of charities and causes, whereas conservatives donate to fewer. Using my moral map, MMM, the researchers found that the difference between breadth (liberals) and depth (conservatives) of giving was accounted for by the respective Social Justice and Social Order orientations of the donors.[6]

Both liberals and conservatives are charitable and aim to help others, but they differ in how they go about it. Conservatives are likely to choose familiar causes and churches, populated by people like them. This correspondence in identity is less important for liberals, who are more apt to choose charities based on correspondence in goals—that of helping vulnerable or less privileged groups attain a greater share of society's benefits. These choices reflect differences in their fundamental motivation—to protect the group or provide for its members—and also tell us something important about how each defines its own "group."

How Important Is Common Identity?

For conservatives, tradition, conformity, and threat sensitivity all serve communal stability and security. To protect the group, Social Order morality calls for vigilance regarding potential threats. From this perspective it is critical to identify who is in the group and who is not. The more "like me" another is, the less threatening. A Social Order morality fosters particularized trust, which is limited to family, friends, and those who share one's social identity (one's tribe or ethnic group). Social Justice, associated with psychological openness, encourages generalized trust.[7] These differences are apparent in each side's charitable contributions.

Social Order binds people into relatively homogeneous groups with strong boundaries, because common social identity is an important feature of membership. These are the people regarded as "safe." Social Justice binds people into more heterogeneous groups with relatively permeable boundaries. Here the most important characteristic is not identity but rather interdependence based on shared goals. For both groups, binding is less about physical communities than psychological ones—that is, perceptions of who belongs in my circle of moral concern.

These differences correspond to distinctions first drawn by Émile Durkheim, whose doctoral dissertation and first book, *The Division of Labour in Society*, was published in France in 1893. Durkheim distinguished between two means of unifying societies—mechanical and organic solidarity. Mechanical solidarity characterizes societies in which people resemble each other; they are similar in traditions and beliefs and are connected by personal ties. These groups share a "collective consciousness." In contrast, "likeness" is not the basis for organic solidarity. Instead, the basis is mutual need; people need to rely on each other to minimize competition and maintain group harmony. Durkheim argued that societies characterized by mechanical solidarity feature greater individual self-sufficiency, whereas societies characterized by organic solidarity contain more interdependence and cooperation.[8] He also proposed that law operates differently in the two types of societies. In mechanical societies, the law emphasizes punishment, whereas in organic societies, the law's primary role is to remedy damage done to the community. These differences between what Durkheim called repressive and restitutive sanctions map onto the proscriptive versus prescriptive nature of Social Order and Social Justice, respectively.

Durkheim's descriptions of mechanical and organic solidarity characterize the differences between groups based in Social Order and those based in Social Justice, with their focuses on common social identity and interdependence, respectively. Recent studies by social psychologists echo these distinctions in identifying two ways that a group of people becomes an "entity" rather than merely a collection of individuals. Group identity can come from "essence," or shared attributes, or from "agency," or shared goals.[9]

Social Order morality, which encourages groups based on common identity, employs the resemblance criteria of mechanical solidarity and essence-based groups. In contrast, Social Justice morality fosters groups based on the interdependence and common goals of organic solidarity and agency.[10] Metaphorically, we might think of a thick band surrounding the Social Order collective, uniting group members who resemble one another into a tightly bound psychological community. In the case of the Social Justice collective, instead of a band encircling the group, we might think of a strong thread that runs from person to person within the group, tying them together through mutual responsibility. Both moralities bind the group, but they have different implications for inclusivity and exclusivity and for how group membership is perceived.

Peter Singer's conception of moral circles is informative here. People differ, he writes, in how broadly we engage in altruism and benevolence. Singer represents these differences as a series of concentric circles, with the self in the center and moving outward through family and friends to an outermost circle that encompasses all humans. The psychologist Susan Opotow has used the phrase "moral exclusion" to describe how some people and groups perceived as falling outside the boundaries of our moral consideration, beyond the "scope of justice," are more vulnerable to mistreatment and exploitation.[11]

We know from years of research that people prefer others like themselves. Ingroup favoritism is a robust phenomenon. People favor their own group when they allocate resources, even when the basis for the group is completely arbitrary.[12] Studies with young children have found that infants as young as a year prefer puppets that help similar others and hinder dissimilar others. These studies used infants' food preferences and mitten color to manipulate similarity. The similar puppet preferred the same food or wore the same mitten as the infant, and the dissimilar puppet preferred a different food or wore a different mitten color. The infants showed a decided preference for others with similar social preferences. Infants as young as six months old have been found to look longer at a native speaker and disfavor those with a foreign accent; at ten months they prefer toys from a person without a foreign accent. Children, before they can even talk, favor people who sound like familiar others. We seem to have an innate or early developing tendency to prefer those who are like us.[13]

This tendency to favor others like us has been called "parochial altruism."[14] But the question of openness to others remains. How likely are we to consider people members of our psychological community and include them in our circle of moral concern? Given conservatives' emphasis on security and their sensitivity to threat, it is not surprising that recent research has shown that they have less expansive moral circles than liberals. The findings regarding charitable contributions, discussed above, are suggestive of these differences.

Jesse Graham and colleagues have distinguished between centrifugal and centripetal forces in our moral circle. The centrifugal force pushes outward, from family and local community to the outermost circles, whereas the centripetal force pulls us inward to family, kin, and tribe. The centripetal force leads us to care for those close to us, whereas the centrifugal force widens our circle of moral concern to include strangers. In describing the group-based moralities in my moral map, Graham and colleagues concluded, "While social justice concerns are primarily centrifugal . . . (urging for expansion of moral regard, as in women's rights, civil rights, and gay rights movements), social order concerns are primarily centripetal (urging for protecting ingroups and maintaining hierarchies)."[15]

Liberals' psychological openness suggests that their moral circles will likely be extensive, promoted by centrifugal forces pushing the boundaries outward. For some, this is a process based in empathy, rooted in emotional connections.[16] But it is not a necessary path, and it may in fact be a route less traveled. Both psychologists and philosophers have called empathy an inappropriate guide to morality, because empathy is naturally parochial, favoring those closest and most similar to us. Paul Bloom argues for "rational compassion," and Steven Pinker writes of the need for reason's "universalizing boost," which moves us away from tribalism and purity to humanism and human rights. For liberals, the morality of Social Justice pushes the moral circle outward. This may involve empathy, rationality, or both.[17]

The Social Order focus on keeping the group safe produces a relatively insular outlook, with a morality centered on "people like me"— family, friends, and similar others. The Social Justice focus on communal sharing and equality produces a more inclusive morality focused on a wider, heterogeneous community. The "us-them" boundary for Social Order morality is strong and relatively impermeable, whereas the boundary for Social Justice morality is more permeable. These differences are clearly reflected in the two sides' different reactions to immigration.

The Politics of Immigration

Other than the 2 percent of the population that is Native American, people in the United States are descended from people who came from elsewhere. Some came against their will as slaves, the rest as immigrants seeking a better life. According to a Pew Research Center report conducted in 2020, immigrants make up about 14 percent of the U.S. population (approximately 45 million persons). The undocumented portion of this population is currently about 11 million, of whom more than half have lived in the United States for over a decade. Given that so much of the effort to curb illegal entry focuses on border security, it is noteworthy that almost half of the undocumented population arrived in the country legally and have overstayed their visas.[18]

Immigration has been an intensely controversial issue throughout much of the nation's history. As early as 1880, laws severely restricted immigration from Asia, and between 1921 and 1965 the national-origins formula based immigration on the proportion of population from each country already in the United States. This had the intended effect of limiting immigration from eastern Europe, southern Europe, and Asia while keeping entry for Protestant western Europeans relatively easy. Politicians on both the left and right continue to propose policies to remedy immigration-associated issues. President Obama established the Deferred Action for Childhood Arrivals (DACA) program to help those who arrived unlawfully in the United States as children and have no criminal records, and he tried to extend the program to undocumented parents of U.S. citizens and permanent residents (Deferred Action for Parents of Americans, or DAPA). A number of states sued, and in 2016 the DAPA program was killed by the Supreme Court.[19]

As a candidate in 2016, Donald Trump ran on promises to curb immigration by building a wall on the border with Mexico, ban entry by Muslims, and deport millions of undocumented immigrants, all of which he persistently pursued as president while also cruelly separating families at the border. The Trump administration tried to eliminate DACA, but in June 2020 the Supreme Court issued a decision upholding the program. High-decibel political debates continue in and out of government, with no progress toward comprehensive immigration reform.

Liberals and conservatives bring to these debates different perceptions of their psychological ingroups and distinct perspectives on providing, protecting, and vigilance toward outsiders. Not surprisingly, then, the left and right have different attitudes toward immigrants to the United States, with liberal attitudes far more favorable than conservative attitudes. For example, 88 percent of Democrats and Democratic-leaning independents believe that immigrants strengthen the country with their hard work and talents, but this number drops to 41 percent for Republicans and Republican-leaning independents. Only 8 percent of the Democratic group view immigration as a burden, compared with 44 percent of the Republican group. Regarding undocumented immigrants in particular, shortly before the midterms in 2018, 75 percent of registered voters who planned to vote for a Republican in Congress viewed "illegal immigration" as a very big problem in the country, compared with just 19 percent of those who planned to vote for a Democrat.[20]

In a survey conducted in 2020, participants were asked about critical threats to the United States' vital interests in the next ten years. Republicans rated "large numbers of immigrants and refugees coming into the U.S." as the third greatest threat to the nation, outdone only by "the development of China as a world power" (number 1) and "international terrorism" (number 2). The threat of immigrants and refugees did not even appear on the Democrats' list, which was headed by "the Covid-19 pandemic" (number 1), "climate change" (number 2), and "racial inequality in the U.S." (number 3).[21] These dramatically different lists clearly illustrate the distinct moralities of each group. Concerns about public health, welfare, and equality are hallmarks of the Democrats' Social Justice interests, whereas an emphasis on safety and security pervades the Social Order concerns of Republicans.

Interestingly, on the right, invaders of a different sort have served as a powerful metaphor promoting anti-immigrant attitudes. Immigrants have long been associated with disease and have often been described as germs contaminating and infecting the body politic. As Howard Markel and Alexandra Minna Stern write, "Anti-immigrant rhetoric and policy have often been framed by an explicitly medical language . . . in which the line between perceived and actual threat is slippery and prone to hysteria and hyperbole."[22] Perhaps not surprisingly, disgust sensitivity is positively correlated with anti-immigration attitudes, and as we saw, conservatives score higher on disgust sensitivity.

In general, the more dissimilar—culturally, linguistically, religiously—an immigrant group is to a nation's dominant group, the greater the disapproval.[23] And when immigrants do not resemble the dominant group, the difference between liberals and conservatives is particularly marked. For example, when Arabic or Hispanic names were cued in research, conservatives reacted far more negatively than liberals to the prospect of those groups immigrating to the United States.[24] Compared with liberals, conservatives have greater distrust of outgroups to begin with, and perceiving greater differences in identity maximizes moral exclusion on the right.

With their sensitivity to threat and their Social Order morality reflected in strong group boundaries, conservatives would be likely to argue that immigration presents real dangers and that people who are in the country illegally are a particular danger. Liberals, with their permeable group boundaries and greater inclusiveness, are likely to include immigrants within their circle of moral concern. In recent research, we explored reactions to undocumented immigrants and found that political orientation was predictably linked to support for policies that punish (conservatism) or help (liberalism) undocumented immigrants. Reflecting the work of Kurt Gray and Dan Wegner on moral typecasting, participants viewed the undocumented either as victims or as harm doers.[25]

When undocumented immigrants were viewed as agents of harm, five themes emerged: they take undeserved benefits, take jobs from Americans, don't pay taxes, threaten the safety of Americans, and make entry by legal immigrants more difficult. When they were viewed as victims, three themes emerged: they fled bad circumstances, are exploited in the United States, and deserve basic human rights that they may be denied in the United States. Perceiving them as agents of harm produced elevated levels of disgust and anger, which in turn was associated with support for punishing policies. Perceiving them as victims increased levels of sadness, guilt, and empathy, which in turn led to support for policies that helped the immigrants.[26]

A sense of shared humanity and community was reflected in compassionate feelings and a willingness to support public policies that help undocumented immigrants. In contrast, those who supported punishment viewed the immigrants as "others" and were more likely to feel anger and disgust than sadness and empathy. These differences map onto Social Justice and Social Order moralities and their differences in openness to outsiders and distrust of them. Conservatives are likely to focus on their outsider status, liberals on their common humanity; conservatives focus on securing intergroup boundaries, liberals on intragroup cooperation and responsibility. Echoing their respective moralities, conservatives take a restrictive position toward immigrants and liberals take an enabling position.

Donald Trump's xenophobic focus on an invasion of criminals, thugs, and terrorists played on conservatives' restrictive attitudes with alarmist falsehoods. Immigrants are actually less likely to commit crimes than native-born Americans.[27] Research on the impact of low-skilled workers is more mixed, but a recent report from the National Academy of Sciences, Engineering, and Medicine concluded that over the long term, immigration has a net positive impact on economic growth and innovation. The study also reported that "there is little evidence that immigration significantly affects the overall employment levels of native-born workers" and that any impact on wages is "very small." As for its fiscal impact on state budgets, immigration has a negative fiscal effect when the cost of educating immigrant children is included, but these "children of immigrants, on average, go on to be the most positive fiscal contributors in the population."[28]

The labor market competition hypothesis argues that people who compete with immigrants for jobs are more anti-immigration than those who do not. But this hypothesis "has repeatedly failed to find empirical support, making it something of a zombie theory."[29] It does not appear to be job competition that turns people against immigrants.

And it is not government benefits that bring immigrants to America. The "welfare magnet hypothesis," developed in the late 1990s by economist George Borjas, has been popular on the right but is not supported by research. Most immigrants to the United States are not interested in living on the dole. Rather, they are drawn to the country by social networks and jobs and are driven from their native countries by political persecution, violence, natural disasters, and poverty.[30]

Hierarchy and Status Threat

Explicit immigrant-based fears are typically related to crime, jobs, and resources, but conservatives are often concerned about a very different type of threat. This is the threat they perceive to their own group's status and standing, arising from their own discomfort with "outsiders" and dissimilar others.

From the perspective of the common identity valued in Social

Order–based groups, the nation has changed a great deal in recent decades. In 1950, about 10 percent of the country was non-white. By 2014 this number was 38 percent. The large wave of immigration began in the 1960s, with people coming first from Latin American and then from Asia. Although Mexico is now the country of origin of the greatest number of U.S. immigrants, immigration from Mexico has slowed in recent years, and more are coming from Asia and Central America. The Pew Research Center projects that by 2055, Asians will surpass Hispanics as the largest immigrant group in the country. The U.S. census projects that by 2044, the majority of the U.S. population will be non-white.[31]

Social psychologists Maureen Craig and Jennifer Richeson conducted a series of studies on the impact of the predicted majority-minority in the future United States. They found that when they pointed out that demographic shift to white participants, it moved them to express greater political conservatism and endorse more conservative policies, including positions regarding immigration, affirmative action, and health care reform. In an extension of this research, Brenda Major and colleagues found a similar conservative shift, but only in participants for whom race or ethnicity was central to their identity. For these highly identified whites, reminders that non-white racial groups will outnumber whites by midcentury led them to express concern about the declining influence and status of their (white) group, which in turn led to greater support of anti-immigration policies and of Donald Trump specifically. Given the importance of common group identity for conservatives, coupled with the threat of "outsiders," the strong identification in the study's white participants was unsurprisingly associated with political party. The higher the white racial or ethnic identification, the greater the likelihood of Republican affiliation.[32]

As the country's racial and ethnic makeup has changed, the gap in the two parties' relative diversity has grown. According to the Pew Research Center, 40 percent of registered Democratic voters were non-white in 2020, compared with only 17 percent of registered Republicans. As Alan Abramowitz makes clear in *The Great Alignment,* since the 1980s the non-white share of the population has increasingly identified with the Democratic Party, and the shrinking white share of the population has increasingly identified as Republican. Religious whites in particular have become more conservative and a major force in the Republican Party.[33]

Social Justice morality promotes group heterogeneity, whereas Social Order morality promotes group homogeneity. Democrats have become increasingly heterogeneous while Republicans have remained largely homogeneous. For two centuries, white Christians have been dominant in the United States, economically, culturally, and politically, as they have constituted the majority of the electorate. Now many of them feel threatened by the changes in society and their declining numbers. They see themselves—and others like them—as endangered "real Americans" and view the country they grew up in disappearing. Trump's message of "Make America Great Again" speaks to this group. It is a veiled promise to ensure that white Christians remain dominant—to make America remain *their* country. Research shows that in the election of 2016, Trump voters were motivated primarily by anxiety around status loss rather than economic insecurity.[34]

Conservatives' anxiety about losing their standing and influence to "outsiders" is magnified by the importance they place on hierarchy. Social psychologists Jim Sidanius and Felicia Pratto have done important research on social dominance orientation, a measure of a person's belief in the desirability of hierarchy and their support for the domination of certain groups over other groups. The conservative interest in Social Order suggests the appeal of an ordered ranking of groups, a hierarchy. It is therefore not surprising that political conservatism is positively correlated with social dominance orientation. Sidanius and Pratto have also found that this measure is a powerful predictor of racial and ethnic prejudice, including denigration of Blacks, Hispanics, Asians, Arabs, Jews, Muslims, and immigrants and refugees generally. Regarding Blacks in particular, they found a "robust" positive relation between social dominance orientation and anti-Black racism, with strong correlations found within every U.S. sample studied.[35]

The social hierarchy serves a dual purpose for conservatives: it maintains order and stability in that people "know their place," and it reinforces conservatives' perception that they deserve dominant status in a changing world.[36] For many, the shifting face of America has created deep feelings of social threat and resentment. The election of President Obama was cause for disquiet, rather than celebration and pride as it was on the left. That the highest office in the land was occupied by a Black man raised alarm bells for many on the right about their own group's continued dominance.

This resentment is all too apparent in the grievance-sodden, hate-filled white supremacists who came out of the shadows, encouraged and buoyed by Trump's racist and xenophobic rhetoric and anti-democratic policies. Their objective is social dominance and, in particular, the subjugation of Blacks and Jews. Yet the response to perceived group status threat exists in a less virulent form among many white Christians who believe they have lost their long-held place in America.

Perhaps nowhere is this more apparent than in rural America, where residents believe that "others," particularly Blacks, are to blame for their economic stagnation. In *Strangers in Their Own Land,* Arlie Hochschild tells this powerful "deep story" on the right; it is the story of rural America. Using the metaphor of standing in a long line running uphill with the American dream on the other side of it, she describes the sentiments of the rural Americans she got to know. They are white Christians who believe they deserve the American dream but feel they are being held back by others who are unlike them. Race is a key element in this story.

> You have shown moral character through trial by fire, and the American Dream of prosperity and security is a reward for all this, showing who you have been and are—a badge of honor. . . . You haven't gotten a raise in years and there is no talk of one. . . . You're not a complainer. You count your blessings. You wish you could help your family and church more, because that's where your heart is. . . . But this line isn't moving. And after all your intense effort, all your sacrifice, you're beginning to feel stuck. . . . Look! You see people *cutting in line ahead of you!* You're following the rules. They aren't. As they cut in, it feels like you are being moved back. How can they just do that?

There is a desperation in much of rural America, a desperation that was visible long before the pandemic in abandoned factories, collapsed barns, and empty storefronts across the landscape. This is what falling behind looks like. Rural white Americans harbor a deep distrust of outsiders and of government spending on services, which they believe benefits the "line-cutters" who cheat the system.

Rural Versus Urban America

Geography has become a marker for political identity. In the 1950s, nearly 80 percent of the American electorate were married white Christians, and they were more or less equally divided between the two parties. By the 2000s, the same demographic constituted barely

40 percent of the electorate.[37] And the change did not come to rural and urban communities equally. The countryside remains predominantly white and Christian, and our cities are a mix of races, religions, and ethnicities. Rural residents live predominantly in homogeneous white communities, whereas urban dwellers live in heterogeneous communities. The parochialism of rural America and cosmopolitanism of urban America have fueled their divergent political orientations.

Distrust and resentment have characterized the rural-urban relationship from our nation's earliest days. In a letter to James Madison in 1787, Thomas Jefferson wrote, "I think our governments will remain virtuous for many centuries; as long as they are chiefly agricultural. . . . When they get piled upon one another in large cities, as in Europe, they will become corrupt as in Europe."[38] In Jefferson's time, farmers and others living in the countryside made up the bulk of the population, and they viewed cities as places filled with immigrants, the poor, and the corrupt.

Rural residents no longer make up 95 percent of the population, as they did when the Constitution was written. The shift to a majority urban population happened in 1920, and now just one in five Americans lives in a rural setting. But the early distrust of cities and their residents was written into the Constitution, which favors nonurban America by providing two senators for every state—meaning that Wyoming, with 580,000 residents, has the same power in the Senate as California, with 40 million. Theoretically today, states with only 17 percent of the national population can elect a Senate majority.[39] The Electoral College, too, established a strong pro-rural bias. In seven of the last eight elections, the Democratic candidate won the popular vote, but in two of those elections the candidate with the most votes (Al Gore and Hillary Clinton) did not become president.

The United States is a patchwork of religions, ethnicities, races, and countries of origin, but societal groups are not randomly distributed.

Our political orientations are influenced by the size, density, and diversity of our communities. As the journalist Josh Kron has written,

> The new political divide is a stark division between cities and what remains of the countryside. Not just some cities and rural areas, either—virtually every major city (100,000-plus population) in the United States of America has a different outlook from the less populous areas that are closest to it. The difference is no longer about *where* people live, it's about *how* people live: in spread-out, open, low-density privacy— or amid rough-and-tumble, in-your-face population density and diverse communities that enforce a lower-common denominator of tolerance among inhabitants.[40]

Rural American towns are red and cities are blue. Some of the most liberal cities in the country are in conservative red states. Every major city in Texas, for example—Austin, Dallas, Houston, and San Antonio—voted Democratic in the past four presidential elections. Joe Biden won the 2020 presidential election not by flipping red counties but by exceeding Hillary Clinton's win margins in urban and suburban areas. Among cities, the larger the population and the higher the density and level of education, the more likely it is the city votes Democratic.[41]

These rural-urban divergences have been called the density divide, reflecting the differences between dense diverse populations and sparse white populations. Our low-density rural areas are conservative and vote Republican. Thus Trump was able to win 80 percent of U.S. counties in the 2016 election, but they contained less than half the U.S. population and accounted for only a third of the nation's gross domestic product.[42]

There are liberals in our small towns and conservatives in our cities, but if you live in a city you are more likely to be liberal, and if you live in rural America you are more likely to be conservative. There is certainly some self-sorting involved, with conservatives choosing small towns and liberals moving to cities; people often choose to live in communities where others share their beliefs, politics, and general outlook.[43]

But places also influence people's politics. "The voting data," Kron writes, "suggest that people don't make cities liberal—cities make people liberal."[44] If you are not liberal when you move to the city, you're likely to become more liberal over time, and more conservative if you move to rural America. The imperceptible norms of your environs have a power all their own, as illustrated in the words of a city dweller regarding immigration:

> In the country . . . chances are pretty good that all your friends and neighbors look and sound just like you. That's because people who live in small towns are mostly born there, and it's pretty rare that anyone new moves in. So when people talk about illegal immigrants coming to America to live large on our welfare system, it's easy to believe whatever you hear and even easier to demonize them because you've never had a conversation with one. . . . But in the city . . . suddenly multiculturalism isn't some failed, politically correct agenda, it's just your neighborhood. Cities are diverse because this is where people come to find jobs, and the vast majority of immigrants, both legal and illegal, live in them. By the time you show up in town, this huge kumbaya-world stew has already been boiling for ages. When you live around people from all over the world, you get to see first hand that most immigrants are normal, hard-working people, just with cool accents and better food.[45]

A *Washington Post*–Kaiser Family Foundation survey showed that attitudes toward immigrants form one of the "widest gulfs" between urban and rural communities. Rural residents are three times more likely than city dwellers to view immigrants as a burden to the United States.[46] Interactions with others who differ by race, ethnicity, nationality, or religion is very limited in our rural towns, and negative stereotypes and prejudices prevail most where homogeneity also prevails.

In relating the racial resentment of bayou country Louisianans, Hochschild makes clear that these rural residents didn't have Black neighbors or colleagues. Instead, Black people entered their lives on the television screen or in newspaper stories, either as criminals and welfare recipients or as rich celebrities. "Missing from the image of blacks in most of the minds of those I came to know was a man or woman standing patiently in line next to them waiting for a well-deserved reward."[47] Missing, too, were Black co-workers, church members, or parents of children in the local school—that is, opportunities in daily life to see similarities. The conservative preference for common identity is satisfied in rural America by the absence of cross-race interactions. The white grievance that has increasingly defined contemporary conservatism is abetted by the demographics of the rural-urban divide.

The Benefits of Contact

The positive impact of intergroup contact in reducing prejudice, particularly between racial and ethnic groups, is a well-documented finding in social science research. Thomas Pettigrew and Linda Tropp conducted a meta-analysis to evaluate the contact hypothesis. A meta-analysis is a statistical technique that enables researchers to combine the results of multiple studies. Pettigrew and Tropp's meta-analysis was based on 515 separate studies, and the combined findings support the debiasing effects of intergroup contact.[48]

In an early formulation of the contact hypothesis, Gordon Allport claimed in *The Nature of Prejudice* (1954) that contact reduces prejudice when it occurs between groups of equal status, in noncompetitive pursuit of common goals, and when supported by authority or custom. Yet Pettigrew and Tropp's meta-analysis found that these factors, though facilitative, are not necessary for the reduction of prejudice. Face-to-face contact reduces prejudice, and the more contact, the less prejudice there is. In a separate meta-analysis focused on what might account for the change, they also found that emotions play a particularly important role.[49] Contact serves to reduce anxiety and increase comfort around cross-race interactions, and it also increases the likelihood that one may take the other group's perspective and empathize with its concerns.

Work by Xuechunzi Bai, Miguel Ramos, and Susan Fiske provides an additional perspective on the positive impact of contact on intergroup perceptions and relationships.[50] The researchers examined the effects of diversity on people's stereotypes of other groups and found that the more diversity they experienced, the more people perceived other ethnic groups as similar to their own. People with the least exposure to multiple ethnicities stereotyped other groups the most and saw them as most dissimilar to themselves. This research provides an important lens on the cognitive impact of diversity; contact with ethnically dissimilar others promotes a perception of greater commonality.

When intergroup contact occurs between people with common goals or engaged in cooperative tasks, it is all the more effective at counteracting biases. When people of different races, religions, ethnicities, sexual orientations, or countries of origin find themselves working together on the same community board, job-related task, or neighborhood event, they get to know one another as multidimensional people rather than "others"—as humans who may have different perspectives born of different life experiences but who also share common human concerns, emotions, problems, and joys.

Yet even without extended interactions, contact expands our moral circles as dissimilar others become more familiar. We see them walking down the street, standing at the checkout counter, sitting on the bus, standing on the subway. These are only surface contacts, yet they can have a positive impact on our views of dissimilar others. They are neutral yet frequent, and they permit a familiarity one could not experience in a homogeneous environment. The positive impact of these thin contacts may be a consequence of the "mere exposure effect." Social psychologists have found that liking increases with familiarity: the more familiar we are with something, the more we like it. For example, when white research participants were exposed to other-race faces, Asian faces in one study and Black faces in another, they showed increased liking for strangers of the same race. In cities, with their considerable diversity, this growing familiarity may happen outside our awareness and yet positively affect our attitudes toward other groups.[51]

The urban landscape is not white, as it is in rural America, but Black and white with every shade in between. Certainly not all of our intergroup interactions are positive, but the diversity of our cities, in race, religion, ethnicity, sexual preference, country of origin, and other characteristics, means that urban dwellers inevitably come into contact with people different from themselves. "For most of us," writes Justin Davidson,

> living in cities means living close to those who are both like us and not. Even just walking down a city block means having no idea who will cross your path, what they believe, or

how they will behave. Strolling is a succession of chance meetings, the vast majority of them superficial. At times, a dense neighborhood can feel like a village, where you bump into friends or revive dormant acquaintances. At other times, it means confronting a vast and entrenched homeless population. Urbanites take this haphazardness for granted. We have the ingrained habit of sharing space, of encountering differences, of swimming in the collective soup.[52]

The collective soup brings urbanites into contact with dissimilar others. And this contact fuels greater inclusion.

The moral underpinning of conservative, rural America is Social Order. Conforming to the community's strict norms demonstrates group allegiance, and strong deviance regulation produces conformity with traditional lifestyles and social roles. Religion plays an important part in reinforcing traditional roles and regulating personal conduct. In the countryside, residents rely on their shared identities and traditions to maximize group solidarity; it is relatively easy to coordinate community efforts. Members of the community generally trust their neighbors because these are typically people "like me." But they distrust outsiders, particularly others who differ in race, sexual orientation, religion, or ethnicity. These outsiders are generally invisible within the community and are largely perceived as threats to the group. Special attention is given to ingroup-outgroup boundaries, or us-them distinctions, and "us" is narrowly defined to include only those who most resemble the community's residents.[53]

Cities are core constituencies of the left. The moral underpinning of liberal, urban America, Social Justice, flourishes in the mix of races, religions, ethnicities, and lifestyles found in cities. Historically, the very location of cities increased the likelihood of a heterogeneous social environment. From the earliest time, urban centers developed along major waterways because these were the sites where goods could be brought for exchange. Waterborne trade inevitably brought people from different cultures and nations into contact with each other. The large populations and density of cities preclude solidarity based on a common social identity. Instead, as Durkheim proposed, solidarity rests on recognizing that the group's success depends on people working together toward common goals.[54]

The opportunities for meaningful interactions, and the countless times people of every color pass each other unbothered on the street, provide the basis for recognition and inclusion in the urbanite's moral community. This is certainly not to argue that either liberals or city dwellers are free of racism. The cities of the northern United States had their own versions of Jim Crow for many decades before these attitudes became socially unacceptable. Even today, when many urbanites abhor the thought of racial prejudice, the vast literature and research on implicit racism makes it clear that the majority of white Americans have non-conscious negative biases and negative stereotypes about Blacks—as we would expect in a society pervaded by systemic racism.[55]

The implicit association test, the primary assessment tool for implicit bias, finds bias when participants more quickly associate Black names or faces with negative words (such as *rotten* or *poison*) and white faces more quickly with positive words (such as *happy* or *love*).

There are questions about how best to interpret implicit association test results given problems with test-retest reliability and the low correlations between test scores and actual behavior.[56] In large part this is because people can "correct" for these biases and strive to act in non-racist ways when engaging in intentional, deliberative acts. Implicit prejudices are most apt to be associated with spontaneous and non-deliberative actions such as non-verbal behavior. Nevertheless, awareness of our implicit biases informs us of our personal responsibility in perpetuating racism and our responsibility as well to work for change, both interpersonal and structural.

The intergroup contact provided by diverse urban settings can reduce these biases—not only our explicit prejudices, which are strongly associated with our intentional actions, but our implicit biases as well. As Nilanjana Dasgupta concluded from multiple studies, "being embedded in naturally existing local environments that facilitate positive contact with members of stereotyped groups creates and reinforces positive implicit associations, thereby counteracting implicit bias."[57] Reducing implicit beliefs is likely a long-term process, but in homogeneous communities where "stereotyped groups" are absent or invisible, it cannot even begin.

There is much talk these days about humanity's tribalism, but there is strong reason to believe that our success as a species has a lot to do with our interactions with other groups. We know, for example, that genetic variability attained through mating with dissimilar others gives our species a biological advantage. Other advantages from contact with dissimilar others include increased skills, talents, and knowledge.

It is in our cities that intergroup contact is greatest—whether we are talking about race, religion, national origin, ethnicity, or sexual orientation. People in cities are apt to have expanded circles of moral concern that reflect the heterogeneity of their environment. And it is in cities that we find liberalism thriving. As Ivo Daalder has pointed out, "The history of liberalism is . . . the history of the city. Since at least the Dutch Golden Age, cities have been the locus of liberalism. . . . While the hinterlands have tended the flames of conservatism and tradition, urban centres have experimented with new political and economic freedoms and liberties. From globalisation to gay rights, most of the major transformations in our modern world began as urban novelties."[58]

PART TWO

Politics, Parties, and Policies

• • •

6

Party Politics and Policy Preferences

Despite cities' openness to multiple "others," the inclusiveness of urbanites does not extend to political orientation. Urban liberals are prejudiced against conservatives just as rural conservatives are against liberals. Republicans are prejudiced against Democrats, and Democrats are prejudiced against Republicans. There is disagreement about which group—liberals or conservatives—is more politically biased against the other, but it is clear that there is plenty of bias to go around and that these biases are not limited to a particular group or demographic.[1] It is fueled by potent policy differences that reflect deeper moral perspectives about how we should live together—about our priorities and obligations to one another.

Ideologies of Liberalism and Conservatism

Left and right, or liberal and conservative, are meaningful labels because they are associated with distinct ideologies. But what is an ideology? The political scientists Robert Erikson and Kent Tedin defined ideology as a "set of beliefs about the proper order of society and how it can be achieved."[2] This line from beliefs to actuality suggests the importance of policies to realize goals. According to Hans Noel, an ideology is a creative combination of ideas and policies that structures our positions on issues. Most simply, it is a "shared set of policy preferences" such that our beliefs about one issue can predict our beliefs about other issues. An ideology is thus a kind of constraint: it tells us what positions go together. "We know," Noel writes, "that favoring progressive taxation and abortion rights are both liberal positions because most people who are liberal agree on both of them. So ideology requires two things. It requires connections among opinions, and that the pattern among those connections be observed across many actors."[3]

In an ambitious empirical project aimed at uncovering the ideologies of the left and right or, more specifically, the policies that cohere on each side of the political spectrum, Noel created an extensive data set of political opinions in twenty-year intervals from 1850 to 1990. He drew these opinions from more than twenty-five politically relevant publications, including the *Atlantic, Harper's,* the *New Republic, National Review,* the *Nation, North American Review,* the *New York Times,* the *Wall Street Journal,* and the *Washington Post,* and coded more than 7,800 opinions for support or opposition to the issue discussed.[4] He was looking for coherence in the contributors' positions as evidence of ideology.

The most recent years in his data—1970 and 1990—contain the issues that continue to go together on the left and right. Among the causes favored by liberals were education spending, environmentalism, gun control, legal abortion, labor unions, legal aid for the poor, gay rights, low-income housing, affirmative action, and universal health care—all causes opposed by conservatives. Conservatives favored crime bills, military spending, privatizing Social Security, school choice, the death penalty, religion in public life, the drug war, and the free market, all of which were opposed by liberals. Overall, liberals supported policies that addressed social inequalities, and conservatives were in favor of those that preserved existing arrangements, both domestically and internationally—specifically a hawkish foreign policy, few economic regulations, and protection of the traditional family and religion.

The left's favored issues continue to reflect many of the economic beliefs of the early twentieth-century Progressive movement. Although many Progressives supported the social Darwinism of the late 1800s, others did not. People like Lester Ward, Josiah Royce, and Charles Peirce argued for a strong role for government in addressing inequality, which they believed was associated with other social problems. Herbert Croly in 1909 popularized these views in *The Promise of American Life,* in which he argued for a strong central government that could improve the lives of disadvantaged citizens through economic intervention. The launch of the *New Republic* in 1914 reflected the efforts of Croly, Walter Lippman, Walter Weyl, and others to create a guide for liberal ideas. Despite some trying times around World War I, the progressive ideas of liberalism became the ideology of the New Deal, and they continue to inform the left's policy focus on addressing societal inequalities.

The conservative focus on traditionalism, a hawkish foreign policy, and free-market capitalism found by Noel is the "three-legged stool" of conservatism that was codified in the mid-twentieth century by William F. Buckley and other key figures such as James Burnham, Russell Kirk, and Frank S. Meyer.[5] Buckley's book *God and Man at Yale* (1951) popularized conservative ideas; his attack on academics was also an argument for the dual values of market individualism and strong religious faith. But it was in *National Review,* the magazine he founded in 1955, that Buckley created a platform for these three strands of conservatism. *National Review* was the conservative counterpart of the *New Republic,* and it continues to serve as a forum and clearinghouse for conservative ideas.

The distinct ideological positions of liberals and conservatives are

POLITICS, PARTIES, AND POLICIES

apparent in their responses to attitudinal surveys. For example, John Jost, Brian Nosek, and Samuel Gosling found that liberals are more favorable toward welfare, same-sex marriage, feminists, environmentalists, and universal health care. Conservatives are more favorable toward the military, big corporations, and traditional sex roles ("the idea of women staying home")—attitudes that reflect their ideology's three-legged stool.[6]

Parties and Ideologies

In the United States today, political ideologies are more than ever associated with political parties. Ideologies entail mutually dependent policy preferences, whereas political parties are organized groups of political actors who want to control government in order to influence policy.[7] They are essentially coalitions trying to enact policies that reflect their own group's interests. Today the Democrats so strongly reflect a liberal ideology, and Republicans a conservative one, that the parties can basically stand in for liberal and conservative. This wasn't always the case. Parties strive to build coalitions to win elections, and historically this has led to ideological differences within each party.

The ideological diversity within the parties in the mid-twentieth century certainly belies any belief that ideology and party are one. Conservative Democrats, largely from the party's southern wing, included such segregationists as Strom Thurmond, Lester Maddox, and George Wallace. The moderate or liberal Republicans included such key political figures as Nelson Rockefeller, Thomas Dewey, Mark Hatfield, Charles Mathias, Jacob Javits, and Charles Percy. Party was not shorthand for liberal or conservative. The realignment began to take hold with the Civil Rights Act of 1964 and the Voting Rights Act of 1965, which began the conversion of conservative southern Democrats and the white working class to the Republican Party and of college-educated professionals to the Democratic Party. Yet in the case of the Civil Rights Act, Everett Dirksen, the Republican minority leader, worked with Mike Mansfield, the Democratic majority leader, to overcome a filibuster by southern Democrats. This ideological diversity has since disappeared. Ideology and party are now closely aligned, and liberal Republicans and conservative Democrats are essentially extinct species.[8]

The alignment means that compromise, discussion, and dissension within parties are much reduced and polarization between parties is far greater. Politics in the United States has always been a negotiation between the two moralities, but the two major parties have never been as monolithic in their moral convictions about the right and wrong way to regulate society. Social psychologists have found that there is something unique about convictions rooted in morality, as opposed to other strong attitudes, which more closely resemble preferences or tastes.

As Linda Skitka and her colleagues have demonstrated, moral convictions not only arouse strong emotions but are viewed as absolute and universal—or, more accurately, positions we believe should be universal. We know that others hold different views, but on moral questions we believe that they *should* share ours. We see moral convictions as more akin to facts, truths that are obviously right or wrong. There seems to be no continuum of "rightness" with morality but only two possibilities: right and wrong. If my moral view is right and you disagree, then your position is wrong. Perhaps not surprisingly, research has shown that we are intolerant of those with different moral convictions. In laboratory settings, participants who disagree morally even try to distance themselves physically.[9]

There is also something unique about groups that are based on moral convictions. In our own research we have found that when group memberships are rooted in morality, outgroup "hate" naturally occurs with ingroup "love." Our identification with groups not rooted in morality (such as our favored sports team) is primarily based on our positive attitudes toward our own group, even when there is a strong rival. But with groups rooted in morality, our identification is not based predominantly on our positive attitudes toward our own group but rests on our strong negative attitudes toward the outgroup as well.[10]

These unique characteristics of moral convictions and morality-based groups contribute to the polarization of our politics. In the first months of the Biden administration, the Democratic-controlled Congress passed President Joe Biden's $1.9 trillion stimulus package to address the economic needs of a nation suffering from the Covid-19 pandemic. The American Rescue Plan included direct checks to Americans, funding for states and schools, child tax benefits, and health care subsidies—a stimulus plan that was entirely an expression of Social Justice morality.

Not a single Republican voted for the bill. Republicans' major legislative efforts were taking place in statehouses, where they focused on voter suppression in the guise of preserving election integrity. Responding to historic voter turnout in the election of 2020, in which they lost the presidency and the Senate, Republicans in thirty-three states presented bills to restrict voting with new ID requirements as well as limits on early voting and mail-in voting in particular. A law passed in Georgia even banned anyone from sharing food or water with people standing in line to vote—lines that are notoriously far longer in Black voting districts than in majority-white districts. As Thomas Patterson noted, "If your base is ninety per cent white, and you're losing Asian-Americans by two to one, the Black vote by nine to one, and the Hispanics by two to one, voter suppression becomes the only viable strategic option."[11]

These weaponized election strategies exist atop the traditional three-legged stool of conservative policy preferences that continue to dominate the Republican Party. Thus, for example, although Trump's xenophobic rhetoric was meant to appeal to white grievances and to blue-collar workers in particular, he actually did little for American workers. His policy accomplishments were straightforward conservative fare. His two signature achievements were his tax bill, which greatly favored the wealthy, and his court appointments, which filled U.S. courts, from the Supreme Court on down, with Federalist Society–approved judges who were strongly pro-business and anti-abortion.

In his book *Partisan Politics,* Patrick Egan showed that the issues "owned" by each of the political parties have remained remarkably consistent over the past fifty years. From voters to party elites, Democratic and Republican partisans list their party's owned issues as those to which they give higher priorities than other issues; when the parties have power in Washington, they govern with these high-priority issues in mind. The top priorities consistently mentioned by Republicans are domestic security, the military, immigration, and taxes. The top priorities consistently mentioned by Democrats are education, energy, the environment, health care, jobs, and poverty.[12] Interestingly, Egan found no relation between a party's priorities and its success in addressing those issues when it was in control of government. Nevertheless, the parties' respective owned issues are quite stable.

Collective Morality and Individualism on the Left and Right

It is because issue positions are not mutually independent that we can meaningfully draw a liberal-conservative distinction. Every position conveys information about its adherents' other policy preferences. Some of these, however, are puzzling at first glance. Why would anti-choice abortion attitudes go with support for unfettered free-market capitalism? Why does support for religion in public life go with efforts to privatize Social Security? And what does support for same-sex marriage and abortion rights have to do with support for environmental regulation? The answers lie in the group-based moralities of Social Order and Social Justice.

Sometimes it appears that the policy positions of liberals and conservatives are simply opposites: whatever one group favors, the other opposes. This no doubt accounts for the common assumption among political scientists that ideology exists along a single dimension, ranging from liberal to conservative.[13] Although there is some usefulness to thinking of ideology this way, it obscures important differences between liberalism and conservatism, differences that reflect their moral underpinnings.

To understand the coherence of policies on each side of the political spectrum, we need to recall the features and aims of each collective morality. Social Order aims to protect the group from threats, both internal and external, and this is accomplished by maintaining a strong defense and by demanding adherence to strict norms and traditional roles in order to insure societal stability and security. Social Justice, meanwhile, aims to provide for the group. It accomplishes this by distributing resources to assure the well-being of group members and to attain greater societal equality.

A closer look at the two moralities suggests different views about what we should regulate as a society. For Social Order it is the social domain, where adherence to group norms takes place. For Social Justice it is the economic domain, where resources are distributed. Economic issues include taxation, market regulation, universal health care, education spending, and Social Security. Social issues include abortion, same-sex marriage, contraception, doctor-assisted suicide, gun control, drug policy, and embryonic stem-cell research.[14] In their respective domains of emphasis, the left and right both seek government intervention and regulation. In the opposite domains—the eco-

nomic domain for conservatives and the social domain for liberals—
the right and left value autonomy. These preferences account for the
coherence of policies on each side of the political spectrum.

In the election of 2004, votes based on social issues, especially opposition to legal abortion and to same-sex marriage, came to be known
as the "moral values vote." Twenty-two percent of the voters in that
election regarded these moral values as that year's most important
issue, and of this group fully 80 percent voted for George W. Bush.
Many reviews of the election concluded that Bush's win hinged on
this moral values vote.[15] For liberals, of course, this represented a mis-
use of the term *morality*, for their "moral values vote" meant something very different. It was based in greater equality and on economic
issues—on Social Justice rather than Social Order concerns.

In unpacking the political ideologies of the left and right it is
important to distinguish not only each group's political attitudes but
how they view regulation by the state. When do we want government involved? Which political positions should have the power of
state enforcement behind them, and which should be left to the individual? The laws and policies favored by liberals and conservatives
reflect their views about the appropriate place of government in people's lives.

Providing naturally involves directing resources to help others,
and therefore the economic domain is where the left seeks government intervention. Liberals favor strong regulation of the free market to prevent monopolies, punish fraud, ensure the safety of workers
and consumers, and prevent environmental degradation, as well as
universal health care, education spending, a higher minimum wage,
higher taxes on the wealthy, and strong safety nets in the form of Social Security, food stamps, and other social programs. These policies
reflect a sense of communal responsibility and interdependence; they
involve a commitment to greater equality and a belief that govern-

ment has an obligation to help vulnerable members of the community. Liberals seek government intervention in caring for the welfare of the nation.

Yet on social issues such as abortion and same-sex marriage, contraception and doctor-assisted suicide, liberals want the government to stay out of their lives. The social domain is neither the focus of their collective morality nor the appropriate domain for government intervention. The left views these as domains of individual autonomy, believing that people should be free to control their own bodies and pursue personal behaviors and lifestyles of their own choosing. The feminist mantra "Keep your laws off my body" reflects this commitment to personal freedom.

Conservatives, in their desire to protect the group, strive to maintain stability, security and the status quo; they value adherence to behavioral norms and traditional social positions. The Social Order morality naturally implicates social issues and favors government intervention into personal and social behaviors, including sexuality and family roles. The right wants the government to involve itself in such matters as abortion, same-sex marriage, doctor-assisted suicide, and what public bathrooms transgender people may use.

Yet in the economic domain, the right rejects government intervention and prefers unfettered individual freedom. Conservatives basically do not want the government involved in economic matters. Their pro-business position argues for competitive capitalism with state involvement limited to the bare minimum needed to keep markets functional: enforcement of contracts and prevention of fraud and theft. Within these bounds they favor a free market where people essentially prosper or fail on their own, and this means deregulation as well as no so-called government handouts. Most regulation in the economic domain is regarded as overregulation that will hobble economic growth.

Believing that the accumulation and distribution of resources are best left to the individual, conservatives favor lower taxes and oppose what they often call big government spending on social programs. They argue for fiscal responsibility and apply this to spending on health care, welfare, and safety nets more generally—in other words, "providing" by the left. When it comes to protective functions such as defense and policing, the right's concerns about fiscal responsibility dissipate. Budget deficits didn't seem to be a problem when conservatives were passing the Tax Cuts and Jobs Act of 2017, which the Congressional Budget Office predicted would increase the deficit by $1.9 trillion.[16] In the Senate, not a single Republican voted against the bill and not a single Democrat voted for it.

The protect and provide motives of the collective moralities tell us where each political group seeks government support and enforcement—where each seeks strong regulation and where it does not. The collective morality Social Justice is not concerned with consensual sexual conduct, but it seeks government regulation of areas having to do with relative wealth and the distribution of resources. The protect motive of Social Order morality is not concerned with resource distribution but instead seeks government intervention into the social behaviors that are believed to ensure societal stability.

In the domains that are not the concern of each collective morality—social issues for liberals and economic issues for conservatives—individual freedom and autonomy hold sway. In these domains we are expected to be moral, but the relevant motives are not those of the collective moralities. Instead they are the other motives of the moral map, especially the fundamental default morality of not harming. As John Stuart Mill noted in the first chapter of *On Liberty*, freedom involves "doing as we like, subject to such consequences as may follow; without impediment from our fellow-creatures, so long as what we do does not harm them even though they should think our conduct fool-

Domain:	Liberalism (Social Justice- Provide)	Conservatism (Social Order- Protect)
Regulation (government intervention)	**Economic Issues** e.g., free market, health care	**Social Issues** e.g., abortion, same-sex marriage
Autonomy (individual freedom)	**Social Issues** e.g., abortion, same-sex marriage	**Economic Issues** e.g., free market, health care

Domains of autonomy and regulation on the left and right

ish, perverse, or wrong." Neither the left nor the right has a lock on advocating individualism, freedom, and liberty. Each has its domain of autonomy and its domain of government involvement.

Michael Walzer notes that the U.S. Constitution provides the following list of public "goods": justice, tranquility, defense, welfare, and liberty.[17] Reflecting their distinct moralities, the left focuses on justice and welfare, the right on tranquility and defense. Both emphasize liberty, but in different domains.

The Fallacy of One-Sided Limited Government

The left's and right's preferred areas of government involvement suggest different forms of regulation. Conservatives' regulation of the social domain is restrictive. From abortion to drug use to same-sex marriage, the focus is on prohibiting behaviors. Liberals' regulation of the economic domain is enabling. From education to health to wel-fare, the focus is on activating resources to promote greater equality. These differences echo the proscriptive and prescriptive nature of So-cial Order and Social Justice, respectively. Recall that in its focus on avoidance, proscriptive morality involves the inhibition of behavior—avoiding an undesirable outcome. Prescriptive morality involves the activation of behavior—moving toward a desirable outcome. These differences are reflected in the dominant form of regulation each side pursues when it wants state intervention.

The combination of domain (economic or social) and form of regulation (activation- or inhibition-based) tells us general patterns of policy preferences on the left and right, but these are not etched in stone. When issues arise that directly implicate either protecting or providing, these moral motives are strongly determinative and over-ride the regulatory orientation. For example, on the left acceptance of government restraint and control in the social domain is evident in its strong advocacy of anti-discrimination laws that criminalize behaviors based on group prejudice and intolerance. The right typi-cally abhors large outlays of government money yet nevertheless seeks greater spending on the military, border control, and police, all of which are directly associated with protection, specifically defense. These are economic matters where, despite a professed desire for lim-ited government, they seek active government involvement. As Peter Ditto and Brittany Liu note, "Politicians of the left and right argue about runaway spending or intrusive regulation, framing them as gen-eral principles of effective governing, but a close look reveals that both sides are more than happy to spend money on government programs they see as moral (e.g., Democrats on social welfare, Republicans on defense)."[18]

It is conventional wisdom that conservatives favor limited government and liberals do not. Yet both groups seek government intervention; neither wants limited government in its domain of regulation, and both seek it in their domains of autonomy. If we judge limited government in terms of spending, liberal preferences for social safety nets and increased social welfare certainly suggest that they do not favor limited government. But conservatives absolutely want the government involved in banning abortion, same-sex marriage, and transgender bathroom use. They are decidedly not anti-government when it comes to personal choice in social domains that include sexuality and the family. This government-supported control in the social domain extends to policing of behavior outside the home as well, consistent with the protect aims of a Social Order morality.

Cognitive Consistency and Policy Positions

The policy positions on the left and right begin to cohere when we recognize their respective domains of government regulation and autonomy. We can make sense of liberals' simultaneous support for strong safety nets and abortion rights, or universal health care and same-sex marriage, and of conservatives' opposition to abortion and same-sex marriage while supporting deregulation in the marketplace. We need not agree with these positions to understand how the issue positions group themselves.

As noted above, the issues owned by each political party have remained stable for decades. The top issues for Republicans have been taxes, domestic security, the military, and immigration, and the top issues for Democrats have been poverty, jobs, health care, the environment, education, and energy.[19] Identifying with a political party presumably means that one supports its positions on the issues. Yet research has found that when study participants are asked to evaluate political issues that are supported by one or the other political party, the support of their preferred party, rather than the merits of the issue, is the primary determinant of their assessment. For example, in a well-cited study by Geoffrey Cohen, self-identified liberal and conservative participants read about a welfare policy—either an extremely generous policy or a stingy one.[20] Half of each group were told that the policy was supported by 95 percent of Democrats, the other half that it was supported by 95 percent of Republicans. Cohen found that the effect of party support overrode policy content and the participants' own ideological beliefs. Liberals supported a harsh policy if they thought it was favored by most Democrats, and conservatives supported a very generous policy if they thought it was favored by most Republicans.

These findings show the overwhelming power of party identity, but we must also recognize that the major parties have owned their policy positions for decades. Party support *should* tell us a great deal about an issue, particularly when we have little other information about it. In Cohen's research, the findings were driven in large part by a change in the assumed factual content of the welfare policies. In other words, study participants altered their perceptions of the welfare policies to make them more consistent with the parties' known ideologies.

In social psychology there is a long history of research on our penchant for cognitive consistency. From early work on cognitive dissonance to later work on motivated reasoning, study after study has shown that we interpret and remember events so as to support our preexisting beliefs and identities, and we also do this with our partisan identities. This is especially evident in the moral domain, where we not only selectively attend to supportive information but selectively interpret information to make it maximally consistent with our partisan views.[21] Although we believe ourselves to be purely rational animals, all too often we are rationalizing animals. Rather than deliberate from first principles, we typically recruit evidence that supports our positions, moving from conclusions to evidence rather than the other way around. We operate more like intuitive lawyers than intuitive scientists.[22]

A classic study of biased cognition, conducted in the early 1950s, showed that undergraduates at Dartmouth College and Princeton University seemed to actually see different games when viewing a contentious football game between the two schools, particularly when it came to "unsportsmanlike conduct." Similarly, when Democrats and Republicans view events with political relevance, we perceive different events. The left, for example, sees Black Lives Matter protesters as peaceful demonstrators, whereas the right sees them as dangerous agitators. In recent research by Dan Kahan and colleagues, participants viewed a video of a political protest and were told that the demonstrators were protesting against abortion outside an abortion clinic. Those with opposing partisan views of abortion disagreed considerably on key "facts," especially whether the protesters threatened and obstructed pedestrians.[23]

As partisans, we not only selectively attend to supportive information, as is evident in people's choices of social media sites and television news programs, but also selectively interpret information so as to be maximally consistent with our views. These selective exposure and interpretation processes serve to confirm our political perspectives and surely contribute to the polarization of partisan positions.

Beware of Labels

Liberals and conservatives, the left and right of the political spectrum, are the focus of this book. Yet labels can sometimes be confusing. Particularly unfortunate is the label "neoliberalism," which suggests an affinity with political liberalism when it is in fact a conservative ideology. Originated by Milton Friedman and the Chicago School, and secured in the elections of Ronald Reagan in the United States and Margaret Thatcher in the United Kingdom, the neoliberal position reflects foundational economic beliefs of political conservatism in arguing for economic freedom, competitive capitalism, and opposition to government regulation of economic activity. It favors reduced taxation and cuts to welfare and social safety nets. In other words, it is the conservative position on economics.[24]

"Classical liberalism" is not the same as political liberalism, or the left. As a political philosophy, classical liberalism broadly refers to freedom from constraints. Both the left and right favor individual freedom and autonomy, but in different domains. Classical liberalism values freedom and autonomy regardless of domain and is therefore more akin to libertarianism than liberalism. Whereas the moral positions of the left and right are both based in a collective morality— Social Justice for liberals and Social Order for conservatives—as we saw in chapter 3, there is a group without a collective morality, and that is libertarians. Libertarian morality is wholly individualistic, based on maximizing individual freedom and eschewing collective concerns. Libertarians espouse autonomy and oppose government intervention in both the economic and social domains. They are therefore likely to support an unfettered free market as well as same-sex marriage and a woman's right to choose abortion. In any given election they could vote for Democrats or Republicans, depending upon which domain is most salient to them at the time.

What about the group labeled "economic conservatives"? Like conservatives, this group is committed to a free market and limited government when it comes to economic regulation. In this sense they don't differ from other conservatives.[25] Yet they are likely to look more like liberals regarding social issues such as abortion or same-sex marriage. But their overriding interests are clearly economic and not social.

Social Justice

	low	high
low	libertarians	LIBERALS
high	CONSERVATIVES	communitarians

Social Order

More nuanced political labels. Economic conservatives belong in the upper left cell. They focus on economics but lack a group morality and are therefore more accurately described as economic libertarians.

They believe strongly in competitive capitalism and fiscal responsibility, at least when it comes to government spending on entitlements and welfare programs; consequently they will vote for conservative candidates who share their economic orientation. In other words, they favor autonomy in the economic domain. Yet they also favor autonomy in the social domain. Economic conservatives are actually libertarians with a marked economic focus. Importantly, they lack a collective morality, whereas conservatism, like liberalism, is based in a binding group morality. Thus a more accurate label for this group would be "economic libertarians."

There is a group, however, whose morality we might consider supercollective, and this is the communitarians. They are particularly group-focused and are motivated by both Social Order and Social Justice concerns; their political perspective incorporates both binding moralities. They regard the community as a source of moral suasion, authority, and stability, and they typically espouse traditional values associated with family and religion.[26] They are likely to favor government interventions that fund social safety nets as well as government prohibitions on abortion and same-sex marriage. Religious conservatives who are focused on both increasing equality and relieving societal poverty are essentially communitarians. Other communitarians, who endorse restrictions on both a free market and social behavior, could vote with the left or right. When abortion and so-called family values dominate their concerns, they will choose a conservative candidate, and when Social Justice concerns are dominant they will vote for a liberal candidate.

"Populist" has become an increasingly popular political label, but it is difficult to place populists as a group because they appear on both the left and the right; there are both liberal and conservative populists. Their similarity lies in their antagonism toward the elites, whom they regard as corrupt and self-serving, unlike the people, who are decent and good. Depending on the populists in question, the "people" could be defined along class, racial, or national lines, but the elite are always the politicians, executives, intelligentsia, and media establishment.

Left-wing populists are likely to define themselves in terms of class and focus on social justice and anti-capitalism. They want to tax the rich, regulate economic activity, and redistribute wealth down the economic ladder. Right-wing populists are apt to define themselves in terms of race or national origin, and they are likely to oppose immigration, the welfare state, and spending on the social safety net. These populists may want to tax the rich, but they oppose what they regard as government handouts to the poor. In the end, populism tells us about attitudes toward the elite, but the label alone doesn't tell us much unless we know whether the populists in question support an ideology on the left or right. Underneath the populist label, liberalism and conservatism remain the dominant political ideologies.

Politics is more nuanced than the two categories of liberals and conservatives. Libertarians and economic conservatives look like liberals when we consider Social Order concerns and like conservatives when we consider Social Justice concerns. Communitarians look like liberals when we consider Social Justice concerns and like conservatives when we consider Social Order concerns.[27] Liberalism and conservatism, based respectively in the two collective moralities—Social Justice and Social Order—constitute the two largest and most significant classifications of political ideology, and their moral bases can provide an understanding of the more nuanced political landscape.

7

What Conservatives Are Protecting

Many issues have fervent proponents and detractors, perhaps none more than guns, same-sex marriage, and abortion. Conservatives favor gun rights and oppose same-sex marriage and legal abortion, whereas liberals support gun control, marriage equality, and abortion rights. These are defining issues for Social Order–based politics. Conservatives' emphasis on protecting underlies their positions on each issue, but who or what is being protected? It is different in each case, ranging from physical protection to defense of traditional institutions and social roles. The conservative position on abortion has two foci of protection, one that is explicitly advanced, the other implicit and often unrecognized. Always, though, the Social Order morality is reflected in conservatives' heightened concern about security and societal stability.

Guns

Conservative advocacy of gun rights seems to defy their proscriptive, restrictive orientation in the social domain. Yet recall that when issues arise that directly implicate either protecting on the right or providing on the left, it is these moral motives that determine one's stance. Guns are one such issue for the right; they implicate the Social Order morality via a protect motive.

In 1993, the *New England Journal of Medicine* published a study by Arthur Kellerman and colleagues reporting that guns at home increased the risk of homicide in the home. The study was funded by the Centers for Disease Control (CDC)'s National Center for Injury Prevention and Control, and the immediate response of the National Rifle Association (NRA) was to lobby for the elimination of the center. The Republican-controlled Congress passed the Dickey Amendment, which banned the use of CDC funds to promote or advocate gun control. This effectively ended the agency's funding for research on gun violence. As Kellerman wrote in 2012, "Precisely what was or was not permitted under the clause was unclear. But no federal employee was willing to risk his or her career or the agency's funding to find out. Extramural support for firearm injury prevention research quickly dried up."[1]

Today the United States is unique among high-income countries in its rate of gun deaths. Americans have both the highest per capita rate of police officers and the highest per capita rate of gun ownership—as well as the highest per capita rate of gun violence.[2] Almost forty thousand people are killed by guns each year in the United States—about 40 percent by another person and 60 percent by suicide. A review of gun deaths across twenty-seven industrialized countries showed that 82 percent of these deaths were American, and the U.S. gun homicide rate was twenty-five times higher than the average rate of the other twenty-six countries. The United States has 5 percent of the world's population yet owns 45 percent of the world's civilian-owned guns: approximately 1.2 guns for every man, woman, and child in the country.[3] Yet the Dickey Amendment of 1996 essentially shut down the National Center for Injury Prevention and Control, which had funded research on gun violence. Congress chose not to know how gun ownership affects us.

The conservative argument is that it is people, not guns, who do harm—but clearly people without guns are far less likely to kill. People in other industrialized countries also get angry and feel vengeful, but they are far less likely to kill others. Liberals witness gun-induced carnage, contend that guns make us all more vulnerable, and argue that guns undermine well-being in a caring society. The left therefore seeks government regulation, including new laws to require background checks and waiting periods, banning of assault weapons, and liability for gun manufacturers.

The conservative attitude toward guns is cloaked in the language of rights and freedom, as are all issues where people favor autonomy. But on the right, there is a belief that guns protect.[4] Conservatives believe that gun regulation minimizes their means of defense. Compared with liberals, they see the world as a dangerous place and distrust unknown others; they feel safer with a gun. The feeling that they are protected overrides what liberals would regard as normal safety precautions, such as child safety locks on guns. The NRA, for example, has argued that these locks could prevent gun owners from protecting their families in emergencies like robberies.[5]

Conservatives, who particularly revere strength, see guns as personally empowering. Although they regard guns as protecting their physical safety and the safety of those close to them, guns are actually used defensively in fewer than 1 percent of reported crimes involving a victim and a perpetrator.[6] Yet in a world of strangers, conservatives feel safer with guns and believe that one way to address the increase in mass killings is to arm more people so that they can intervene. Liberals, who value interdependence, see guns as a danger to all, and they emphasize the need for gun safety measures to curb rampant gun deaths.

The epidemic of gun violence in the United States continues, and increasingly experts in the field are arguing for good research that can inform policies and prevent the carnage guns have wrought. Mark Rosenberg, who helped establish the National Center for Injury Prevention and Control, put it this way: "It's not either, 'Keep your guns or prevent gun violence.' There's a strategy that science can help us define where you can do both—you can protect the rights of law-abiding gun owners and at the very same time reduce the toll of gun violence."[7] Of course, this requires an openness to science.

Years of condemnation of the Dickey Amendment by virtually every medical society in the United States as well as Democrats in Congress, and continuing cases of catastrophic mass shootings, finally led congressional negotiators to reach a deal in 2018. The Centers for Disease Control could fund research, but government funds could not be used to advocate specifically for gun control. Although the words didn't seem very different from the original amendment, now some funding was once again available. And even without support from the CDC, some research on gun violence has been conducted. In 2020 the Rand Corporation attempted to summarize the research findings to date but noted the paucity of good research. Basing its conclusions on only methodologically strong studies, Rand found evidence that stand-your-ground laws increase firearm homicides, whereas waiting periods and background checks decrease firearm homicides.[8]

An emphasis on gun safety rather than gun control, while acknowledging the Second Amendment right to own a gun, may help move us forward. Importantly, the political landscape has shifted in the past decade, particularly following the mass shooting in Newtown, Connecticut, in which twenty-six people died, including twenty children between six and seven years old. A gun-control movement on the left took shape and became increasingly organized and well funded. Although clearly outspent by gun rights groups ($155 million to $48 million for lobbying over the past decade) there is now strong, vocal advocacy for gun control and gun safety measures.[9] Changes have occurred at the state level—blue states enacting safety measures (background checks) and red states expanding gun rights (open carry laws). Following years of mass shootings, Congress finally acted after the massacre in Uvalde, Texas, that killed nineteen schoolchildren and two teachers. Fifteen Republican senators joined the fifty Democrats to pass a bill that included background checks for buyers under twenty-one years old, and millions of dollars for expanded mental health services. Although less than the Democrats would have liked, it was the first federal gun safety legislation in almost three decades. Future responses to the plague of gun violence will have to consider both the individual's right to own a gun and the well-being of society at large, concerns that are respectively emphasized by the right and the left. In the meantime, mass shootings and gun-related deaths continue to ravage the nation.

Same-Sex Marriage

The issue of same-sex marriage, or marriage equality, returns us to the more typical restrictive moral orientation of the right in the social domain. The moral motive for conservatives remains protection; now, however, it is not people's physical safety that is believed to be at stake but the traditional family, associated with Social Order and the perceived stability of society. The Republican platform for 2016, adopted again without change in 2020, endorsed strict views of the family, gender, and homosexuality, as well as the importance of Christianity as a guide and teaching the Bible in public schools. Regarding marriage, the platform read:

> Our laws and our government's regulations should recognize marriage as the union of one man and one woman and actively promote married family life as the basis of a stable and prosperous society. For that reason, as explained elsewhere in this platform, we do not accept the Supreme Court's redefinition of marriage and we urge its reversal, whether through

judicial reconsideration or a constitutional amendment returning control over marriage to the states.

Interestingly, "married family life" is seen as the basis of a stable society, but marriage between two men or two women is viewed as a threat—to the institution of marriage and traditional family values more generally. For the left, on the other hand, same-sex marriage is a matter of equality, of providing the LGBTQ community the same civil rights as heterosexuals.

Across the United States, there has been a sea change in attitudes toward gay rights in the past fifty years. In 1969 homosexuality was illegal in every state except Illinois. In that year a police raid on the Stonewall Inn in Greenwich Village in New York incited a three-day riot that electrified the gay community and spurred a movement for gay rights across the United States. Almost half of the states decriminalized homosexuality within the next dozen years, and the Supreme Court, in *Lawrence v. Texas* (2003), overturned an anti-sodomy statute in Texas.

Twelve years later, in 2015, the Court ruled that the right to marry is guaranteed to same-sex couples, based on both the due process and equal protection clauses of the Fourteenth Amendment of the Constitution. The two sides of the debate—liberal and conservative—are apparent in the majority and dissenting opinions of the Court, respectively. The vote was five to four, with the majority opinion written by Justice Anthony Kennedy and joined by the four liberal justices (Stephen Breyer, Ruth Bader Ginsburg, Elena Kagan, and Sonia Sotomayor). The opinion specifically noted that the personal choice to marry is "inherent in the concept of individual autonomy," echoing the importance on the left of autonomy and freedom in the social domain.

The four conservative justices (Samuel Alito, John Roberts, Antonin Scalia, and Clarence Thomas) each wrote a dissenting opinion. In one of them, Chief Justice Roberts (joined by Justices Scalia and Thomas) noted that no earlier opinion had changed the core nature of marriage as between a man and a woman and argued that bans on same-sex marriage served a legitimate government interest in preserving the traditional definition of marriage. He asserted that the "universal definition of marriage"—between a man and a woman—was intended to guarantee successful childrearing.

Justice Alito also wrote a dissenting opinion (joined by Scalia and Thomas), in which he, too, argued that the rights and liberties protected by the due process clause are those that are "deeply rooted in this Nation's history and tradition," and these did not include a right to same-sex marriage. He also noted that same-sex marriage bans promote procreation and the optimal environment for childrearing.

Of course, using childbearing and childrearing as justifications for marriage is a problem, given that we would not deny the right to marry to couples who do not want to have children, are infertile, or are past childbearing age when they marry. And the conservative justices' statements about optimal childrearing were not supported by the research. The major medical and psychological societies in the United States, including the American Medical Association, the American Academy of Pediatrics, the American Psychological Association, the American Academy of Family Physicians, and the American Psychiatric Association, submitted a brief to the Court on behalf of the plaintiffs in the case in which they rebutted the conservatives' arguments:

> Scientific evidence strongly supports the conclusion that homosexuality is a normal expression of human sexuality; that gay men and lesbians form stable, committed relationships that are equivalent to heterosexual relationships in essential respects; that same-sex couples are no less fit than heterosex-

ual parents to raise children, and their children are no less psychologically healthy and well-adjusted; and that denying same-sex couples access to marriage is both an instance of institutional stigma and a contributor to the negative treatment of lesbian, gay, and bisexual people. In short, the claim that allowing same-sex couples to marry undermines the institution of marriage and harms children is inconsistent with the scientific evidence.[10]

In his majority opinion, Justice Kennedy directly responded to the conservatives' Social Order concerns. The opinion noted that marriage "safeguards children and families" and "is a keystone of our social order" and, echoing the medical and psychological societies' amici briefs, asserted that "there is no difference between same-and opposite-sex couples with respect to this principle; consequently, preventing same-sex couples from marrying puts them at odds with society, denies them countless benefits of marriage, and introduces instability into their relationships for no justifiable reason."

So same-sex marriage was legalized throughout the United States in June 2015. This decision applied to civil, not religious, services, and some denominations—including the Roman Catholic Church and the Southern Baptist Convention—have declined to sanctify same-sex marriage. Others, including the Episcopal Church and certain branches of Judaism, have sanctified the unions.

The perceived threat to the traditional family underscores the perceived importance, for conservatives, of so-called appropriate behavior for men and women. In a county-level analysis of attitudes toward same-sex marriage, sociologists found that opposition was strongest in communities where traditional family roles and family structure make up a large portion of the population. Other research has shown that support and opposition to same-sex marriage is strongly related to attitudes about promiscuity—their comfort with causal sex, with having different partners over time, and with sex outside a long-term relationship. Participants' attitudes about promiscuity, together with their beliefs about the promiscuity of gay men and lesbian women, were very strong predictors of attitudes toward same-sex marriage. Opposition was greatest among those who strongly disapproved of casual sex and believed that gays and lesbians are far more promiscuous than heterosexual men and women.[11] One of the ways these respondents believed that same-sex marriage threatened marriage as an institution was that it would undermine marital fidelity.

Yet the nation has moved strongly toward favoring marriage equality over the past two decades. According to the Pew Research Center, in 2004, Americans opposed same-sex marriage by a margin of 60 percent to 31 percent. By 2019, the pattern reversed: 61 percent of Americans approved of same-sex marriage, and 31 percent disapproved. Large differences appear across age groups, with 74 percent of millennials (born 1981–96) favoring same-sex marriage, compared with 51 percent of baby boomers (1946–64) and 45 percent of the silent generation (1928–45). And large partisan differences remain, with 71 percent of Democrats favoring same-sex marriage compared to 37 percent of Republicans.[12]

Legal marriage affords same-sex couples greater equality in society. It also moves them into a traditional institution (marriage) and so could be regarded as a conservative change. While this may help account for the relatively rapid change in attitudes toward same-sex marriage, the increased acceptance is primarily attributable to people's (especially the younger generation's) greater familiarity with members of the LGBTQ community. Over the past fifty years, as they have increasingly come out to family and friends, gays and lesbians have ceased to be others for many Americans but instead sons and daughters, brothers and sisters, close friends and acquaintances. The importance of familiarity is epitomized by Dick Cheney's support of same-sex marriage amid his otherwise strong political conservatism. Cheney is anti-abortion, pro-gun, a supporter of military intervention overseas, anti-tax, and against entitlements. Yet he openly supported same-sex marriage in 2009 after he learned that his own daughter Mary is a lesbian; Mary is married to another woman and has two children—his grandchildren.

The widespread openness of gay men and lesbians has clearly contributed to conservatives' greater ease in accepting their participation in an institution that Social Order morality otherwise strongly supports.

Abortion

In the same decades during which same-sex marriage has gained acceptance, abortion has become more closeted, and many Americans are unaware that their mothers, sisters, daughters, and friends have had abortions.[13] Abortion arouses passions on both sides of the political spectrum and is one of the most difficult issues on which to have a respectful dialogue between left and right. People on each side of the debate find it difficult to accept that there are well-intentioned, sincere people on the other side. For those on the right, abortion is murder, and one cannot be open-minded about murder. For those on the left, abortion bans violate women's right to control their own bodies and ultimately their lives. For conservatives, government intervention and regulation are appropriate in the social domain, and efforts to ban abortion are therefore a wholly legitimate exercise of government authority. For the left, this is the domain of autonomy and freedom, and women's choices are to be respected.

On this issue, the right's focus on protecting is evident at two levels. The most apparent is anti-abortionists' efforts to protect life in

the womb. Less evident, but extremely powerful, is the desire to protect established gender roles and hierarchy. In the right's Social Order
morality, collective stability is thought to depend on traditional roles
and institutions. This is not to question many anti-abortionists' very
real concern for the embryo or fetus but rather to make explicit what
has too often been implicit in the anti-abortion movement, which
has everything to do with women's place in society.

First, it is important to note how common the procedure is. Almost a million abortions are performed each year in the United States.
According to the Guttmacher Institute's fact sheet from 2018, 1.06
million abortions were performed in 2011 and 862,000 in 2017. Fully
59 percent of women obtaining abortions are already mothers. Almost half (45 percent) of all pregnancies in the United States are
unintended, and in about 40 percent of these pregnancies, women
chose an abortion. In 2017, 18 percent of pregnancies (excluding mis-
carriages) ended in abortion. About one in four women has had an
abortion; the Guttmacher Institute estimates that 24 percent of American women will have had at least one abortion by age forty-five.[14]

Although many women keep their abortions secret, it is likely
that virtually all of us have a family member or friend who has had
one. The conservative senators and representatives who have fought
for abortion bans and restrictions are overwhelmingly white men. Yet
women they are close to—their mothers, sisters, or daughters—likely
have had abortions.

Roe v. Wade and Its Aftermath

In its landmark ruling in *Roe v. Wade* in 1973, the Supreme Court
made abortion legal in the United States on the ground that the Fourteenth Amendment's due process clause creates a right to privacy, and
this includes a woman's right to have an abortion. While not attempt-

ing to resolve the issue of when life begins, the Court stated that previous English and American common law and statutes have not regarded the "unborn" as a person and therefore that the rights enumerated in the Fourteenth Amendment do not extend to the fetus. The Court also argued that the right to abortion is not absolute but must be balanced against the state's interest in the "potentiality of life."[15]

Given current U.S. politics, it is worth recognizing that five of the seven justices who were in the majority and supported abortion rights were nominated by Republican presidents—judicial nominations were not yet politicized as they are today. Richard Nixon nominated Justices Harry Blackmun, Warren Burger, and Lewis Powell, and Dwight Eisenhower nominated Justices William Brennan and Potter Stewart. The two justices nominated by Democratic presidents were William O. Douglas (by FDR) and Thurgood Marshall (by Lyndon Johnson). Nor did views on abortion fall along party lines in the 1970s. President Gerald Ford, a Republican, opposed *Roe v. Wade,* but his First Lady, Betty Ford, was a supporter of abortion rights, and Vice President Nelson Rockefeller had overseen the repeal of abortion restrictions when he was governor of New York. The political sorting of opinions on the subject is apparent in Ronald Reagan's career. As governor of California he signed a law loosening abortion restrictions, but his presidential campaign of 1980 explicitly called for the appointment of anti-abortion judges.

Interestingly, Ruth Bader Ginsburg, a strong supporter of abortion rights, felt that the *Roe* decision was a mistake because it stopped a political process that was moving toward the elimination of restrictions. In 1992, she wrote that the decision "prolonged divisiveness and deferred stable settlement of the issue."[16]

Since *Roe v. Wade* was handed down, conservatives have persisted in trying to restrict where, when, and how women can obtain an abortion. Consistent with their constraint-based morality, they have set gestational limits, prohibited public funding, restricted coverage in private insurance plans, established onerous requirements on doctors and hospitals, required parental involvement for minors, allowed health care providers to refuse to perform abortions, and required women seeking abortions to undergo ultrasound examinations, counseling, and waiting periods. Six-week abortion bans have become increasingly common; these are particularly insidious because at six weeks many women do not even know they are pregnant.

States passed 1,271 abortion restrictions between 1973 and 2019; 792 were enacted in the thirty-eight years between 1973 and 2011, but in just the first five months of 2019, 378 abortion restrictions were introduced across the United States, 40 percent of them outright bans. Between January and mid-May 2021, 549 bills restricting abortion were introduced in forty-seven states, including 165 complete bans; of these, 69, including 9 bans, were enacted into law across fourteen states. The Guttmacher Institute noted that 2021 was on track to become "the most devastating anti-abortion state legislative session in decades."[17]

A recent salvo from the right has been the passage of heartbeat abortion bills, which ban abortion when the fetal heartbeat can be detected by ultrasound. This happens as early as six weeks. At six weeks, the embryo (which will not be called a fetus until the eleventh week) is the size of a pea, and the electric pulsing detected on ultrasound is not the pumping of blood but electric activity in what will later become a fetus's heart.[18] Heartbeat bills have passed in North Dakota, Arkansas, Iowa, Kentucky, Mississippi, and Ohio, although most of them have been blocked by the courts. In September 2021, Texas passed a law that bans abortion after six weeks and offers a $10,000 bounty to any person who successfully brings a suit against anyone—the abortion provider or a cab driver who drives a woman to the clinic—who aids or abets in the process of getting an abortion. Crafted to make it difficult to challenge in court, the law leaves enforcement to private citizens.

These harsh restrictions on abortion whittle away abortion rights. Many such measures are what are called TRAP laws—targeted regulation of abortion providers. Their purpose is to shut down abortion clinics by requiring compliance with regulations that don't apply to medical professionals engaging in comparable care, including requiring hospital admitting privileges for doctors performing abortions and prohibitively expensive building standards.[19]

The American Medical Association and the American College of Obstetricians and Gynecologists argue that TRAP laws are medically unnecessary and don't improve safety. Instead they harm women's health by limiting access to safe, legal abortion. In two recent cases, *Whole Woman's Health v. Hellerstedt* (2016, from Texas) and *June Medical Services v. Gee* (2019, from Louisiana), the Supreme Court struck down the TRAP abortion restrictions. Yet it is worth noting that roughly 80 percent of the Republicans in Congress signed the "friend of the court" brief prepared by Americans United for Life in the *June Medical Services* case. The brief also asked the judges to overturn *Roe v. Wade*.

Another example of a medically unnecessary constraint on women's health is the now-reversed federal requirement that the first of two pills in a medication abortion be administered in person by a specially certified doctor or medical provider. Research attests to the safety of medication abortion, and the president of the American College of Obstetricians and Gynecologists noted that the in-person requirement was arbitrary and did not make an already safe medicine safer. The Biden administration made the decision to allow women to receive both pills by mail. Medication abortion now accounts for more than half of all U.S. abortions (54 percent), up from 24 percent in 2011.[20]

A medication abortion can be completed in the privacy of one's home, and pills can be sent through the mail. A medical setting is not required, which largely accounts for its increased incidence, as almost 90 percent of U.S. counties currently lack even one abortion clinic.[21] Yet a large network of 2,500 crisis pregnancy centers has been established across the United States, actively discouraging women from having abortions. Many states fund them directly; Texas, for instance, reduced family planning funding by two-thirds in 2011 while increasing funding for these anti-abortion centers.[22]

In May 2021, the Supreme Court announced that it would review a restrictive Mississippi law that would ban abortions after fifteen weeks of pregnancy. During oral arguments the Court's conservative justices made it clear that they were open to reversing or weakening *Roe v. Wade.* A draft opinion written by Justice Alito was leaked in early May 2022 striking down *Roe.*[23] Within forty-eight hours the Louisiana legislature introduced a bill that would classify abortion as homicide and give prosecutors the right to charge patients with murder.

In July 2022, the U.S. Supreme Court overturned *Roe v. Wade.* Abortion laws are now to be left up to the states. According to the Guttmacher Institute, abortion will likely be banned in twenty-six states.[24] Eighteen of these have a trigger law tied to the death of *Roe* or an abortion ban on the books that predates *Roe,* making abortion illegal immediately. In contrast, sixteen states and the District of Columbia have policies in place that recognize a women's right to abortion, and several are "sanctuary states" where abortion would be extended to women in other states. For women living in much of the Midwest and South, abortion access will depend on their having the money and time to travel to another state.[25]

While many states are restricting the abortion rights women have had for more than fifty years, a network of abortion activists is responding to a post-*Roe* United States. From providing pills and information about self-managed abortions to the creation of abortion funds to pay for procedures, this growing movement will likely have a major impact on the future of abortion and women's health in the United States.[26]

Religious Mobilization on the Right

After the decision in *Roe v. Wade,* religious conservatives became energized and joined the Republican Party, creating the anti-abortion conservative movement.[27] That decision, by majority Republican appointees, reflected a different time from today, before the alignment of morality, party, and policy preference. It was also a time before the coalition of the religious right and the Republican Party. In the years before *Roe v. Wade,* the United States Council of Catholic Bishops and its Family Life Bureau presented the only coordinated opposition to abortion. By 1980, evangelical leaders had joined with Catholic bishops to create the backbone of the Christian right and its anti-abortion mobilization.[28] The Christian right became a powerful force in the Republican Party, as Jerry Falwell and others urged conservative Christians to get involved in politics. The success of this new coalition was apparent in 1980, when the Republican Party platform first included anti-abortion planks and a call for a Human Life Amendment to the Constitution to ban abortion.

Jerry Falwell was a Baptist pastor at the time. Interestingly, before 1980 the Southern Baptist Convention actually advocated for loosening abortion restrictions, and in the *Baptist Press,* W. Barry Garrett published an article praising *Roe v. Wade:* "Religious liberty, human equality and justice," he wrote, "are advanced by the . . . decision."[29]

Making abortion illegal became a rallying cry for conservative Christians. Pat Robertson's Christian Coalition became an important anti-abortion organization in the early 1990s. At a meeting of Black journalists in 2005, at which panelists argued that fighting poverty and racism were the most urgent societal issues calling for church involvement, Richard Land, the president of the Southern Baptist Convention's Ethics and Religious Liberty Commission of America, stated that there was no more important issue than making abortion illegal.

Given that the religious right is the muscle behind the anti-abortion movement, it is curious to note that the Bible does not explicitly condemn or even mention abortion. The sixth commandment is "Thou shalt not kill," but nothing in the Bible says that abortion is equivalent to the killing of a human being; and in any case, exceptions are often made in the case of war, self-defense, and, for many (who are likely to oppose abortion), capital punishment.[30]

The passage most often cited as indicating disapproval of abortion is Exodus 21:22–25, which discusses what happens when a woman gets involved in a fight between her husband and another man. "If people are fighting and hit a pregnant woman and she gives birth prematurely but there is no serious injury, the offender must be fined whatever the woman's husband demands and the court allows. But if there is serious injury, you are to take life for life." Opponents of abortion claim that "life for a life" refers to the life of the fetus. Rabbinical history for more than a thousand years has interpreted the passage to mean that the life is that of the pregnant woman, not the unborn. If the author of Exodus intended to condemn abortion, one wonders why it would be done so obscurely. The New Testament tells us a great deal about sex and marriage, but abortion is never mentioned. The Bible is not shy about offering proscriptions regarding women's bodies: infertility, menstruation, rape, infidelity, and prostitution are all addressed. But it does not mention abortion.

The lack of biblical injunctions notwithstanding, the major forces behind the anti-abortion movement are conservative churches, particularly the Roman Catholic Church and evangelical Christian churches.[31] The LDS Church (the Mormon Church) also strongly supports the movement, as do the Lutheran Church–Missouri Synod, the Wisconsin Evangelical Lutheran Synod, and the Eastern Orthodox Church. Yet many Christian denominations support abortion rights and are not working to overturn *Roe v. Wade.* Among these are mainstream Protestant churches—the Episcopal Church, the Evangelical Lutheran Church in America (a mainline Protestant Lutheran church), the Presbyterian Church (U.S.A.), and the United Church of Christ. Reform and Conservative Judaism also support abortion rights.

Given that there are religious denominations on either side of the abortion debate, it is worth noting that all the churches that power the anti-abortion movement are strongly patriarchal. Men are the church leaders and the major interpreters of texts. Women are subservient in these churches, and this inferior status extends to their role in the home.

The Christian Right and the Role of Women

The Christian right's control of women ranges from subtle shaming to strong directives. In reacting to the religious right's seeming idolization of Amy Coney Barrett during the Supreme Court confirmation process, Katelyn Beaty, managing editor of *Christianity Today,* asked why traditional Christianity doesn't encourage more women to be like her but instead asks women to sacrifice their career ambitions for family life. "Barrett is the exception," she writes, "not the rule, to traditional Christian teachings on women's work and vocation. Most of the 125-plus women I interviewed over two years said they had heard from a peer, pastor or professor that being a wife and mother was, by God's design, their highest calling—and that a career would distract from that. As such, many Christian women with professional ambitions feel less than Christian, or woman, if they follow those ambitions in the way that Judge Barrett has followed her own."[32]

Beaty makes it clear that many of the women she interviewed wanted to have children, but they also wanted to go back to school or start a nonprofit or work to become a CEO. Yet they were made to feel ashamed for having such ambitions.

One woman told Beaty that she was thrilled to have gotten into law school until a pastor told her no Christian man would want to marry a lawyer. Another told her of a megachurch pastor in Seattle who preached that he didn't know a single woman who worked outside the home. These attitudes are not exceptions but the rule in conservative Christian churches, where, Beaty notes, there is a belief "that God designed men to be leaders in the church and home, and that women are to submit to male leadership in these spheres. . . . If a church teaches the essence of femininity is godly submission, it is difficult to then, in turn, encourage women who are called to lead and hold authority at work."[33]

A poll conducted in 2017 by the Barna Group, an evangelical polling firm, showed that evangelicals were particularly uncomfortable—more so than any other group in the sample—with women having power outside the home. They were also the least likely to believe that women face barriers in the working world. Motherhood and family, not employment outside the home, are regarded as a woman's calling in the evangelical world. Echoing Beaty's observations about traditional Christianity, the Barna report notes that "there is a long history among evangelicals of emphasizing motherhood and family as a woman's primary calling. While the broader culture, and much of the Christian church, has shifted away from this, evangelicals seem more reluctant to do so. This reluctance is often tied to a scriptural reading that insists men are to occupy primary leadership positions within the family and church and, by extension, society."[34]

Rest assured my intent is not to demean women's family roles. I feel very fortunate to be a wife, mother, and grandmother, and I value these roles tremendously. The matter at hand is the conservative religious view—primarily Christian in this country, but not exclusively so—that these are the *only* roles appropriate for women and that women should not work outside the home, whether or not they are wives and mothers. This view also bears on women's equality within the home. Americans obviously regard it not only as acceptable but appropriate for men to be husbands, fathers and productive workers outside the family, but many religious conservatives would not accept women in multiple roles.

Benevolent Sexism

The religious right, and conservatives more generally, rely on a particular form of sexism to justify their very traditional attitudes toward women. When we think about sexism, most of us think of openly negative evaluations of women, including stereotypes that women are manipulative, too emotional, and mentally inferior. Yet there are two forms of sexism. According to social psychologists Peter Glick and Susan Fiske, "hostile sexism" is the overtly negative type just noted. "Benevolent sexism" is different: on its face it seems to involve positive rather than negative evaluations of women. Both forms regard women as inferior and relegate them to a lower status than men, but hostile sexism typically involves anger and misogyny (hatred of women), whereas benevolent sexism appears to view women as more like undeveloped adults in need of protection. Women are valued as mothers, wives, and caretakers; they are romanticized as objects of heterosexual affection who are available yet sexually pure.[35]

On its face, benevolent sexism may appear harmless or even praiseworthy, but it restricts women's ambitions and opportunities outside the home. At the root of these beliefs are the assumptions that women are weak and shouldn't deviate from the traditional roles that place them in the home, caring for others and being protected by men. These beliefs reinforce and maintain patriarchal structures that give men power over women and shape our political, economic, and religious institutions.

It should be evident that not only men but women can be benevolent sexists. Conservative activists like Phyllis Schlafly certainly knew how to use benevolent sexism to sell anti-feminist politics to women, focusing on opposition to abortion and the Equal Rights Amendment. Researchers have found that when women were exposed to benevolently sexist comments (such as "Women have a way of caring that men are not capable of in the same way"), they were less likely to declare themselves willing to engage in anti-sexist collective action such as protests and rallies and more likely to assume a passive role. But when exposed to hostile sexist comments (such as "Women are too easily offended"), they reported being more willing to engage in these collective actions.[36] Benevolent sexism can be an effective way to get women to accept subordinate status and reinforce the status quo. To truly value women is to affirm their competence, strength, and ambitions both within the home and outside it.

Abortion and Women's Unequal Status

Embedded in the anti-abortion movement is a deep discomfort with women's independence and freedom. The operative assumption is that women's proper role is to bear children and attend to maternal and marital duties. Abortion threatens this assumption because it gives women control over their own bodies and thus affords them not only sexual freedom but the freedom to move beyond domestic boundaries. Importantly, abortion restrictions are strongly associated with women's unequal status.

Consider these data from the Center for American Progress on "The State of Women in America": Using indices of economic security, leadership, and health—thirty-six factors in all—the report assessed the status and well-being of women in all fifty U.S. states. Not surprisingly, there were great disparities in how women fared. The ten states where women fared worst—those that received a grade of "F"— were also the states with the most onerous abortion restrictions: Alabama, Arkansas, Georgia, Indiana, Louisiana, Mississippi, Oklahoma, South Dakota, Texas, and Utah.[37]

Anti-abortionists are a major constituency of the Republican Party and banning abortion is a major platform of the party. We should note, as well, that the Republican Party has opposed virtually all legislation that would contribute to the increased status of women. This includes the Lilly Ledbetter Act, the Violence Against Women Act, the Paycheck Fairness Act, and the International Convention on the Elimination of All Forms of Discrimination Against Women. The United States is one of only six countries—along with Iran, Palau, Somalia, Sudan, and Tonga—that have not ratified the international convention.[38]

The link between anti-abortion positions and the status of women is apparent from the earliest days of abortion prohibitions. Until about 1880, abortions were widely practiced in the United States and were illegal only after women could feel the fetus moving ("quickening"). As Leslie Reagan, the author of *When Abortion Was a Crime,* writes, "At conception and the earliest stages of pregnancy, before quickening, no one believed that a human life existed; not even the

Catholic Church took this view."[39] Starting in 1880, however, abortions were gradually made illegal except when necessary to save the mother's life. By 1910, they were outlawed in every state except Kentucky. The movement against abortion had little to do with protecting fetuses. One motive had to do with ethnic dominance: increasing numbers of immigrants were entering the country, and anti-abortionists claimed that White Protestant women had a patriotic duty to stay at home and bear more children.

It was not religious or social conservatives who made this case but rather the developing medical establishment, which was then in the process of gaining control over the practice of medicine. In their efforts to establish themselves as the only scientific providers of health care, medical doctors sought to discredit all competing practitioners, including the (almost exclusively female) midwives who cared for pregnant mothers and newborn infants and administered herbal abortifacients when needed. At the same time, women were trying to gain entrance to medical schools, in part to work as obstetricians and gynecologists. As Reagan notes, the crusade by the medical establishment was "anti-feminist at its core," a response to women's rising aspirations.[40]

Contemporary efforts to restrict access to abortion and reverse *Roe v. Wade* reflect similar motivations. Banning abortion helps preserve the social hierarchy and social roles that conservatives consider vital. Any particular behavior may have multiple causes: some overt and immediate, others that are deeper and broader. At the explicit level, opposition to abortion reflects conservatives' convictions about the sacredness of life, but the deeper cause involves the fear of women rebelling against their traditional social roles and a need to keep women in their place by restricting their sexual and economic freedom. The anti-abortion movement is a reaction to women's increasing autonomy and power.

Even conservative women who have had abortions regard women now seeking abortion as loose and irresponsible—not like them. Journalist Darlena Cunha talked with a group of women in Florida who supported Trump in the election. Three of them had abortions when they were younger and admitted that if they had not gotten them, their current lives would not have been attainable. But they were different, they insisted, from the women needing abortions today. "When I was younger," said one woman, "we didn't use abortion as birth control like these girls now. It wasn't like sending back a coffee."[41] They were able to justify their opposition by judging current abortion seekers as irresponsible.

If abortion bans are about protecting life, why hasn't a single abortion law passed in the United States contained any provision to help women raise the children the state has required them to bear? When it comes to helping low-income women raise their children, opponents of abortion are also most likely to cut support for food, housing, and other social services that would benefit these mothers. And if anti-abortionists are interested in life, why do they not care more about life per se? The words of Jerusha Duford, Billy Graham's granddaughter and a committed evangelical, pro-life Christian are instructive: "I genuinely wish the Democratic Party would have a greater value for life inside the womb. Yet I equally wish the Republican Party would place a greater value on life outside the womb. You cannot choose just one and define yourself as pro-life." Sister Mary Traupman, a Catholic nun, in a letter to the *Pittsburgh Post-Gazette,* described denial of health care to the poor, environmental degradation, and family separation at the border and added, "These are not pro-life policies."[42]

Consider, too, the views of Stephanie Ranade Krider, a pro-life evangelical and former executive director of Ohio Right to Life who has spent her career fighting against abortion. She considers pro-life "an ethic committed to protecting the vulnerable, and grounded in the idea that every human deserves dignity, because every human is created in the image of God, including the unborn, Black people, immigrants, the incarcerated and the poor." Unfortunately, she wrote, this was not the view of the pro-life movement: "Throughout my time in the pro-life movement, colleagues have often told me that the movement does not get involved in other human dignity issues like the death penalty, or issues of immigration or race, because it might dilute our messaging. Under [President Trump], it's become resoundingly clear that these matters are no longer considered merely ancillary or a distraction: They are now rejected as outright obstacles on the path to power. Leaders in the pro-life and evangelical movement enabled that trade-off." Krider resigned her leadership position at Ohio Right to Life in late June 2020.[43]

Against Contraception

If abortion restrictions are meant to protect the unborn, why do abortion opponents also oppose comprehensive sex education and family planning to reduce unwanted pregnancies? Why are they increasingly against contraception? If abortion must be prevented at any cost, we would expect broad, even enthusiastic support for contraception as an effective means to this end. This clearly has not been the case on the right. Instead, conservatives have waged a war on contraception.

According to a Population Institute report titled "Senseless: The War on Birth Control" and published in 2017, the attack on abortion has "morphed into a far broader, undeclared war on contraception itself." In recent years, "conservatives sought, on multiple fronts, to deny public funding or support for contraceptive services, whether or not the recipient organization, or its affiliate, provided any abortion services."[44]

The attack on contraception is disheartening to the public health field, which has relied on contraceptive use to prevent both sexually transmitted diseases and unintended pregnancy—which, as noted, constitutes about half of all pregnancies in the United States. For the right, sexual freedom is anathema. R. Albert Mohler Jr., president of the Southern Baptist Theological Seminary and a leading figure of evangelical Christianity, has written, "The effective separation of sex from procreation may be one of the most important defining marks of our age—and one of the most ominous."[45] Conservatives' thoughts about contraception and abortion run on parallel paths, both of which lead to preservation of women's traditional maternal role. For contraception, the reasoning looks like this: sex is for procreation, and having children is women's natural role and duty; restricting access to contraception increases the likelihood that women will have children; therefore, restricting contraception reinforces women's natural maternal role. We might add that conservatives view this maternal role as appropriate solely in the context of marriage. But we could easily substitute "abortion" for "contraception": restricting access to abortion also reinforces "women's natural maternal role."

Conservatives celebrated the Supreme Court's decision in the *Hobby Lobby* case (2015), which allowed the craft store chain and other closely held corporations to be exempt from regulations the owners found objectionable because of their religious beliefs—in this case, coverage of contraception for their female employees under the Affordable Care Act.

As Katha Pollitt notes, "Not one major anti-abortion organization supports making birth control more available, much less educating young people in its use: not Feminists for Life, National Right to Life, or the Susan B. Anthony List; not American Life League, Americans for Life, or Pro-Life Action League, to say nothing of the US Council of Catholic Bishops, Priest for Life, and Sisters for Life. Anti-abortion organizations either openly oppose contraception, or are silent about it."[46]

Anti-abortion advocates claim that they oppose forms of birth control that they believe prevent uterine implantation of the embryo, in particular intrauterine devices and the morning-after pill. Consistent with their belief that life begins at conception, they view these methods as abortifacients. But this reasoning cannot account for conservatives' opposition to other forms of birth control. There is strong scientific evidence that the contraceptive pill prevents pregnancy by suppressing ovulation, and an additional mechanism involves inhibiting the movement of sperm through the genital tract.[47] There is no fertilized egg involved, no interference with implantation. Yet there is considerable opposition to the pill, which is highly effective at preventing pregnancy.

Nor is there any effort to promote forms of birth control that don't inhibit implantation, including condoms, cervical caps, and diaphragms (as well as vasectomies and tubal ligations). In fact there have been active efforts to disparage such methods. Senator Tom Coburn of Oklahoma, who is trained as an obstetrician, led a campaign to force condom manufacturers to include information on their labels indicating that condoms don't prevent certain sexually transmitted diseases, in particular the human papillomavirus. He did this even though the information he wanted the manufacturers to include was contrary to the findings of a National Institutes of Health panel on condoms and sexually transmitted diseases.[48]

In trying to deter contraceptive use, the right actively works against the prevention of pregnancy. Texas and Utah, for example, require parental permission for teenagers to get prescription birth control from state-funded clinics. And the right adamantly opposes sex education, with the single exception of abstinence-only-until-marriage, or AOUM, education. These abstinence programs have received large amounts of federal funding despite ample evidence that they don't work. As researchers concluded in a comprehensive review, "The weight of scientific evidence finds that AOUM programs are not effective in delaying initiation of sexual intercourse or changing other sexual risk behaviors. AOUM programs, as defined by U.S. federal funding requirements, inherently withhold information about human sexuality and may provide medically inaccurate and stigmatizing information."[49] It is worth noting, too, that the abstinence-only programs' goal of delaying sex until marriage becomes more challenging as Americans marry later in life. In the early 1970s, the median age for first marriage was 21 for women and 23 for men. According to the U.S. Census Bureau, the average age in 2017 was 27.4 years for women and 29.5 years for men.

The attack on contraception is about women's sexual freedom. Sex for pleasure and without fear of pregnancy is viewed as a moral calamity on the right, and research has found that attitudes about promiscuity are strong predictors of attitudes toward abortion.[50] Consider the reaction to a Georgetown University law student, Sandra Fluke, following her testimony to a congressional committee in February 2012. She was testifying in support of President Obama's new policy that religiously affiliated institutions like universities and hospitals should provide insurance that covers the cost of contraceptives. Fluke, from a religiously affiliated law school, discussed the financial burden of contraception and said nothing about her sex life or use of contraceptives.

Yet Rush Limbaugh attacked Fluke in the most distorted terms: "What does it say about the college co-ed Susan [sic] Fluke who goes before a congressional committee and essentially says that she must be paid to have sex? It makes her a slut, right? It makes her a prostitute. She wants to be paid to have sex. She's having so much sex she can't afford the contraception. She wants you and me and the taxpayers to pay her to have sex." In response, John DeGioia, the president of Georgetown University, defended Fluke, calling her testimony "a model of civil discourse" and Limbaugh's comments "misogynistic, vitriolic, and a misrepresentation of the position of our student."[51]

Abortion and Misinformation

By opposing both abortion and contraception, the anti-abortion forces lend support to the view that the fundamental threat they are fighting against is the freeing of women from their roles as bearers and caregivers of children. To promote their agenda, abortion opponents relied on an additional weapon—false information about abortion's health consequences. This misinformation campaign was largely the brainchild of David Reardon, an electrical engineer and anti-abortion activist who believed that the anti-abortion movement couldn't win over a majority of the populace with arguments about the life of the unborn fetus. In his book *Making Abortion Rare* (2006), he argued that the anti-abortion movement should instead focus on harm to women: "We must change the abortion debate so that we are arguing with our opponents on their own turf, on the issue of defending the interests of women."[52] The anti-abortion movement embraced this recommendation, and false information is now rampant on the right. Liberals, meanwhile, with research on their side, are trying to provide accurate information to women so they can make informed decisions about their pregnancies.

The right's misinformation campaign has two components: abortion causes psychological damage, and abortion is bad for a woman's physical health. Those who oppose abortion claim that women who have had abortions are more likely to become depressed and suicidal; abortion thus increases their risk of psychological problems. Yet researchers representing the American Psychological Association, the Academy of Medical Royal Colleges, and Johns Hopkins Bloomberg School of Public Health have all concluded that the proposed link between abortion and mental health problems is unfounded. A recent study of four hundred thousand women, published in *JAMA Psychiatry,* concluded that having an abortion does not increase a woman's risk of depression. Research simply does not support the abortion opponents' mental health claims.[53] In fact, the most common emotion in the aftermath of an abortion is relief.

As for physical health consequences, the anti-abortion movement asserts that abortion causes a risk of future infertility and a greater likelihood of breast cancer. To examine these claims, the National Cancer Institute convened a group of more than a hundred leading experts on pregnancy and breast cancer risk. Based on a review of all available research, they concluded that neither abortion nor miscarriage increases a woman's risk of developing breast cancer.[54] The claim is also refuted by the American College of Obstetricians and Gynecologists and the American Cancer Society.

Nor is there any link between abortion and subsequent fertility, provided that the abortion is a safe, legal one.[55] Of particular interest, and not included in the anti-abortion armament, are the findings about physical safety more generally. A study in *Obstetrics and Gynecology* reported that the risk of dying from giving birth (8.8 in 10,000) is about fourteen times greater than the risk of dying from abortion (0.6 in 10,000). According to the American Medical Association and the American College of Obstetricians and Gynecologists, "Abortion is one of the safest medical procedures performed in the United States." The mortality rate of a colonoscopy is about forty times greater than the mortality rate of an abortion.[56] When abortion is debated on women's own turf, as Reardon recommended, only pseudoscience and misinformation support the anti-abortion side. Science and accurate information unequivocally support those who defend abortion rights.

When people express a deep concern based on demonstrably false information and then refuse to change their views when the information is shown to be false, we can safely conclude that the expressed concern is not what is really on their minds. This is what we see with abortion opponents and women's health: their opposition is not about women's health but about something else.

Women's Freedom and Equality

On the left, abortion is about rights—women's freedom to control their own bodies and lives. Women should be able to have children when they feel they can best raise and support them. It is not the maternal role that is opposed but the imposition of that role by others. On the right, abortion is part of a constellation of behaviors representing a new sexual permissiveness that threatens the social order.

Assisted reproductive technologies, particularly in vitro fertilization, are increasingly common as a path to pregnancy. Fertility clinics often discard unneeded or defective embryos. Parents sometimes make this request, and at other times the embryos deteriorate. Although the Catholic Church and conservative evangelical churches oppose this as "baby killing," they are surprisingly silent about it. We don't see protests in front of fertility clinics or active efforts to shame women who are trying to get pregnant. This discrepancy makes sense if the most important factor is that these women are choosing the maternal role rather than delaying or rejecting it. Embryos are being

POLITICS, PARTIES, AND POLICIES

destroyed, but the traditional role of women as mothers and caregivers is being preserved.

A number of highly respected legal scholars have argued that *Roe v. Wade* should have been decided on the basis of equality, not privacy—more specifically, on the basis of the equal citizenship guarantees of the Fourteenth and Nineteenth Amendments. Such an argument would have recognized what is really at stake in the abortion controversy. As law professor Reva Siegel has written,

> States will punish pregnant women who have "voluntarily" engaged in sex by making them bear children, even though the state has imposed no similar duties, burdens, or sanctions on the men who were coparticipants in the act of conception. The state does not hold the pregnant woman's partner accountable for sharing the work of parenting, nor does it alter the sex-based citizenship consequences of performing the work: during pregnancy and then for some two decades after, a woman will face severe restrictions on her ability to participate in education, employment, or politics—restrictions the society is only now beginning to ameliorate.[57]

Had *Roe v. Wade* been decided on the basis of equality, it might have placed the status of women at the center of the abortion debate and forced abortion opponents to be more forthright in linking their position to women's subordinate social roles. Ruth Bader Ginsburg said during Senate confirmation hearings in 1993 for her nomination to the Supreme Court: "It is essential to woman's equality with man that she be the decisionmaker, that her choice be controlling. If you impose restraints that impede her choice, you are disadvantaging her because of her sex."

For those on the right, Social Order morality is based in protecting society not only from outside threats but from threats arising within the group. Maintenance of traditional social roles is regarded as essential for stability. Benefits accrue to men from women's subordinate status in these traditional roles, but benevolent sexism on the right, manifested clearly in conservative religions, masks the view of women as inferior. Control of women—control of their bodies and thus the course of their lives—serves to keep women in their traditional roles. On its face, the abortion debate is about the life of the unborn, and this concern is no doubt important to abortion opponents. But at a deeper level that is seldom acknowledged, the abortion debate is about women's place in society.

8

What Liberals Are Providing

The social sphere—the realm of guns, same-sex marriage, and abortion—is where conservatives' Social Order morality is most visible. In contrast, liberals' Social Justice morality, focused on providing, expresses itself mainly in economic matters, specifically regarding government efforts to further equality. Entitlements in particular illuminate the difference between the politics of left and right, because the very word *entitled* sends us in two different directions. One meaning tells us that a person has a right to something, as in a legal right to a house or compensation. The other is pejorative and tells us that a person unjustly feels deserving of special treatment or privileges. In the former case the entitlement is deserved, whereas in the latter it is not. In the former the person is to get what she or he is due, whereas in the latter the person is seeking more than his or her due.

These differences parallel the divergent views of liberals and conservatives on the distribution or redistribution of public goods. The two sides have very different reactions to entitlements, government programs that provide resources and a safety net for members of society. Well-known entitlement programs include Medicare, Social Security, Medicaid, unemployment, welfare, and food stamps, and the political battles surrounding each of these have drawn strong opposing reactions on the left and right.[1] Liberals' and conservatives' views on entitlements reflect divergent beliefs regarding deservingness and legitimacy that are anchored in the distinct moralities of the left and right.

Social Security is the most popular program in America, yet the Republican Party has been opposed to it from its inception. In 1935, when it was first passed by Congress, Republicans voiced concerns that the program would "discourage thrift," stifle individual responsibility, and prevent business recovery. Ronald Reagan famously noted in 1964 that he switched from the Democratic Party to the Republican Party because of his opposition to Social Security and Medicare.[2] Over the following decades, shrinking Social Security through privatization became a primary objective of conservatives, and in 2005, President George W. Bush tried to replace it with private investment accounts. Despite strong Republican support, the effort failed. Not a single Democrat voted for it.

Medicare, passed in 1965, was reviled by major voices on the right. In his Senate campaign in 1964, George H. W. Bush called it socialized medicine and ridiculed his opponent for supporting medical care for the aged. Ronald Reagan warned that if Medicare was not stopped, "one of these days you and I are going to spend our sunset years telling our children and our children's children what it once was like in America when men were free." Barry Goldwater asked, "Having given our pensioners their medical care in kind, why not food baskets, why not public housing accommodations, why not vacation resorts, why not a ration of cigarettes for those who smoke and of beer for those who drink?"[3]

Compare these reactions on the right with the view of President Franklin Roosevelt in his speech accepting the Democratic nomination for his reelection in June 1936: "Better the occasional faults of a government that lives in a spirit of charity than the consistent omissions of a government frozen in the ice of its own indifference."

Social Security, Medicare, and the other government entitlement programs that constitute our American safety net have long been associated with support on the left and antipathy on the right. These differences reflect the distinct moral underpinnings of the respective political ideologies and the contrasting views of inclusiveness and deservingness that follow from each. These divergent perspectives are readily apparent in reactions to the more recent Patient Protection and Affordable Care Act, or Obamacare, which *Forbes* magazine labeled "America's last entitlement."[4]

The Affordable Care Act

A decade before the Covid-19 pandemic, the tremendous needs and inequities in our nation's health care system were already all too apparent. The Affordable Care Act was an attempt to begin to address these concerns. As soon as President Obama signed it into law, in March 2010, conservatives began an all-out effort to bring it down by any means necessary. They called it Obamacare to ensure its connection to a president they despised, yet both supporters and detractors quickly embraced the name. Obama himself said, "I have no problem with people saying Obama cares. I do care."[5]

The Affordable Care Act represented a major reform of a health care system that had essentially been unchanged since the passage of Medicare. It greatly expanded health care coverage and instituted a number of requirements for insurers. Insurers were no longer allowed to deny coverage due to preexisting conditions, all applicants had to be accepted, and premiums could not vary based on preexisting conditions. No longer could copayments or deductibles apply to preventive care such as vaccinations and medical screenings such as mammograms, colonoscopies, and HIV screening. Lifetime coverage caps were eliminated. Children were permitted to stay on their parents' insurance plans until the age of twenty-six even if they did not live with their parents or were not claimed as dependents on taxes, and insurers could not drop policyholders if they got sick. Obamacare also required that insurers spend 80 to 85 percent of all premiums on health care costs. The major provisions of Obamacare went into effect in 2014, and the Department of Health and Human Services reported that by early 2016, the number of uninsured Americans had been cut by more than 40 percent; some twenty million more people now had health insurance.[6]

Obamacare increased coverage by changing insurance markets for individuals. States were now required to provide insurance exchanges, usually online, where people could purchase their health insurance. People with incomes between 100 percent and 400 percent of the federal poverty level could receive federal subsidies to enable them to buy insurance through the exchanges. In a concession to conservatives, only U.S. citizens or those with proof of legal residency were eligible to receive these benefits.

Obamacare also expanded Medicaid eligibility for all U.S. citizens and legal residents. Starting in 2014, those with incomes up to 133 percent of the federal poverty level now qualified. The federal government agreed to pay states 100 percent of the increased costs from 2014 through 2016, a subsidy that gradually dropped to 90 by 2020 and all years to follow. By the end of 2019, thirty-seven states and Washington, D.C., had embraced the Medicaid extension.[7]

From the start, the right viewed Obamacare as a threat to the nation. The overheated rhetoric on conservative talk radio, cable television, blogs, and social media left no doubt that liberals were destroying the country. There have been eight challenges to Obamacare in the Supreme Court, over 1,700 cases in lower courts, numerous Trump administration executive orders attempting to undermine it, and more than sixty efforts by congressional Republicans to repeal all or part of the law. Even before passage of the bill, the right's talk of "death panels" was intended to poison the public's view of the Affordable Care Act. Sarah Palin pioneered the phrase, which promoted the idea that panels established under Obamacare would not only deny care to seniors because of their age but advise them to end their lives rather than get end-of-life care. Although these assertions were regularly repeated on the right, no such panels were included in Obamacare, and PolitiFact selected death panels as its Lie of the Year for 2009. The Lie of the Year for 2010 was the claim by some opponents that Obamacare represented a "government takeover of health care." PolitiFact called this a lie because all health insurance remained in the hands of private insurers.

In 2011, the Congressional Budget Office estimated that between 2012 and 2021 the Affordable Care Act would reduce the deficit by $210 billion.[8] Conservatives, however, were less disturbed by the costs of Obamacare than by what the spending was for. Here was another government handout—an entitlement for the unentitled. One feature that particularly galled conservatives was the individual mandate, which required people to either have health insurance or pay a penalty. This measure was meant to ensure that healthy and younger Americans, who might otherwise opt out of insurance, would get insurance. The individual mandate would prevent people from gaming the system by waiting until they got sick to get insurance, since insurers are required to accept all applicants. It was also needed to spread the costs of health care throughout the population, so that premiums would stay affordable. As Jonathan Cohen wrote in the *New Republic:*

> There are other reasons to support a mandate. One is explicitly about redistribution—from the medically lucky to the medically unlucky. At any one time, only a very small per-

centage of the population will have major health problems. The rough rule of thumb is that 20 percent of the people are responsible for about 80 percent of the costs in the system. But fortune (and misfortune) plays a huge role in determining who ends up as part of that 20 percent—all it takes is contracting a serious disease, having a debilitating accident or developing an acute condition. Rather than force this unlucky 20 percent to bear the burden of their medical expenses alone, you can ask everybody else—the people lucky enough to be in good health—to help shoulder that burden.[9]

The individual mandate reflects the Social Justice motive to provide for all group members.

In a vote on the bill in 2009, every Republican senator voted to call the individual mandate "unconstitutional." And on the day Obama signed the act into law—March 23, 2010—fourteen state attorneys general filed suit claiming that the individual mandate was unconstitutional.[10]

Conservatives viewed the mandate as an affront to individual liberty. In Social Order morality, freedom and autonomy reign supreme in the economic domain. Obamacare, however, would require people not only to pay for their own insurance but to help pay other people's health care costs. A Republican voter in Florida, railing to a journalist that he didn't want to pay to help other people who didn't deserve it, said he had once used duct tape to close a cut on his arm because he couldn't afford stitches. "I'd rather take care of my own self with tape," he declared, "than be stuck in a system where I pay for everyone else."[11]

The individual mandate was challenged in the courts multiple times, but ultimately the Supreme Court deemed it constitutional.[12] Yet in 2017, as part of the Tax Cuts and Jobs Act, Congress effectively eliminated the individual mandate by reducing the payment required of those refusing to get insurance to zero. Citing the Congressional Budget Office's prediction that thirteen million people would lose health insurance by 2027, liberals ranted about the right's selfishness. For the left, the fact that the new act's tax cuts would go overwhelmingly to the wealthy was further evidence of conservative greed, as well as a betrayal of American values.

In the same case that upheld the constitutionality of the individual mandate, *National Federation of Independent Business v. Sibelius* (2012), the Supreme Court also found that Obamacare's Medicaid expansion was coercive because states had to accept it or lose their Medicaid funding. The decision allowed states to opt out of the expansion without losing Medicaid funding.

The court battles over Obamacare continued.[13] In February 2018, Texas and nineteen other states went to court to argue that Obamacare was no longer constitutional because Congress's elimination of the penalty for refusing the individual mandate meant that the mandate could no longer be considered a tax, and there was no other provision in the Constitution authorizing it. Thus, the plaintiffs argued, the act as a whole was not constitutional.[14] The Justice Department under President Trump refused to defend the law, but California and thirteen other states stepped in to provide a defense. The Supreme Court once again heard arguments on Obamacare on November 10, 2020, one week after the presidential election, and once again declined to strike down the law.

During the pandemic, eleven years after its passage, Obamacare became somewhat less controversial. In the first two weeks of an open enrollment period created by President Biden, more than two hundred thousand people signed up for health insurance through the act's online marketplace, and the 2021 stimulus law greatly expanded subsidies to make insurance more affordable.[15] Yet the fight over health care is unlikely to end, because the differences between the left and right over Obamacare represent far more than divergent opinions about health care. They reflect fundamental disagreements over government's responsibilities toward its constituents—differences based in their binding moralities.

Binding Moralities, Poverty, and Perceived Responsibility

Appearing before a group of Milwaukee high school students in 2017, Republican senator Ron Johnson was asked whether he considered health care a right or a privilege. He responded, "I think it's probably more of a privilege. Do you consider food a right? Do you consider clothing a right? Do you consider shelter a right? What we have as rights is life, liberty, and the pursuit of happiness. Past that point, we have the right to freedom. Past that point everything else is a limited resource that we have to use our opportunities given to us to afford those things."[16]

For liberals, health care is a right; for conservatives, it is a privilege. When health care is viewed as a right, all are entitled to it.[17] Here liberals' expansive circle of moral concern is apparent: health care, in their view, is a community resource that should be available to all members of society. When viewed as a privilege, however, it must be earned, and individuals are responsible for their own health care. Clearly evident here are the divergent political views regarding the roles of autonomy and government involvement. The political ideology of the left, based in Social Justice and an enabling morality, embraces government funding of health care; the monetary costs are what a just society takes on to care for its members. For liberals, all people deserve adequate health care; their status as members of society, constituents of a nation, render them deserving. The political ideology of the right, based in Social Order, espouses autonomy and self-determination in this domain and reserves government intervention, particularly restrictive regulation, for areas related to social roles and social behaviors. In the economic realm, where spending on public goods such as health care, housing, and education reside, autonomy and freedom reign, and responsibility is assigned to individuals.

Similarly, when in the first months of his term President Biden proposed government-funded day care, universal prekindergarten for young children, and free community college for all Americans, conservatives immediately balked. They vehemently opposed Biden's proposals and called for fiscal responsibility. Yet Biden and his advisers had proposed a way to pay for these benefits, a plan that included reversing the tax cuts the conservatives had pushed through Congress in 2017. It is not that his proposal was not fiscally responsible but rather that it was not fiscally responsible in the way conservatives preferred—that is, no spending on education or family benefits if it involved higher taxes, even if the higher taxes are limited to the very richest among us. On the right, day care and additional education are individual responsibilities, whereas to the left, education and family benefits are shared responsibilities. These differences have very distinct implications for people's welfare, especially those who are most disadvantaged.

The question of social versus individual responsibility reflects different views of deservingness. For social psychologists, this question is informed by years of research on attributions—people's causal perceptions. Given that the expenditures for health care and most entitlement programs are primarily aimed at helping the poor, the work on attributions for poverty is particularly relevant.

In understanding how people assign causes for others' behaviors and outcomes, social psychologists make a basic distinction between internal and external attributions—that is, attributions to the person or the situation. When we locate the causes of behavior in the person, we are focusing on an individual's personal attributes or efforts. When we locate the causes of behavior in the situation, we are focusing on the environment or larger social forces. Thus in the simple case of someone tripping on the sidewalk, we can believe that the person is clumsy or was distracted (internal attributions), or we can believe that the sidewalk was uneven and poorly maintained (external attributions). In the former instance we see the person as responsible, whereas in the latter we regard situational factors as responsible.

This basic distinction can be applied to all sorts of behaviors and outcomes, including poverty. And when we turn to the work on attributions for poverty, we find differences that correlate with political orientation. Conservatives are more likely to endorse internal causes of poverty, whereas liberals are more likely to endorse external causes.[18]

Bernard Weiner, an attribution researcher who has studied beliefs about poverty, makes an additional distinction between controllable and uncontrollable attributions. Uncontrollable internal attributions include people's abilities, disabilities, and characteristics that a person has little control over; controllable internal attributions focus on people's conscious efforts. External attributions can also be uncontrollable, occurring through luck or chance, or controllable, as in situational factors such as a poorly maintained sidewalk.

Weiner has found that the perceived controllability of internal causes of poverty is critical to understanding people's beliefs about it. Conservatives attribute the internal causes of poverty to personally controllable causes such as laziness and drug use. In other words, if you are poor it's because you don't put in the effort to make a decent living. In attributing poverty to the poor themselves, conservatives are able to justify and thus perpetuate the current wealth hierarchy.[19]

Liberals largely attribute the causes of poverty to controllable external factors, including systemic and structural factors related to educational and job opportunities, housing and lending, and criminal justice. The sociologist Mark Rank notes such factors when he writes that "poverty is the result of an economy producing more and more low-wage jobs combined with an extremely weak social welfare state. Approximately 44 percent of all jobs in the United States are low-paying without benefits; many poor people hold several simultaneously (subverting the notion of their laziness)."[20] Here poverty is not the fault of the poor, and the appropriate response then is social change in the interests of Social Justice.

Weiner and his colleagues have also found that the different attributions for poverty draw distinct emotional and behavioral responses. People viewed as responsible for their financial hardship elicit anger, whereas those seen as not responsible for their plight elicit sympathy. In turn, when it comes to actually responding, anger leads to neglect, whereas sympathy leads to giving assistance.

These differences in attributions and aid reflect the distinct moralities of the left and right. Entitlements, our current focus, reside in the economic domain; government programs from Obamacare to welfare provide resources to those who are most vulnerable. Liberals' binding morality, Social Justice, operates here, with its emphasis on interdependence and equality. But in this domain, conservatives' binding morality—Social Order—is not operative. This does not mean that conservatives' positions are not based in morality. But lacking a collective morality for distributing resources, conservatives rely on an individuated, interpersonal morality—perceived Fairness.

The policy preferences of the left and right regarding entitlements and economics return us to a consideration of Social Justice and Fairness and the difference between interpersonal (individualized) and collective morality. The major conflicts between liberals and conservatives over health care, welfare, and public assistance reflect fundamental differences in the application of the Fairness and Social Justice moral motives. Liberals prefer government intervention to assure the well-being of all group members and greater equality of outcomes across society. In the absence of an operative group-based *provide* morality (Social Justice), the right relies on an individualized prescriptive morality—Fairness—in deciding how goods and resources should be distributed.[21]

Fairness involves matching outcomes with inputs. It therefore requires a determination of inputs. But with the poor and vulnerable, while we know the outcomes—poverty and need—we seldom know much about people's input behaviors. If you believe that wealth comes from hard work and a virtuous life, it is easy to assume that poverty comes from laziness, drug use, and other internal, controllable factors. On the right, deservingness is based on individuals' efforts, not on shared humanity or shared societal bonds: you make your own bed and must lie in it, and if you're poor it's your fault. Whereas liberals view entitlements as socially just, conservatives view them as unfair. They see the government taking their wealth and giving it to the undeserving.

Conservatives engage in attributions of blame: if you're in need, it's because you haven't worked hard enough to move up the economic ladder. You need to pull yourself up by your own bootstraps. What is missing here is that some people don't have boots. As Martin Luther King said, "It's all right to tell a man to lift himself by his own bootstraps, but it is cruel jest to say to a bootless man that he ought to lift himself by his own bootstraps." And some boots are so worn they can't bear the lifting.

The claim that government welfare undermines personal responsibility must also be considered in light of evidence that we can predict children's outcomes based on their Zip codes.[22] When a Zip code can predict a child's future earnings and likelihood of incarceration, we need to reconsider whether poverty can be attributed to personal versus situational factors. Zip codes, as stand-ins for local environments, argue strongly for the powerful role of external factors in poverty.

The right also maintains that entitlement programs themselves inhibit personal responsibility and self-reliance. In the words of the former Republican Speaker of the House Paul Ryan, "We, right now, are trapping people in poverty. And it's basically trapping people on welfare programs, which prevents them from hitting their potential and getting them in the workforce."[23]

These dependency arguments continued even after President Clinton changed welfare requirements in 1996 to address such concerns by putting strict time limits on cash aid and requiring welfare recipients, even single mothers, to work. Following the elections of 1994, the Republican-controlled Congress passed two major welfare reform bills, both of which Clinton vetoed. But then, concerned about re-election, he negotiated with House Speaker Newt Gingrich and ultimately signed the Personal Responsibility and Work Opportunity Reconciliation Act of 1996. This measure dramatically reduced the number of people receiving federal welfare, an outcome long sought by conservatives.

President Biden's American Rescue Plan revived Democratic efforts to provide no-strings-attached help to needy Americans. In addition to doubling the child tax credit and making virtually all families eligible, the plan expanded and extended unemployment benefits, made large new investments in food assistance, expanded health coverage, increased housing assistance, and provided aid to states. Not a single Republican in Congress voted for it, and not a single Democrat voted against it. Under the pandemic conditions of 2021, the left no longer feared pushback from conservatives about welfare dependency.

In any case, research strongly challenges the assumption that welfare payments remove the incentive to work. As Esther Duflo and

Abhijit Banerjee, recipients of the Nobel Prize in economics in 2019, conclude, "40 years of evidence shows that the poor do not stop working when welfare becomes more generous." They note the results of the negative income tax experiments in the 1970s, in which "participants were guaranteed a minimum income that was taxed away as they earned more, effectively taxing extra earnings at rates ranging from 30 percent to 70 percent, and yet men's labor hours went down by less than 10 percent."[24]

Compared with other developed countries, the share of Americans who work is low, and some have questioned whether generous welfare payments are responsible. The chair of the Federal Reserve Board, Jerome Powell, a Republican, has refuted this view, noting that when adjusted for inflation, people's benefits have actually gone down as labor force participation has declined. It has also become increasingly difficult to receive welfare money unless you're working or disabled. Moreover, in contrast to the falling U.S. labor force (before the pandemic), European nations with far more generous safety nets have seen increases in labor force participation.[25] In the United States, our safety nets are weaker and our poverty rates higher than in other wealthy countries. Yet conservatives continue to attack entitlement programs, from Social Security and Medicare to welfare and Obamacare, as providing government aid to undeserving recipients.

The Racialization of Poverty

The "undeservingness" associated with entitlements has also become racialized, and this helps account for the negative reaction by conservatives in particular. In the mid-twentieth century, media images of poverty focused on white Appalachian farmers and white workers whose factories closed, but over the next few decades poor and Black became increasingly linked, and poor urban Blacks in particular became the face of poverty. This led the American public to a dramatic overestimation of the percentage of Blacks versus whites on welfare.[26] Entitlements, particularly welfare and food stamp programs, have probably never recovered from President Reagan's promotion of "welfare queens driving Cadillacs," which delegitimized recipients in an explicitly racialized way.

The term *welfare queen* originated in 1974 in a *Chicago Tribune* story by George Bliss about one woman, Linda Taylor, who defrauded the welfare system. The welfare queen, a derogatory stereotype aimed primarily at Black single mothers, reinforced the belief that welfare recipients were gaming the system. They were not only getting help they didn't deserve but were doing nothing and living far better than most taxpaying Americans. Yet as Christopher Borrelli wrote in the *Tribune* decades later,

> Arguably it's Ronald Reagan who gained the most. He rarely said "welfare queen" in public. He referred to Taylor as merely "a woman in Chicago." But her public-assistance crimes—which Reagan read about in news reports, then fastened into a fixture of stump speeches during the 1976 and 1980 presidential campaigns—became his go-to, ready-baked cautionary tale. Public assistance, he said, was wasteful, run by do-nothing bureaucrats. And the people it served? *They* were out there buying steaks and lobsters with food stamps. *They* were living in housing projects as plush as country clubs. And how were the '70s treating you, struggling middle-class voter? Were you as well off as *those* people getting something for nothing? As well as *that woman in Chicago?*[27]

The welfare queen became a symbolically powerful image that reinforced the link between poverty and race, and between entitlement

programs and undeserving recipients. Consistent with the racialization of poverty, research has shown that racial prejudice predicts
opposition to Obamacare.[28]

The racialization of poverty has also brought a broader demonizing of so-called Black culture. The response to problems in inner-city
Black communities has often been to blame Black culture for drug
use and family breakdown.[29] These are damaged communities, the
reasoning goes, whose values encourage a lack of personal responsibility. Powerful external factors, most importantly drug and incarceration policies as well as joblessness, are ignored.

President Nixon officially declared a War on Drugs in 1971. A top
aide, John Ehrlichman, explained that Nixon had two enemies: Blacks
and the antiwar left. "We knew we couldn't make it illegal to be either against the war or black, but by getting the public to associate
the hippies with marijuana and blacks with heroin, and then crimi-
nalizing both heavily, we could disrupt those communities. We could
arrest their leaders, raid their homes, break up their meetings, and
vilify them night after night on the evening news. Did we know we
were lying about the drugs? Of course we did."[30]

Reagan expanded on the drug war and its anti-Black foundations.
When crack cocaine began to spread across American cities during
the 1980s, he hired staff to publicize its use in order to gain support
for the war against drugs. "The media campaign was an extraordinary success," Michelle Alexander writes in *The New Jim Crow.* "Almost overnight, the media was saturated with images of Black 'crack
whores,' 'crack dealers,' and 'crack babies'—images that seemed to
confirm the worst negative racial stereotypes about impoverished
inner-city residents."[31] Soon Congress passed the Anti-Drug Abuse
Act of 1986, which contained an enormous sentencing disparity between crack cocaine, associated with Blacks, and powder cocaine,
associated with whites. A person in possession of five grams of crack

cocaine got a mandatory sentence of five years, but to get the same mandatory sentence for powder cocaine, a person had to be holding five hundred grams. This was effectively a one-hundred-times harsher sentencing rule for crack than powder cocaine. Not surprisingly, the new law had a disproportionate impact on young Black men.

There was no scientific justification for the disparity. The supposed greater danger of crack cocaine in terms of addiction and violence was purely mythical, and there is strong evidence that Blacks and whites use drugs at very similar rates.[32] In 2010, Congress passed the Fair Sentencing Act, which reduced the sentencing disparity for crack versus powder cocaine to eighteen to one. Cocaine is only one example of racial differences in criminal justice. From enforcement to sentencing, the drug war has had an immensely disproportionate impact on the Black community. As Alexander writes in *The New Jim Crow:*

> More African American adults are under correctional control today—in prison or jail, on probation or parole—than were enslaved in 1850, a decade before the Civil War. The mass incarceration of people of color is a big part of the reason that a black child born today is less likely to be raised by both parents than a black child during slavery. The absence of black fathers from families across America is not simply a function of laziness, immaturity, or too much time watching Sport Center. Thousands of black men have disappeared into prison and jails, locked away for drug crimes that are largely ignored when committed by whites.[33]

In addition to the dire impact of incarceration on Black families, other external factors also belie blame of Black culture. Joblessness is particularly notable. In his book *When Work Disappears,* the sociologist William Julius Wilson describes the devastating impact of dwindling work opportunities on the inner city.[34] The disappearance of unskilled factory jobs, which once sustained America's urban centers, left inner-city Blacks without the anchor of decent employment in the closing decades of the twentieth century. Wilson also maintains that poor public transportation to factories outside the city, coupled with employers' negative stereotypes of poor Blacks, further promote chronic joblessness, which is associated with drug use and family breakdown.

Now we are seeing joblessness, drug use, and family breakdown in rural white communities. As Nicholas Kristof and Sheryl WuDunn note, "When good jobs left white towns . . . because of globalization and automation, the same pathologies unfolded there. Men in particular felt the loss not only of income but also of dignity that accompanied a good job. Lonely and troubled, they self-medicated with alcohol or drugs, and they accumulated criminal records that left them less employable and less marriageable. Family structure collapsed."[35]

Incarceration has not been regarded as the answer for these white communities, and many people continue to associate poverty with Blacks. Yet many rural towns have seen an increase in resentment toward "lazy" white neighbors, community members who are believed to be on drugs and collecting benefits. This is the very group largely affected by the recent opioid epidemic. In places like Pike County in eastern Kentucky, an area devastated by the collapse of the coal industry, people are angry about the dependency they see in many of those around them, neighbors and even family members who they believe are living too well on government benefits. "It's Cousin Bobby—'he's on Oxy and he's on the draw and we're paying for him.'"[36] Eastern Kentucky had been a Democratic stronghold and is currently highly dependent on public benefits. Nevertheless, Republicans are winning by large margins here, as people view the Democratic agenda, with its entitlements, as good for other people and not themselves. It was here that Republican senator Rand Paul warned about intergenerational welfare and the culture of dependency, speaking to an audience all too willing to agree with him.

As Arlie Hochschild has shown, these people feel betrayed by the federal government because they think it is on the side of undeserving beneficiaries. These rural residents are strong advocates of the free market, which they believe supports people who work hard for the American dream. Hochschild writes, "In the undeclared class war, expressed through the weary, aggravating, and ultimately enraging wait for the American Dream, those I came to know developed a visceral hate for the ally of the 'enemy' cutters in line—the federal government. They hated other people for needing it. They rejected their own need of it—even to help clean up the pollution in their backyard."[37] Their disdain for government handouts, particularly for the so-called undeserving, has steered them away from Democrats and toward Republicans, which many note is working against their economic interests.

Republicans are far less likely than Democrats to believe government should play a major role in providing health care or helping people out of poverty. The long and continuing battle over Obamacare and entitlements is a fight over the government's proper role in providing for people's well-being. It reflects fundamental differences in binding moralities, only one of which, Social Justice, is concerned with providing for the larger community. Social Order, with its interest in maintaining stability, does not see a major role for government in increasing equality or addressing the needs of society's most vulnerable. Here the free market rules, and Fairness, based in their own judgments of others' inputs, is conservatives' operative morality.

Climate Change and the Role of Government

The right's aversion to government involvement in alleviating poverty and expanding access to health care is a consequence of conservatives' emphasis on autonomy in the economic domain. Whether the subject is entitlements or the competitive market, they believe the appropriate role for government is non-interventionist. This hands-off preference is apparent with climate change as well. In one sense, climate change is about protecting the earth and its inhabitants; in another it is about taking care of each other and our most valued public good—our earth—for the benefit of all. Given the grave costs climate change poses for society, we should all be responding, just as in the case of a fire we would all choose to extinguish it. When it comes to climate change, then, the question is not why liberals have embraced the science of climate change and have chosen to respond but why conservatives have not.

Climate change is clearly recognized as a rapidly increasing threat to humanity by virtually all members of the scientific community. The Intergovernmental Panel on Climate Change has concluded that it is real and its main cause is human activity. The national science academies of our major industrial nations all support these findings. Given the unequivocal threat, we might expect the threat sensitivity of conservatives to make them particularly responsive to the dangers posed by global warming. Clearly, however, this is not the case.

Research on perceived risk alerts us to our shared psychological tendency to underestimate threats we see as distant and remote. Here feelings such as fear and anxiety are relatively weak, and we must rely on analysis that is typically less powerful.[38] The scientific community has offered such analysis for many years. NASA, for example, provides evidence of climate change and global warming online for the general public, including the rise in surface temperature, the warming ocean, shrinking ice sheets, glacial retreat, sea level rise, declining

Arctic sea ice, and extreme weather events.[39] Extreme weather conditions in particular have become more apparent—whether in the form of powerful hurricanes, out-of-control fires, coastal flooding, or severe droughts—and have made the effects of climate change more immediate for many people. Again, we might expect both the left and the right to acknowledge the threat confronting us.

Yet this acknowledgment seems to be limited largely to one side of the political spectrum. According to a recent Pew Research Center survey, the fraction of Americans who believe that climate change is a "major threat to the well-being of the United States" grew from 40 percent to 57 percent between 2013 and 2019, but the increased concern came almost entirely from Democrats. Fully 84 percent of Democrats and Democratic-leaning independents agreed that climate change is a major threat to the country (compared with 58 percent in 2013), but Republicans' concerns have changed very little and remain quite low (22 percent in 2013 and 27 percent in 2019).[40] Rand Paul called U.S. efforts to cooperate with global responses to climate change "anti-American and anti-freedom."[41] His words reflect not only conservatives' response to international cooperation on the issue but their response to climate change more broadly. Many believe that climate change is not a problem and therefore requires no response. Republican senator James Inhofe even published a book in 2012 entitled *The Greatest Hoax: How the Global Warming Conspiracy Threatens Your Future.* Inhofe served as chair of the Senate Committee on Environment and Public Works from 2003 to 2007 and again from 2015 to 2017. Yet he is an extreme climate change denier; he rejects the science behind global warming and thinks that there is a pro-environment conspiracy on the left.

In addition to encouraging acceptance of the scientific consensus, liberals' Social Justice morality may promote recognition of our interdependence with others on this planet and our responsibility to fellow humans (including future generations) and other life. But a crucial difference in climate-related positions on the left and right can be explained by the right's interpretation of climate change as an economic issue rather than a social survival issue. The right has chosen to focus on climate regulation as a perceived threat to free markets, where the Social Order morality opposes government intervention, and it is this economic lens that defines the conservative response— or lack of response—to climate change.

The right's denial of climate change is a continuation of conservatives' anti-environmentalism over the past decades. In the 1980s, after a decade of ambitious environmental legislation, Republicans adopted a strategy of nominating anti-environmentalists to lead environmental agencies. President Reagan appointed James Watt, a leader of the Sagebrush Rebellion, an effort to turn federal lands in the Western states over to local control for development and resource extraction, to the position of secretary of the interior. Anne Gorsuch, whom he made head of the Environmental Protection Agency, slashed the agency's budget, reduced suits against polluters, and eliminated many pro-environment regulations. In the 2000s, President George W. Bush appointed a Watt protégé, Gail Norton, as secretary of the interior, and President Trump regularly chose pro-business, anti-regulation, anti-environmentalist activists for regulatory posts. The right's reaction to climate change fits neatly into this pattern of favoring unfettered markets over regulations aimed at environmental protection.

Jim Manzi and Peter Wehner write of this position that Republicans "fear, at least implicitly, that the politics of climate change is just a twisted road with a known destination: supporting new carbon taxes, a cap-and-trade system, or other statist means of energy rationing, and in the process ceding yet another key economic sector to government control. Conservatives seem to be on the horns of a dilemma: They will have to either continue to ignore real scientific findings or accept higher taxes, energy rationing, and increased regulation."[42]

The mainstream media have not helped. In an attempt to counteract conservative attacks about liberal bias, journalists have often opted for parity in articles about climate change, giving equal weight to scientific studies and papers by conservative think tanks written by so-called experts with funding support from fossil-fuel companies and others with a financial interest in the findings. As the left has become increasingly concerned and active, the right has grown increasingly committed to disputing the science regarding carbon dioxide emissions and global warming.

There are important parallels between the right's response to global warming and its response to Covid-19. Closing non-essential businesses in an effort to control the virus led to feverish accusations about attacks on personal freedom—on the economic autonomy so valued by the Social Order morality. Had more closures and lockdowns been in place nationally early on, especially before vaccines were available, the country would likely have avoided some fraction of the millions of cases and hundreds of thousands of deaths it suffered. But rather than acknowledge the seriousness of the public health threat, the right again chose to regard the virus through the lens of the economy, the domain where personal freedom reigns supreme. Consequently, when it came to responding to the deadly virus, the advice of public health experts was all too often ignored or belittled, exacerbating the toll of the disease.

President Trump also sidelined science experts when he withdrew the United States from the Paris Agreement to limit global warming, claiming that the agreement would put the nation at a disadvantage by undermining the U.S. economy while requiring far less sacrifice from other nations. Conservatives interpret climate change mitigation efforts as a threat to the nation's economy. In contrast, liberals focus on the costs of not addressing climate change, and they see mitigation efforts as investments that will bring prosperity to large numbers of Americans. In the Social Order morality, climate change may be costly—perhaps hugely so—but it doesn't obviously threaten the social *order*, the hierarchy on which conservatives' sense of society depends. A massive investment in reorienting the economy away from fossil fuels and pollutants inevitably brings wealth and power to new people and is therefore much more to be feared. For the Social Justice morality, that broadening of wealth and power is a feature, not a bug—so liberals are much more enthusiastic about the economic opportunities inherent in climate mitigation efforts.

Republicans were therefore willing to live with some parts of the $2 trillion infrastructure package that President Biden introduced a few weeks after taking office. Repairing roads and bridges, and even building a few new tunnels, restores functionality to the existing order. It was the spending that would change the social order, such as free community college, universal pre-K child care, and anything that evoked the dreaded phrase "Green New Deal," that conservatives found unaffordable and socialistic. But even though the various proposals were known by their price tags—the $1 trillion plan, the $3.5 trillion plan, and so on—the dispute was never about the money. For both liberals and conservatives, the massive spending plans promised a reorientation of the U.S. economy.[43] Social Justice morality welcomes that reorientation for its opportunities, Social Order morality views it as a threat. The battle, as always, pits a hands-off policy against government intervention in economic matters, protecting the status quo versus providing the resources for social change. It is an inconvenient truth, however, that the right's efforts to protect the social order against perceived threats have themselves become a threat to the social order.

9

Social Justice and the Bane of Inequality

In 2019, the U.S. Census Bureau reported that income inequality in the nation had reached the highest level since the bureau began tracking the data, more than five decades ago.[1] As conservatives have successfully pushed for individual economic autonomy and deregulation, the wealthy have benefited while those lower down on the economic ladder have increasingly struggled. As the left calls for Social Justice and greater equality of outcomes, the right fights liberal attempts at redistribution and argues for equal opportunity instead. Yet unequal outcomes foreclose any possibility of equal opportunity. As we'll see below, opportunities today are primarily based on what you already have. The Social Order morality, which attempts to preserve the existing social hierarchy, now finds itself defending a hierarchy of wealth that has grown increasingly unequal. We have enormous inequality and very little social mobility.

"Immoderate" Social Justice

In the bulk of this chapter we'll address economic inequality in the United States, a problem that suggests we currently have too little Social Justice. But before going there, let's consider the opposite problem: the belief among conservatives that we have "too much" Social Justice or that our society has gone too far in pursuing Social Justice. The entitlements and government intervention discussed in chapter 8 would qualify, but there are other examples as well. One is the movement on the left to "defund the police," which has raised hackles among conservatives who take the phrase literally. The ill-advised word *defund* suggests that the goal is to eliminate police departments by purging their budgets. In fact, the proposal typically involves shifting some taxpayer funds from the police to social services, whose workers are better equipped to address such community problems as addiction, homelessness, and mental health. The intention is to reallocate money to help with problems the police often confront but are not trained to handle. The support of social services would presumably help the police, too.

Sixty years of data have shown that increasing police funding does not necessarily bring a decrease in crime.[2] Moving police funds is intended to help communities deal with problems that are themselves associated with crime. For the right, the phrase "defund the police" raises the frightening prospect of unchecked crime after police departments have been eliminated. Media sound bites using the phrase without context may have contributed to the Democratic loss of House seats in the election of 2020.

But the movement to defund the police has begun to divide liberals as well. Many on the left believe the movement has gone too far, especially given the increase in violent crime during the pandemic. In Minneapolis, where George Floyd was murdered by a police officer, residents agree that police reform is needed, but the overwhelmingly Democratic city is divided on the way to accomplish this. A ballot question in November 2021 would have replaced the Minneapolis Police Department with a Department of Public Safety overseen by the city council and the mayor. Mental health workers and violence prevention efforts were important aspects of the proposed department, and although there likely would have been armed police officers, a minimum number would not have been required. The ballot language simply read that the Department of Safety "could include" police officers "if necessary."

The ballot question was defeated (56 percent to 44 percent). In the city's Black communities a generational divide was apparent in younger activists' support of the ballot and older leaders' opposition. Some Black leaders claimed that the ballot question received a lot of support from liberal whites who wanted to be better allies in the aftermath of George Floyd's murder, but live in relatively safe neighborhoods. The ballot question pitted community leaders on the left against each other, including Black activists on both sides of the issue. Some, like JaNaé Bates, a Black reverend and leader of a coalition of religious, racial, and labor groups that wrote the question, believe that the change would have given the city more flexibility in addressing community safety. Others, like the Black activist Sondra Samuels, believe that the wording was too vague and really about defunding and abolishing the police, which would have endangered the community.[3]

Efforts to restrict the size and scope of police departments are responses to the biases and mistreatment that people, particularly people of color, have experienced at the hands of police. They are also embedded in a wokeness orientation that involves being attentive to racism and social injustice. Initially used by Black activists after the rise of the Black Lives Matter movement, wokeness and cancel culture have become Republican rallying cries aimed at increasing white resentment.[4] But they are also far from universally approved on the left.

John McWhorter, a linguist who describes himself as a "cranky liberal Democrat," notes that because he is Black many might see him as traitorous.[5] He claims that this "Third Wave Antiracism" exploits whites' fear of being thought racist to push a cultural reprogramming with "contemptuous indignation." He contends that innocent people are losing jobs and academic inquiry is being strangled, as its adherents have become inquisitors on this narrow range of issues.[6]

Some on the left view cancel culture as illiberal. Others disagree and feel that this negative attitude reflects critics' elitism and privilege. These differences were apparent in 2020 in an exchange in *Harper's Magazine*. A letter signed by 153 public figures, including Noam Chomsky, Gloria Steinem, Margaret Atwood, Wynton Marsalis, and Salman Rushdie, argued against stifling free speech and specifically against "an intolerance of opposing views, a vogue for public shaming and ostracism, and the tendency to dissolve complex policy issues in a blinding moral certainty." In response, 160 members of academia and the media argued that the earlier letter was an appeal by successful people with large media platforms to exclude those who had been "cancelled for generations."

In his final opinion as a columnist for the *New York Times* (although he remains a contributing opinion writer), Frank Bruni lamented the absence of nuance in today's toxic political environment:

> Take the overlapping issues of cancel culture and free speech. Much of what I read is absolutist: Agonized laments about cancel culture are a cynically overblown right-wing diversion from grave injustice. Or woke zealots are conducting a quasi-religious purge. I think either can be true—depending on the circumstances and the details, which vary from case to case and prevent any summary judgment. . . . I think that campuses have gone way too far in quashing speech they don't like, but I also think that some speech is so intentionally injurious and flamboyantly cruel that refusing to showcase it isn't the defeat of constitutional principles; it's the triumph of empathy.[7]

The debate over cancel culture is important to have—especially on the left, where attitudes toward free speech can be understood in the context of a shared commitment to Social Justice. Both free speech and police reform are connected to Social Justice through the ideas of victimhood and identity politics. With its goal of greater equality, Social Justice naturally engenders an assessment of which societal members are disadvantaged and a focus on groups (rather than individuals) that experience the injustices of subordinate status. Identity-based groups strengthen and amplify appeals for equality. Race, gender, religion, ethnicity, sexual orientation, disability status, national origin, and other identifying factors become the bases for political agendas and political action. Identity politics likely increases social activism and can create greater recognition of the injustices experienced by non-dominant groups. These are important benefits when, as in the United States, there are entrenched structural inequalities.

At the same time, identity politics has shortcomings. In their pursuit of equality, marginalized groups may engage in competitive victimhood, claiming greater suffering than other groups. Whenever access to resources is difficult—which is true of disadvantaged groups by definition—distinct victim groups will vie with each other for a larger share.[8] Claiming greater victimization, while justified when the comparison is with dominant societal groups, can be problematic when the comparison is with other groups that have also suffered injustice and discrimination. There is much research showing that the perception of discrimination against one's own minority group is sometimes associated with more negative attitudes toward other minorities.[9] Competitive victimhood can lead to tensions between marginalized groups, which only serves the dominant group that largely controls society's resources.

A second problem with identity-based politics is that in a fragmented society such as ours, reinforcing subgroup identities contributes to a lack of unity. As Arthur Schlesinger stated in 1991 in *The Disuniting of America,* a focus on ethnic differences with little attention to similarities can fracture the civil polity. Social psychologists note that the remedy for this splintering is a common group identity, essentially a superordinate identity (such as American) that can be embraced by all and can coexist with the different subgroup identities. In fact, researchers have found that there are benefits to having *both* a superordinate identity and a subgroup identity.[10] The goal, then, is to get all members of society to adopt a meaningful identity like "American" that is valued by all, a difficult feat in these days of bitterly divided politics.

Since the 1970s, as ethnic and racial diversity has increased in the United States, identity politics has grown as well. During this same period, the bottom half of the income distribution in the United States has seen stagnant wages and decreased job security. Although racial diversity and economic insecurity are not causally related, they are nevertheless seen as such by many white working-class Americans. They see a Social Justice agenda on the left focused primarily on racial equality, based in an identity politics that fails to include them.[11]

Government entitlements typically concentrate on the poor, not the working class, and the racialization of poverty has led to a view on the right that Blacks and people of color are getting more than their fair share of resources. The left's advocacy of race-based justice reinforces this perception. The original sin of racism has certainly not been adequately addressed in this country, but this does not preclude the white working class from feeling that they have been ignored. Unfortunately classism and elitism, born of educational achievement and economic security, often taint the left's views of this class. For their part, many white workers' embrace of the politics of hate and division more than justifies the left's negative views. Nevertheless, the strained relationship between liberals and the white working class has not benefited either group.

The mutual disdain recalls Hillary Clinton's use of "deplorables" to describe supporters of Donald Trump: "You could put half of Trump's supporters into what I call the basket of deplorables. . . . The racist, sexist, homophobic, xenophobic, Islamophobic—you name it. And unfortunately there are people like that." Many people forget, however, that she described the other half of Trump supporters as people who "feel that the government has let them down" and are "desperate for change. . . . Those are people we have to understand and empathize with as well."[12]

In the years following World War II, the white working class was able to count on raises in income and living standards from one generation to the next. But with the decline of manufacturing in recent years, this trajectory has turned downward for those without a college education. How far the working class has fallen can be seen in the findings of a major study by the Federal Reserve Bank of St. Louis. In 1989, white college graduates and working-class whites owned the same share of wealth in the United States—46 percent and 45 percent, respectively. By 2016 this had changed dramatically. White college graduates owned three times the share of the white working class— 67 percent to 22 percent.[13]

Those stark numbers tell us that the white working class is justified in feeling overlooked. The stable, good-paying full-time jobs that were once a staple of American life are at the heart of Trump's slogan "Make America Great Again." Also inherent in this nostalgia, sadly, is an image of America in which Blacks are largely out of sight, away from comfortable suburbs and prestigious schools, working in menial jobs, and never in positions of authority. Now that that status is changing, many in the white working class believe that Blacks and people of color have become the takers in a zero-sum game, pushing white people out of well-deserved jobs and homes—and, further, that liberals are abetting this process for nefarious reasons. While this myth is widespread on the right, the true beneficiaries of U.S. economic policy over the past fifty years have not been Blacks, Indigenous people, or Latinos, but the wealthy. The Federal Reserve of St. Louis found that even given the decreasing wealth of working-class whites, it still far surpasses that of non-whites. White working-class families have nine times more wealth than their Black counterparts.[14] The economic inequality in this country is astounding, as is the lack of social mobility, as we'll see below. We are now the most unequal major industrial nation in the Western world, and the problem lies at the top of the economic ladder, not with the people of color struggling on the bottom rungs.

How Little We Know: Wealth and Race

Are Americans aware of the country's wealth inequality? The social psychologists Michael Norton and Dan Ariely asked a nationally representative sample about wealth distribution in the United States and found that survey participants dramatically underestimated the nation's level of inequality. Yet they preferred distributions that were far more equitable than what they thought existed. Although Republicans and the wealthy in the sample desired a less equal distribution than Democrats and the poor, all demographic groups wanted a more equal distribution than what currently exists. Few recognized the true extent of inequality in America today.

Perceptions of wealth inequality are particularly inaccurate when it comes to race. One team of social psychologists looked at how a national sample of Americans estimated the Black-white wealth gap.[15] They found that racial wealth inequality was vastly underestimated. Respondents believed that Black households have $90 for every $100 held by white households. Yet the median wealth of white households in 2019 was $188,200, and median wealth of Black households was $24,100, less than 15 percent that of whites.[16] There is a general perception that discrimination has been overcome and the United States is approaching racial equality, but the economic data powerfully tell us otherwise.

Even before the coronavirus pandemic made the disparities even worse, people of color were at a great economic disadvantage. Over the past thirty years, the average wealth of white families has grown by 84 percent: three times that of Black families. Over the same thirty-year period, the wealth of the four hundred richest Americans grew by an average of 736 percent, twenty-seven times the rate of growth for the Black population and ten times the rate of growth for the Latino population. If Black wealth continues to grow at the pace of the past 30 years, it will take another 228 years for the average Black family to amass the same amount of wealth the average white family now has. It will take Latino families 84 years.[17]

For white and Black families with children living at home, Black households have one cent for every dollar held by white (non-Hispanic) households. One-third of Black families have zero or negative wealth, compared with 15 percent of white families, so the consequences of medical emergencies, divorce, and job loss are often disastrous.[18]

Home ownership has been a major way to build wealth in America, but Blacks have been locked out of this opportunity. Wealth of parents or grandparents facilitates a first home purchase, but this family financial help has generally not been available to Blacks. Government help has also not been available to Blacks. In 1934, Congress created the Federal Housing Administration (FHA), which insured private mortgages and resulted in lower interest rates and smaller down payments on homes. But the administration based its loans on maps that essentially denied this financial backing to Blacks. As Ta-Nehisi Coates writes in the *Atlantic,*

On the maps, green areas, rated "A," indicated "in demand" neighborhoods that, as one appraiser put it, lacked "a single foreigner or Negro." These neighborhoods were considered excellent prospects for insurance. Neighborhoods where black people lived were rated "D" and were usually considered ineligible for FHA backing. They were colored in red. Neither the percentage of black people living there nor their social class mattered. Black people were viewed as a contagion. Redlining went beyond FHA-backed loans and spread to the entire mortgage industry, which was already rife with racism, excluding black people from most legitimate means of obtaining a mortgage.[19]

The Federal Housing Administration is often credited with building the modern American middle class. Yet between 1934 and 1962, fully 98 percent of FHA-insured loans went to white Americans.[20] It is as if the federal government engineered the wealth gap. When Blacks purchased a home, their mortgage rates were typically higher than the rates for whites of equal creditworthiness. And their houses have not appreciated as well as homes owned by whites because prices have remained stubbornly tied to the racial makeup of neighborhoods.

Other government programs were also crafted to help whites and not Blacks. Through the Social Security Act of 1935, insurance for old age and unemployment specifically excluded domestics and farmworkers, two job categories that were heavily occupied by Blacks. At the time, the NAACP (National Association for the Advancement of Colored People) called this new safety net "a sieve with holes just big enough for the majority of Negroes to fall through."[21]

For Black Americans, enormous roadblocks have been placed in the path of wealth accumulation, a process that accrues over generations. Whites have been the beneficiaries of government assistance, helping to create a white middle class. "Wealth begets wealth," Nikole Hannah-Jones writes in the *New York Times Magazine,* "and white Americans have had centuries of government assistance to accumulate wealth, while the government has for the vast history of this country worked against black Americans doing the same."[22]

Desperately Seeking Social Justice

If white working-class resentment of Blacks is misplaced, we need to take a closer look at inequality in America to see where the real problem lies. The job market has changed, with more automation and artificial intelligence technologies creating job losses, particularly for those with less education. But we should also be very aware of who has benefited from the vast and growing inequality in the country. During the Covid-19 pandemic, as millions of Americans lost their jobs and financial security, not only did the rich not experience financial losses—they got richer. In the eight months between March 18 and November 24, 2020, the wealth of America's billionaires grew by $1.2 trillion, while millions of other people grew hungry and faced evictions.[23]

Before Covid, though, it already looked like we had entered a new Gilded Age. The one undeniable fact about economic growth in the United States is that the beneficiaries have overwhelmingly been those already at the top of the economic ladder. We have become a country of dramatic inequality that has only been heightened by the pandemic. Milton Friedman, the guru of conservative economic policies, wrote in 1980 that "the free market system distributes the fruits of economic progress among all people."[24] The past four decades have proved him dead wrong. The conservative push for unfettered capitalism, deregulation, and individual autonomy in the marketplace has not created positive outcomes for all members of society.

As political scientists Jacob Hacker and Paul Pierson write, the rising tide hasn't lifted all boats; instead, "yachts are rising, but dinghies are largely staying put."[25] The middle class has been abandoned and the rich have gotten richer—and, Hacker and Pierson argue, the increasing inequality is the work of political forces, specifically the power of those at the top to institute self-serving policies. In 2019, wealth inequality was not only the highest ever recorded in the United States but far higher than that of any western European country. As the World Inequality Report 2018 shows, the inequality in the United States in 1980 was similar to that of the western European countries but is far greater today. The *income* share of the top 1 percent in 1980 was about 10 percent in both regions. Over the next thirty-five years it rose slightly, to 12 percent, in western Europe but to 20 percent in the United States. The rise in *wealth* inequality has been especially large in the United States, with the top 1 percent increasing their share of the nation's wealth from 22 percent in 1980 to 39 percent in 2014—and with most of that rise going to the top 0.1 percent. Over the same period, the top 1 percent in the United Kingdom increased its share of wealth from 19 percent to 20 percent, and in France from 18 percent to 23 percent. While some point to globalization as the primary engine of inequality, the divergent paths taken by the United States and western Europe—which is no less subject to globalization than America—strongly argue for the primary role of economic and social policies in creating great wealth disparities in the United States. The levels were similar in 1980 but are radically different today.

The top 10 percent of Americans now own 70 percent of the nation's wealth, more than the amount owned by the bottom 90 percent. The four hundred richest Americans have more wealth than the 150 million Americans in the bottom 60 percent of the wealth distribution.[26]

Chief executive pay in the United States is remarkably high as well, averaging $17.2 million at the top 350 firms in 2018—exceeding the typical worker's compensation by 278 to 1. The ratio was fifty-eight to one in 1989 and twenty to one in 1965. From 1978 to 2018, inflation-adjusted CEO compensation grew by 940.3 percent, whereas the typical worker's wages grew by only 11.9 percent.[27] It is highly unlikely that today's CEOs are that much more skilled than their predecessors, and although those at the top want to promote the case that obscene pay packages are essential for retaining the best leaders, there is little support for this argument. As Nobelists Esther Duflo and Abhijit Banerjee maintain, financial incentives are far less power-ful than we think. "No one," they point out, "seriously believes that salary caps lead top athletes to work less hard in the United States than they do in Europe, where there is no cap." Moreover, research has shown that when tax rates go up, the rich don't work less. "Chief executives and top athletes are driven by the desire to win and be the best."[28]

Social psychological research is also unequivocal in showing that we determine our self-worth, including our satisfaction with our mon-etary compensation, by comparing ourselves to others—especially those similar to us.[29] Chief executive officers, for instance, compare their pay with that of other CEOs at comparable firms. In a hypothet-ical world, a chief executive who makes $10 million while comparable CEOs earn $5 million would be more satisfied than one who makes $15 million while others earn $20 million. If chief executive officer compensation had remained at, say, twenty times the average worker's pay, satisfaction would not have suffered. The psychological perks of being at the top would remain, and CEOs would stay on the job.

In addition to compensation, the other major driver of inequality has been the changes in the U.S. tax code since 1970, which have made taxes increasingly less progressive. Americans with the highest incomes now pay barely more, in percentage terms, than those with the lowest incomes. In 2018 the four hundred top earners were taxed at a lower overall rate than working-class Americans. In their book *The Triumph of Injustice,* the economists Emmanuel Saez and Gabriel Zucman show that together, the gain in the top's pretax income and the lower tax rate account for essentially all of current U.S. extreme inequality.[30] In 1950, for example, the wealthiest four hundred earners were taxed at an average rate of 70 percent; in 1980, at 47 percent; and in 2018, at just 23 percent. Among the bottom 50 percent of earners, income after taxes and transfers has grown by just $8,000 in constant dollars since 1970 ($19,000 to $27,000), whereas the average income of the top 1 percent of earners, after taxes and transfers, increased fivefold, from $1 million to $5 million, and the income of the top 0.01 percent went from $3.5 million to $24 million (a sevenfold increase).

While the rich were receiving large tax benefits, the federal minimum wage has not changed from $7.25 in more than a decade, and the small gains by middle- and lower-income workers were offset by far greater gains by the wealthy. In accounting for the great divergence in inequality between western Europe and the United States, the authors of the World Inequality Report 2018 pointed to the decline in tax progressivity and the "massive educational inequalities" in the United States. "Out of a hundred children whose parents are among the bottom 10% of income earners, only twenty to thirty go to college. However, that figure reaches ninety when parents are within the top 10% earners."[31]

These excesses of wealth are not always hidden behind the gates of large country estates or in exclusive clubs or office towers. Sometimes wealth is very public. If you fly out of Los Angeles International

Airport, you can use a deluxe private terminal with an annual membership fee of $4,500 and an additional fee of $3,000 per trip. A $1,000 Legends ticket at Yankee Stadium can buy you a seat in the first few rows at field level and get you escorted into the stadium by a security guard, so you don't have to wait in line with the other fans. During the California fires, as many houses burned to the ground, the superwealthy paid for private firefighters to protect their property.[32]

In his landmark, data-driven book *Capital in the Twenty-First Century*, the economist Thomas Piketty argues that when the economy does well, it disproportionately helps those who already have wealth and capital.[33] One of his key ideas is that invested capital (such as real estate or stock market holdings) grows faster than income, so if you rely on income, in an expanding economy you'll never catch up with those who already have invested capital. And of course to own invested capital, you have to have the money to invest.

Piketty argues that capitalism is working exactly as it is supposed to and therefore that inequality is inevitable in free-market capitalism. The more perfect the market, the higher the rate of return on capital compared with the rate of economic growth. Piketty's remedy is a global progressive tax on wealth—global so that the rich can't move their assets to other countries.[34] There are additional remedies directly aimed at redistribution that would shrink the gap, including more progressive taxes, taxes on financial transactions, raising the minimum wage, strengthening unions through changes in labor laws, and giving workers a say in corporate governance. All of these policies are opposed by most conservatives, who instead favor even lower income and capital-gains taxes and the elimination of the estate tax. These moves would only widen the gap between the wealthy and everyone else.

The substantial disagreements between liberals and conservatives on inequality clearly have the potential to impact the distribution of wealth in the country. A large survey by the Democracy Fund Voter Study Group, a research collaboration of more than two dozen scholars and analysts, found a large political divide on economic issues.[35] Seventy-five percent of Republicans supported reducing regulation, versus 23 percent of Democrats; and 72 percent of Democrats supported making it easier to unionize, compared with just 16 percent of Republicans.

Researchers have also found that the wealthy hold distinct opinions. In a recent study that focused on the policy positions of the top 1 percent, and in particular their differences from the general population, the authors concluded that the very rich are far more conservative regarding economic regulation, taxation, and especially social welfare programs. Wealthy respondents strongly opposed any government action to redistribute income or wealth or to regulate Wall Street or corporations.[36] These policy preferences held among those who had inherited their money and those who were self-made, young and old, male and female, well educated and not, regular attendees at religious services and those who did not attend services. There were two demographic exceptions to this consistency. One was that Jewish respondents were far less likely to want to cut back social welfare programs than non-Jewish respondents. The other was that professionals (primarily doctors and lawyers) were more likely to favor regulation of industries, environmental protections, and some social welfare programs than business owners, business managers, or investors. But the primary differentiating factor was party identification: Republicans were far more conservative than Democrats. This sample of the top 1 percent contained more than twice as many Republicans (58 percent) as Democrats (27 percent), echoing a consistent finding that wealthy Americans are more likely to identify as Republicans than the less affluent.

Attributions, Meritocracy, and Social Mobility

The left-right distinction is also the major factor in differentiating the political preferences of the broader population. When it comes to inequality, liberals and conservatives have diverging views that justify their distinct policy preferences.

The Democracy Fund Voter Study Group asked participants to rate explanations for inequality. Those on the right were more likely than those on the left to credit the rich for their accumulation of wealth and more likely to blame the poor for their poverty.[37] In light of these differences, it is noteworthy that the two sides of the political spectrum focus their anger and resentment on different ends of the economic ladder. Conservatives typically feel that the poor are not working hard and are taking more than they deserve; they view those close to the bottom rungs of the ladder as freeloaders living off government handouts. Liberals typically see those at the top as greedy and responsible for an economic system that overcompensates them and denies resources to those below. While the left seeks more help for those who have not profited from the recent U.S. economic expansion and seeks redistribution, the right seeks to cut entitlements for the poor and lower taxes on corporations and the wealthy.

Each side has its distinct political narrative regarding wealth. To conservatives, the wealthy earned their position through hard work and therefore deserve to keep their assets and earnings. In the economic realm, where Social Order morality endorses freedom and autonomy, these views justify and help perpetuate a society of haves and have nots. Conservatives consider redistribution through the lens of Fairness and focus on their perceptions of individuals' contributions. Liberals take into account systemic factors and, importantly, consider the distribution of wealth across society. The liberal account acknowledges that hard work certainly plays a role in producing economic success, but does not regard it as sufficient.[38] People can work very hard and never move up the economic ladder, and hard work alone cannot account for the riches of those at the top. The left's "provide" morality, based in Social Justice, favors greater equality and is dissatisfied with the large gap between haves and have nots.

As Elizabeth Warren said during her first campaign for the U.S. Senate, "There is nobody in this country who got rich on his own. Nobody. You built a factory out there—good for you. But I want to be clear. You moved your goods to market on the roads the rest of us paid for. You hired workers the rest of us paid to educate. You were safe in your factory because of police forces and fire forces that the rest of us paid for."[39]

During his campaign for reelection in 2012, President Obama built on Warren's words:

> Look, if you've been successful, you didn't get there on your own. . . . There was a great teacher somewhere in your life. Somebody helped to create this unbelievable American system that we have that allowed you to thrive. Somebody invested in roads and bridges. If you've got a business—you didn't build that. Somebody else made that happen. The Internet didn't get invented on its own. Government research created the Internet so that all the companies could make money off the Internet. The point is, is that when we succeed, we succeed because of our individual initiative, but also because we do things together.[40]

The right heard these comments as an assault on hard work and self-reliance. At the Republican Convention in 2012, the phrase "We built it" was everywhere and was mentioned in the major speeches at the multiday event. Conservatives rallied behind their shared belief that people succeed by their own efforts. They fail by their own efforts, too, and that accounts for inequality.

The belief in the efficacy of hard work and self-reliance speaks to the right's continued belief in merit as the basis of the social order. The United States has traditionally been viewed as a land of opportunity whose meritocracy makes success available to all. Here, hard work and self-reliance guarantee success; you reap what you sow. But these days, meritocracy in America is more a legitimizing myth that serves the Social Order morality and less and less a means of actual social mobility.[41] It legitimizes wealth and power while often failing to reward hard-working Americans struggling to move up the ladder.

The meritocracy myth feeds a sense among the economic elite that they earned their positions through their own talents and efforts. Just as Fairness is used to justify poverty at the bottom, so it can be used to justify the accumulation of wealth at the top.

Acceptance of meritocracy also preempts the antipathy that many lower-income Americans might otherwise feel toward the rich. Many people in the middle and lower rungs of the economic ladder are strongly motivated to believe that there is an upward path for them. They embrace the current system rather than acknowledge the dismal alternative—that their prospects are exceedingly dim.[42] Conservatives' emphasis on individual (internal) rather than systemic (situational) attributions for poverty and wealth allows them to continue believing in a functioning meritocracy. It serves as a psychological salve and at the same time reinforces the position of those at the top. In contrast, the liberal emphasis on systemic factors acknowledges meritocracy's illusory promises in America today and focuses on policies that could produce change and reduce societal inequalities.

True meritocracies can exist only when there is equal opportunity.

"Equal opportunity for all" has long been an American mantra, yet it cannot be true when people start with such disparate resources and access to education, income, safety, and employment. Unequal starting points necessarily translate into unequal opportunity. Imagine that getting ahead in society is a hundred-yard dash, but instead of all participants taking their places at the starting line, some get to start many yards in front of the starting line, while others have to start many yards back. This is the United States today, with some people advantaged and others disadvantaged at the starting gate to American success. And yet the belief in a meritocracy too often leads to blaming those who don't win in the rigged competition.

Social Mobility and the Great Gatsby Curve

The test of whether meritocracy is reality or myth in the United States is the country's degree of social mobility, and here the evidence strongly points toward myth. When there is social mobility, you can move up or down the economic ladder based on your own actions rather than your parents' economic standing. Your position at birth does not determine your future prospects. It has gotten very hard to move up in the United States. If you make little money in your first job, you'll probably still be making little decades later. And this lack of social mobility does not depend on whether you have a college degree. If you're not born into the top economic tier, the odds are great that you'll never get there.[43]

In a multination report from the Organisation for Economic Co-operation and Development, the United States fared more poorly on indices of social mobility than almost anywhere else. For example, in a study of twenty-six countries, the percentage of managers whose parents were also managers was higher in the United States than in all other countries. And the United States had the highest percentage of people in the bottom quartile of income whose parents were also in the bottom quartile.[44]

As reported in the *Financial Times,*

> In 1970, 30-year-olds [in the United States] had a 90 per cent chance—almost a guarantee—of earning more than what their parents earned at the same age, adjusted for inflation. Ten years later, a 30-year-old still had an 80 per cent chance of making more money than their parents. . . . In contrast to previous generations, about half of 30-year-olds in 2016 are earning less than their parents earned at the same age. And it is not just something about the age of 30. The trend also holds if you compare today's 40-year-olds to their parents. . . . US social mobility fell by more than 70 per cent in the past half-century.[45]

The chances of improving your own economic position have dramatically declined in the United States. Increasingly there are sticky rungs on the ladder, leaving people more likely to remain where they began. Perhaps not surprisingly, Bong Joon-ho's film *Parasite,* which won the Oscar for best picture for 2019, strongly resonated with American viewers. The film portrays the wide chasm between the worlds of the rich and poor in South Korea, but the same chasm exists in the United States. The poor Kims manage to deviously work their way into the home and lives of the rich Parks and are clearly competent at their jobs. At the end of the movie, following an episode of startling violence, the Kim son presents a plan to get rich and save his father, who is in hiding from the police. As the audience watches, it appears that Kim has been able to fulfill his dream, but the final shot of the movie makes it clear this was only in his imagination, and he is back—and stuck—where he began. *Parasite* is a powerful portrayal of the false hopes conveyed by the myth of meritocracy and the harsh reality of social immobility.

Your parents' economic position has become the primary factor in educational outcomes as well. As Robert Putnam notes, "Now, your family income matters more than your own abilities in terms of whether you complete college. . . . Smart poor kids are less likely to graduate from college now than dumb rich kids. That's not because of the schools, that's because of all the advantages that are available to rich kids."[46]

In *The Tyranny of Merit,* Michael Sandel powerfully exposes the failure of the American promise of equal opportunity, which has created a competition that derogates the losers and unjustly honors the winners. The highly educated now resemble a hereditary aristocracy. In *The Meritocracy Trap,* Daniel Markovits also claims that meritocracy, which once furthered social mobility, paradoxically produced its own poisonous system of privilege and inequality. Meritocracy has created a caste system that restricts access to the best schools and the best jobs and transmits privilege and wealth across generations. In the 1960s, in an effort to increase social mobility, elite universities began to expand admissions beyond the hereditary elite to include candidates chosen on merit. Achievement mattered. Yet today, across the Ivy League, more students come from the top 1 percent than from the entire bottom half of the income distribution.[47]

For past generations, education was the prime mechanism for social mobility, but now educational systems perpetuate the very social inequalities that they should help improve. The Center for Education Policy Analysis at Stanford University has found that racial economic disparities are strong predictors of the racial achievement gap.[48] Poor schools are mostly found in impoverished neighborhoods, while wealthy neighborhoods can pay for far better schools. These inequalities thwart aspirations for moving up. Those with wealth pass their privilege to their children, who move from expensive preschools to $50,000-a-year private schools and after-school enrichment programs and tutoring to costly SAT prep courses and prestigious unpaid summer internships.

Social mobility is at depressingly low levels in the United States while inequality is at record-high levels. And the two are related: the greater the economic inequality, the lower the social mobility. This negative association is known as the Great Gatsby Curve, a term introduced by Alan Krueger, chair of the Council of Economic Advisers, in his President's Economic Report to Congress in 2012. As the rich in America have gotten richer, those in the middle and bottom of the wealth distribution are increasingly stuck as the economic elite move the top rungs of the ladder ever farther out of reach.

Yet just as Americans underestimate the extent of inequality in the United States, they overestimate the degree of social mobility. Social psychologists Shai Davidai and Thomas Gilovich found that people underestimated downward mobility but, to a far greater degree, overestimated upward mobility.[49] Here, political affiliation was important. Conservatives were more likely than liberals to overestimate upward social mobility.

These overestimates are consistent with conservatives' belief that one's station in life—whether rich or poor—is determined by one's individual effort. Psychological research has shown that perceptions of higher economic mobility directly affect people's attitudes toward inequality, and this relationship is mediated by how much one believes that people's economic position is a product of their own efforts.[50] The more a person believes in the possibility of moving up the economic ladder, the more willing they are to accept the unequal distribution of wealth in America. The conservative teaching that hard work and personal responsibility pave the way for unlimited success is precisely the kind of belief that leads people to trust in the possibility of upward mobility and, in turn, to be complacent about vast inequality.

Wealth and the Affordances of Power

Wealth confers power, and in the political arena this means access and influence. In the study of people in the top 1 percent of the economic scale, the researchers found that fully 84 percent of the sample paid attention to politics "most of the time," and 21 percent "bundled" others' political contributions, a very uncommon practice among everyday Americans. The wealthy study participants were also more in touch with politicians, with almost half having contacted their senator or some congressional office. As the study's authors note, fundraising and access are consistent with the findings of others showing that in the United States, political activity, especially donating money (regardless of the amount), is positively associated with wealth.[51]

Many Americans, particularly those on the left, believe that money has far too much influence in politics. In the early months of the presidential campaign of 2016, 158 families donated $176 million to presidential candidates, almost half of all the political donations to those candidates.[52] By a huge margin, the contributions went to Republican candidates (138 of the 158) rather than Democrats (20 of the 158). These donors were overwhelmingly conservative and were most likely to support candidates who pledged to reduce regulation and cut taxes and entitlement programs.

Most of the $176 million was given through channels made legal by the Supreme Court's *Citizens United* decision of 2011. No longer do campaign finance laws limit how much donors can contribute, and now money can be given while the donors' names are shielded from the public. Economic clout has been converted into political clout, and this political clout is far more likely to reflect the ideology of the right than the left. Wealth inequality becomes political inequality, with money being the proxy for power in a market economy and with *Citizens United* providing an easy avenue for money to directly impact political decisions without public accountability. In an economic world driven by individualism, the wealthiest are best able to take advantage of the system—to earn more, protect their assets, and set the rules.[53]

Wealth confers power and with it the ability to have your voice heard. Some might argue that the wealthy are knowledgeable and well informed and therefore *should* have the loudest voice in political decisions. A classic social psychology experiment may serve as a cautionary tale regarding the tendency to overestimate the knowledge of those at the top. Lee Ross, Teresa Amabile, and Julia Steinmetz were interested in the impact of social roles and in our sensitivity to the constraints of these roles.[54] In the context of a general knowledge quiz game, they randomly assigned participants the role of "questioner" or "contestant" by a flip of the coin in their presence.

The questioners were asked to come up with ten "challenging but not impossible" questions from their own general knowledge. They were told to draw from any area in which they had expertise or interest—"for example, movies, books, sports, music, literature, psychology, history, science, etc." The questioners and contestants worked in pairs, and each contestant's task was to answer the ten questions posed by the questioner. The questioner's advantage in asking the questions was soon apparent, as contestants weren't able to answer a number of the relatively esoteric questions. (Examples included "What do the initials W. H. in W. H. Auden's name stand for?" and "What is the longest glacier in the world?") The researchers also created a third group, observers who witnessed the quiz game and subsequently rated the general knowledge of both contestants and questioners.

Clearly the questioners had a *role-conferred advantage,* in that they were the ones asking the questions, which were intended to be very difficult. Yet the observers seemed insensitive to this advantage: they consistently rated the contestants as below average in general intelligence and the questioners as exceptional.[55] However, the researchers administered a general knowledge quiz (fifteen moderately difficult questions drawn from the game show *Jeopardy*) to both contestants and questioners at the conclusion of the study and found no differences between the two groups.

The questioners did not have superior knowledge. The observers, in rating them more intelligent, were responding only to their superior position in the quiz setting. Had the roles been reversed, the contestants could have prepared ten questions that would no doubt have stumped the questioners. The observers were not sufficiently sensitive to the affordances and constraints associated with roles and ranks.[56]

This was a psychology experiment, but there are many contexts outside the laboratory in which social roles also create illusory differences. The power differences between bosses and employees, for instance, also create unequal opportunities for control and advantaged self-presentation. Precisely *because* of the privileged role they occupy, those at the top, who metaphorically "ask the questions," are apt to be perceived as smarter, more knowledgeable, and more deserving of the privileged social role they occupy.

No doubt many will respond that those in powerful roles got there in the first place through their superior talents and hard work. There are clearly very talented, hard-working people in top positions. There are also those who got there not because of talent and hard work but by nepotism, connections, or inherited wealth. More important, there are very talented, hard-working people in relatively powerless positions. And in a society as unequal as ours, the role advantages already conferred on the powerful make it increasingly difficult to move those who are asked the questions into the position of those who ask them. Role-conferred advantage has the unfortunate effect of perpetuating existing power differences.

In addition, regarding the knowledge of the wealthy, it is likely that they know more about the tax code and economic regulations than most Americans, given their interest in retaining a financial advantage. But they surely do not know more about the struggles of the poor. They are not apt to know what it's like to worry about having enough food or a roof over one's head or about forgoing necessary medications to pay bills. They do not know what it's like to send one's children to an underperforming school or to lack the money for child care while holding down one or two low-paying jobs to make ends meet. They did not lose their jobs in the Covid-19 crisis, and their homes were not foreclosed in the aftermath of the Great Recession of 2007–9.

A study reported in the *Proceedings of the National Academy of Sciences* showed that economic inequality has a strong effect on generosity. Relative to their means, the wealthy are less generous than poorer individuals when inequality is high.[57] Inequality provides those at the top with a greater sense of entitlement.

There is a good deal of psychological research on the relation between power and concern for others, particularly those lower in the social hierarchy. In a market economy, wealth translates into power, and researchers have found that greater power is associated with lower levels of distress when confronting another's suffering. The researchers tested different mechanisms that could account for their findings and concluded that the cause is motivational: those with power are less dependent on other people and consequently are less invested in interactions with them. They simply care less.[58]

Other studies have shown that greater power minimizes both perspective-taking and the impact of social disapproval.[59] The powerful are less likely to attend to others in social interactions and are less interested in understanding others' views and emotions. Power affords people the luxury of attending to their own agendas, with minimal constraints imposed by others or external circumstances.

Those at the top are more apt to be conservative than liberal. In addition, decreased compassion is more likely to be found in wealthy conservatives than in wealthy liberals, because conservatives' comfort with social hierarchy and their smaller circle of moral concern translate into diminished empathy for those lower on the economic ladder. In the political marketplace, the policies most strongly promoted by the wealthy tend to support the free market and cuts to government entitlements, increasing economic inequality.

Inequality and Democracy

Several large national surveys have shown that in the four decades between 1972 and 2012 Americans became far less trusting of such institutions as religious organizations, media, government, and business, as well as of each other.[60] The degree of public trust tracked income inequality and poverty; as these increased, public trust declined. Researchers noted that public trust is a key indicator of social capital, the cooperative relationships needed for a functioning democracy in which the few represent the interests of the many.

Although successful societies reward individual effort and ability in the interests of greater societal competencies and advances, their success is also dependent on maintaining social bonds. There is mounting evidence that societal well-being is served by a binding morality based on greater egalitarianism. Equality is associated with greater social harmony, happiness, health, and higher quality of life across all members; inequality is associated with low social capital, low social trust, lower community participation, and higher levels of violent crime.[61]

As a nation, we increasingly seem to lack the sense of communal responsibility and interdependence that is central to a liberal morality. Economic individualism has run rampant at the expense of common concern. The left, with its Social Justice morality, views the extreme wealth inequality in the United States as a national disgrace and failure, and there is a recognition that this inequality is reproduced in education, housing, health care, and other aspects of life. Liberals would agree with the ancient Greek historian Plutarch, who wrote, "An imbalance between rich and poor is the oldest and most fatal ailment of all republics."

The left's Social Justice morality leads it to seek remedies for the fatal ailment of extreme inequality. These include more affordable and accessible child care and health care, greater benefits and wages for workers, and progressive taxation that could reduce some of the nation's current wealth disparities. The Social Order response to inequality, even among those not at the top of the economic ladder, simultaneously justifies wealth accumulation at the top and fosters resentment of others on the bottom. The result is a rising threat to American democracy noted by Plutarch and echoed by the Supreme Court justice Louis Brandeis decades ago: "We can either have democracy in this country or we can have great wealth concentrated in the hands of a few, but we can't have both."

10

Social Order and Authoritarianism

One clear threat to our democracy is undoubtedly the authoritarianism promoted by Donald Trump and his Republican base. Inequality threatens a nation by widening divisions between rich and poor that create distrust in institutions and fray societal bonds. Authoritarianism also creates divisions, but its greatest threat is its opposition to democratic norms and institutions. Although authoritarianism is certainly not a necessary outcome of Social Order morality, there are aspects of Social Order morality that make it vulnerable to anti-democratic sentiments. Authoritarianism is a sign of too much Social Order. Before addressing this relation, though, let's consider a very different concern—the problem of too little Social Order, which is a concern on the right.

Not Enough Social Order

In October 2019, Attorney General William Barr gave a speech at Notre Dame University describing threats to the moral order posed by "secularists and their allies among progressives," whom he blamed for social pathologies ranging from rising illegitimacy rates to the drug epidemic, soaring suicide rates, and destruction of the family. Secular liberals, he charged, were given to "licentiousness—the unbridled pursuit of personal appetites at the expense of the common good," and to oppose them "we should do all we can to promote and support authentic Catholic education at all levels."[1]

In *Why Liberalism Failed,* the political scientist Patrick Deneen also lamented the breakdown of traditional values, although his argument is embedded in a larger critique of classical liberalism. He sees the left and right as having a common focus on individualism, two sides of the same coin. Deneen's strong defense of traditional values as antidotes to social pathologies is evident in his adulation of Christian and Stoical teachings and his aversion to changing social roles. For example, he calls women's entry into the workforce a "highly dubious form of liberation."[2]

The conservative interest in protecting the group naturally focuses attention on indices of disorder and instability. From family dissolution to drug use, violence, and suicides, the right bemoans the breakdown of social norms that bind a community. These are genuine concerns for all members of a society who value its members' well-being. We need look no further than the suicide rate in the United States, the highest of any wealthy country, to recognize that there is a problem.[3]

The breakdown of the family is a particular concern on the right. Conservatives view marriage as essential for a stable, healthy society, although their enthusiasm does not extend to same-sex marriage. Having reviewed the research on marriage, the major U.S. psychological and medical associations—including the American Psychological Association, American Medical Association, American Psychiatric Association, and American Academy of Pediatrics—concluded that married adults have "better physical and mental health than their unmarried counterparts" and "greater well-being than members of comparable cohabiting couples." Assuming marital satisfaction and not marital discord, marriage also enhances children's well-being by strengthening the parents' relationship and reducing the risk of household instability. Single parents can certainly provide the "loving guidance in the context of [a] secure home" so crucial for children's positive adjustment, but the demands of parenthood and work are arduous for one person who has to do it all. "Children benefit when their parents are financially secure, physically and psychologically healthy, and not subjected to high levels of stress"—which, the major societies found, are all benefits of marriage.[4]

Is the Left to Blame?

We should be careful to distinguish between recognizing a social problem, such as family dissolution, and identifying the culprits or causes of the problem. For conservatives, the cause of social breakdown is clear—it is the loss of traditional values and authority, and the culprit, too, is clear: it is society's liberals, whom Barr labeled "militant secularists."

Describing the social disruption associated with changing social roles, Deneen writes that "the norm of stable lifelong marriage is replaced by various arrangements that ensure the autonomy of the individuals, whether married or not."[5] The replacement and breakdown of "stable lifelong marriage" are problems attributable to secular liberals, who are perceived as too interested in autonomy and self-gratification in their interpersonal relationships. Conservatives might be surprised to learn, then, that today the most stable marriages are among these secular liberals. As journalist Thomas Edsall writes, "It is the well-educated, often secular liberal elites so detested by social conservatives who are reviving the traditional two-parent family, with declining divorce rates and a commitment to combine forces to invest in their children."[6]

Marital stability in the United States today is primarily a function of education. Divorce rates are around 16 percent for those with at least a college degree, compared with 46 percent for those with no high school diploma. These groups didn't differ in the 1960s and 1970s, but as social psychologist Eli Finkel notes, "Starting around 1980, . . . when income inequality began to soar, these trajectories diverged sharply. Although the divorce rate continues to climb in the least educated group, it has actually declined sharply in the most educated group." And notably, in the United States the level of education is positively associated with political liberalism.[7]

These demographic trends suggest that autonomy in the social domain need not be associated with disorder and family disruption. As Finkel continues, "Despite their loosened romantic and sexual values, educated liberals became more dedicated to family stability and intensive parenting. They did adopt the beliefs that marriage is optional and divorce is acceptable, but in their personal lives, they also sought to build and sustain an egalitarian, mutually fulfilling marriage. Today, educated liberals certainly value individuality and self-expression, but they tend to pursue family stability as a primary means of realizing those values."[8]

This is the stability drawn from personal commitments. Philip Brickman, in his groundbreaking analysis of commitments, makes it clear that we derive meaning and value in our lives through our commitments. We are never committed to things that are easy. Instead, commitments require the recognition that some sacrifice of time, effort, or other resources is an inherent part of the task. Importantly, they also require some freedom of choice, which implies some degree of autonomy.[9] Commitment can be seen in many people's devotion to marriage and children and the fulfillment of social obligations associated with family roles. It is also evident in dedication to a political cause or religious practice. Increasingly, education has provided people with the economic security, psychological resources, and opportunities to make and keep commitments.

Although demographics regarding education and marital stability are telling, Deneen, Barr, and many on the right believe that religion is the means by which people learn to govern themselves and cultivate restraint. This perspective harkens back to the features of proscriptive morality: the assumption is that marriage may be endangered by people's personal appetites and temptations, and religion teaches restraint and the obligation to remain in a marriage. The emphasis is on avoiding the bad, whereas prescriptive morality focuses on approaching the good. From a prescriptive viewpoint, the key to stability is a focus on the positive rather than avoidance of the negative. Stability is based primarily on a chosen commitment that provides benefits to the marital partners, including fulfillment of, in Finkel's words, "high altitude needs" that include emotional and sexual intimacy, growth, and friendship. The difference is reminiscent of a comment by David Brooks in response to *Why Liberalism Failed.* Brooks wrote, "Every time Deneen writes about virtue it tastes like castor oil—self-denial and joylessness. But the liberal democratic moral order stands for the idea that souls are formed in freedom and not servility, in expansiveness, not in stagnation."[10]

In considering social disruption more broadly, we should also recognize where it is most evident. Here again, Edsall is helpful. It is not liberals, he tells us, but the largely conservative white working class that "is now succumbing to the centrifugal, even anarchic, forces denounced by Barr and other social conservatives."[11]

Similarly, the sociologist Robert Putnam, in congressional testimony in 2017, noted that the family disruption once associated with Black families was now more evident among the white working class. "Most Americans are unaware that the white working class family is today more fragile than the black family was at the time of the famous alarm-sounding 1965 'Report on the Negro Family' by Daniel Patrick Moynihan."[12]

The parts of the nation currently experiencing major social disruption are often rural, conservative areas where joblessness, drug use, and family breakdown are destroying lives and communities. Nicholas Kristof and Sheryl WuDunn tell us that fully a quarter of the kids who rode on Kristof's school bus in Yamhill, Oregon, when he was a child are now dead from drugs, alcohol, or suicide.[13] As we saw in chapter 8, the loss of jobs led to the loss of income and dignity and was followed by drug and alcohol use, often criminal records, and decreased likelihood of marriage.

Is Religion the Answer?

For Barr, Deneen, and others on the right, the erosion of religion and the growth of secularism have led to a grim moral upheaval. In a speech to the National Religious Broadcasters Convention in February 2020, Barr again railed against secular progressives, charging that they advocate "totalitarian democracy, which seeks to submerge the individual in a collectivist agenda." Whereas Deneen blames individualism for society's moral decay, Barr blames the left's collectivism, arguing that "religion tends to temper the passion and intensity of political disputes" and we therefore need more religion in politics.[14]

Is religion the answer to our social problems? Interestingly, a Pew Research survey from 2018 showed that the United States is unique internationally in having high levels of both wealth and religiosity.[15] The United States is far more religious than other wealthy nations, certainly more so than western Europe. And yet western Europe has not seen the same levels of social breakdown, violence, and suicide.

A comparison of countries with the highest and lowest percentages of religious people casts doubt on the idea that religion is the antidote to social problems. In the WIN/Gallup International Survey of people in sixty-eight nations in 2017, the ten most religious countries included the Philippines, Papua New Guinea, and Armenia (which are predominantly Christian), as well as Pakistan, Thailand, India, and Nigeria. The least religious countries included China, Japan, Australia, Sweden, the Czech Republic, the United Kingdom, and Belgium. The least religious nations were much better off across multiple social indicators, including unemployment, poverty, homicide rate, life expectancy, and infant mortality. They also had higher GDPs and better-educated populations.[16]

Another concern is the rising number of children living with single parents. The United States has the highest rate of single-parent households across 130 countries, but a Pew Research Center report from 2019 showed no differences in this rate based on religion. "The study, which analyzed how people's living arrangements differ by religion, . . . found that U.S. children from Christian and religiously unaffiliated families are about equally likely to live in this type of arrangement."[17]

Religion may certainly serve as an effective moral authority for some and afford meaning and purpose to others. Nevertheless it is difficult to conclude that religion is the answer to our social ills. Some have argued that religion creates better people, who are more prosocial and benevolent toward others. This, too, is unsupported by data. Both correlational and experimental studies show that the pattern for religion precisely replicates the pattern for conservatives more generally: common identity characterizes the circle of moral concern. Religious individuals are typically more giving and benevolent toward those who share their religion, but they are more prejudiced than the non-religious toward those outside their religious group.[18]

One benefit of religion that could have a positive impact on social disruption is the sense of community people derive from religious affiliation. Sociologists and social critics have lamented the increasing isolation of Americans over the past decades. Robert Putnam's book

Bowling Alone, published in 2000, for example, shows our increasing disconnection from family, friends, neighbors, and organizations. Social isolation has been shown to be a risk factor for suicide, a key indicator of social breakdown. In two large longitudinal studies, men and women with high levels of social integration were less at risk for suicide than those with less social integration. The authors of both studies recommended strengthening or creating new social networks to counter the risks of isolation.[19]

Religion can provide this social connection, but social integration is neither liberal nor conservative. It can also be attained through engagement with extended family, friends, neighbors, and community groups. The advantage of religion posited by Barr and Deneen is not social integration but the strict, restrictive morality promoted by a traditional Christian education, which they believe protects against social disorder and instability.

Although conservatives may claim that "soaring suicide rates" are a result of the secularist assault on traditional values, economic factors are more likely culprits—in particular increasing inequality coupled with job insecurity and an inadequate social safety net. There is a strong correlation between a nation's income inequality (based on a country's Gini index) and its suicide rate. The European countries that have experienced a drop in suicide rates all have lower inequality and stronger safety nets. The same correlation exists among U.S. states. State per capita spending on welfare and public assistance also predicts suicide rates: the less spending, the more suicides.[20]

The number of people reporting extreme mental and emotional problems has increased in the United States in recent years, and this increase has been particularly apparent among whites with low education. Researchers studying this pattern between 1993 and 2019 found that at the individual level, the best predictor of extreme distress was

"I am unable to find work." At the state level, the best predictor was a decline in the share of manufacturing jobs.[21]

Given these findings, it is noteworthy, as Kristof and WuDunn write, that following plant closings in Canada, the government stepped in to help those affected, whereas the U.S. federal government did little to help workers left unemployed by plant closures at General Motors. Little wonder, Kristof and WuDunn note, that the United States lags other nations on a number of social indices.[22]

Providing for community members can forestall social breakdown by creating greater order and stability. Joseph Margulies's account of policing in Olneyville, a run-down neighborhood in Providence, Rhode Island, supports this point.[23] As he reports in his book *Thanks for Everything, Now Get Out,* when the police in Olneyville used strong authority-based policing, there was continued breakdown of the local community. Police changed their tactics and focused instead on working with community members to purchase neglected real estate and rebuild abandoned blocks of the neighborhood. The result was greater order and a major reduction in crime, and the trust and sense of interdependence that grew from working together promised better crime control going forward.

It seems unlikely that dissolute liberals and absence of religious authority are the primary reasons for our social ills. Rather than a more socially constrained society, it seems that we need a more just, caring, connected society, responsive to the needs of all its members.

Going Full Trump: The Road to Authoritarianism

Given conservatives' longing for an orderly, morally upright nation, it is beyond irony that they chose Donald Trump as their vehicle, a man not only invested in dividing Americans but one who has assaulted women, stiffed workers on his building projects, paid hush money to a porn star, and lied incessantly, topping thirty thousand lies during his four-year term in office.[24] For establishment Republicans, the embrace of Trump was largely transactional, and it seemed to pay off with his two main achievements: a tax cut for the rich and very conservative appointments to the courts. But Trump turned the party into a cult of personality, with the loyalty test being acceptance of the lie that the election of 2020 was stolen from him. The transactional decision proved to be a Faustian bargain. These Republicans lost the party they had known, and the nation has come close to losing its democracy.

As a problem of too much Social Order, authoritarianism relies on extreme forms of restrictive morality's key elements: authority, conformity, loyalty, and veneration of strength and power. Trump's presidency saw no end of anti-democratic, authoritarian actions. From calling the press the "enemy of the people," continually telling Americans that the election of 2020 would be rigged, sucking up to dictators around the world, praising an assault on a reporter, pressuring Ukraine to investigate Biden, failing to disavow white supremacists, criticizing judges for having Mexican ancestry, pardoning a U.S. Navy Seal accused of war crimes, cruelly separating children from their parents at the border, and failing to commit to a smooth transition of power when he was not reelected, Trump moved far beyond the boundaries of appropriate behavior by a democratic leader. According to the Varieties of Democracy Project (V-Dem), which tracks the health of democracies around the world, Trump attacked the very pillars of our constitutional system—including freedom of speech, the right to vote, and the independence of the judiciary.[25]

In *Democracy Rules,* the political scientist Jan-Werner Muller writes that there are two "hard borders" for maintaining a democracy. First, the political standing of other citizens cannot be undermined (as in the case of voting restrictions), and second, people must be "constrained by what we can plausibly call facts."[26] Trump and his minions have failed on both counts.

Record numbers of American voters went to the polls or mailed in their ballots in the presidential election of 2020. The voting went smoothly, but the days passed following Election Day with no winner declared, and anxiety climbed on both sides. On November 10, the race finally ended. Joe Biden was the president-elect. On the left, people poured into streets in an explosion of joy and relief. Yet as celebrations continued into the night and the following day, Trump did not concede but made bold and increasingly wild claims that the election had been stolen. He had lost by more than seven million votes.

Trump tried to overturn the outcome in more than sixty court cases; he lost every time. He contested the votes in multiple cities, especially Detroit, Atlanta, Philadelphia, and Milwaukee. You do not have to be a rocket scientist to see the similarity among these cities; each has a very significant Black population. In Georgia, Trump tried to pressure Brian Kemp, the Republican governor, and the Republican secretary of state, Brad Raffensperger, to alter the results; to their credit, they refused. The election of 2020 was the most secure in American history, according to U.S. election officials and in particular the Department of Homeland Security's Cybersecurity and Infrastructure Security Agency. Biden's win was validated by responsible Republican secretaries of state, and even William Barr, Trump's loyal attorney general, announced that the Justice Department found no evidence of voter fraud that could change the outcome.

Yet Trump, taking a page from propagandists' book, relied on a technique he used many times in his presidency—repeating a lie again and again. The repetition created a false reality, known in psychology as the "illusory truth effect."[27] With the help of the right-wing media megaphone, Trump convinced the majority of Republicans that the

Big Lie was true—that he had won but the election had been stolen from him. He incited an armed insurrection on the U.S. Capitol that threatened the lives of elected representatives, and yet those very same Republican officials supported the lie. In January 2020, 139 Republican House members and 8 Republican senators objected to the results of the election. At Trump's second impeachment trial, held days after the Capitol insurrection of January 6, and with his attack on the election known to all, Trump was found not guilty by fully 197 House Republicans and 43 Republican senators.

By the spring of 2021, only 24 percent of Republicans believed that Joe Biden had legitimately won the election, compared with 94 percent of Democrats; 74 percent of Republicans believed that the election had been stolen.[28] The propaganda playbook was once again successful. For many Republican officials, neither gullibility nor private acceptance of the Big Lie likely explained their support of Trump. Instead they were scared, both of a very vengeful former president and of upcoming election losses if they lost the support of his loyal base. They concluded that Trump now had a stranglehold on the party and that Republicans could not win without his loyal followers in tow. Among the elected representatives in Washington, only a few courageous voices—in particular, Liz Cheney and Adam Kinzinger—stood up to Trump in support of democracy, and for their integrity they were booed at state-level Republican events and regarded as personae non gratae within the new Party of Trump.

The Cult Leader

When Trump ran for reelection in 2020, the Republican Party did not write a new party platform, as is customary, but instead simply reused the platform from 2016. This was implicit recognition that the Republicans were not running on ideas or policies but on Trump himself. The party was now the cult of Trump. The word *cult* is not used lightly, because the basic authoritarian nature of cults now characterized the relationship between Trump and his followers. Surely not all Trump voters were akin to cult members—some viewed their support as transactional, and others would vote Republican, or against Democrats, no matter who was on the ticket. But for many, including many working-class whites, Trump was their supreme leader.

Cults are led by charismatic individuals who attract followers by creating their own reality. Hallmarks of cults include subservience and zealous commitment to a strong, idealized leader. In the cult of Trump, key elements of Social Order—loyalty, authority, and conformity—are pushed to extremes. His followers venerate the strongman and dutifully embrace his web of lies and false promises. Cults push the Social Order focus on common identity and vigilance toward outsiders to extremes. Members are dependent on the group for their identity, and fear and hatred of outsiders are cultivated to bolster cult-based group identity and commitment. Members accept and rigidly follow the dogma propagated by their authoritarian leader, a dogma whose conflict with common wisdom is in some ways the point. The absurdity of the dogma distinguishes the cult's followers, marks them as having superior knowledge not available to believers in ordinary reality, and signifies the loyalty of those who make the effort to commit to it. Trump used his followers' loyalty to ignore democratic norms, create false narratives, and raise the specter of an authoritarian America.

The term *authoritarian* describes an anti-democratic political leader who demands loyalty and obedience, reveres power, and does not see himself as responsible to those he governs. Disinformation and devaluation of a free press, used to create false narratives that strengthen the leader's hold on the populace, are primary tools in the authoritarian armament and Trump's playbook. In her classic work on totalitarianism, Hannah Arendt discussed the need for truth and the dire consequences of failing to distinguish between fact and fiction. As a Jewish intellectual writing about the rise of the Nazis, she emphasized the role of propaganda in demonizing the Jews and noted that the real goal of propaganda "is not persuasion but organization."[29] It's less about what you believe than whose side you're on.

Discussing Arendt's claim, David Luban notes that "persuasion aims at changing someone's belief; organization aims at recruiting them to a tribe, so that belief and truth no longer matter. Or rather, the only truth that matters is truth about tribal identity. What matters isn't factual reality, but the reality of 'us,' the real people, in contrast to the poisonous subtlety of 'them,' the tribal adversary in the body politic."[30] Trump's incessant lies, attacks on the media, propagation of fake news, and racist, xenophobic rhetoric fueled this us-them narrative and created a base of loyal cult followers.

In a canny invocation of Social Order morality, Trump presented himself as the "protector," the nation's savior, in the battle between us and them. In his first television interview after the election in 2020, with Maria Bartiromo on Fox News, he presented himself as the lone safeguard against the "radical left": "Nobody wants to do anything with Antifa except me. If I wasn't here, Antifa would be running this country right now. They'd be running the country. . . . And they club people over the heads when nobody is looking, and then nobody talks about it. It's a disgrace. It's absolutely a disgrace. And if I'm not here—I'm sort of your wall."[31]

Trump's authoritarianism relies on the elements of Social Order— strength, conformity, loyalty, and authority—but unlike traditional conservatives, he seems less interested in creating order and stability than in fomenting disorder. Trump's cult has strong Dionysian features that resemble anarchism more than traditional conservatism— from the ecstatic mass rallies and valorization of outrageous behavior to political violence and the rejection of rationality and legal standards. Trump thrives on adulation, and his zealous supporters fulfill this need. We may never know what Trump really thinks of his followers, but a political pamphlet written by James Fenimore Cooper in 1838 titled *The American Democrat* offers a telling description: "The peculiar office of a demagogue is to advance his own interests, by affecting a deep devotion to the interests of the people." It is a symbiotic relationship in which an anti-democratic leader receives loyalty, deference, and adulation, while his acolytes receive a worldview that depicts them as historically significant and revel in membership in his tribe.

The Cult Followers: Economic Losses as Social Breakdown

Crucial for Trump's success is the continued support of his loyal base, largely members of the white working class. Just as we might ask how establishment Republicans, focused on the country's moral upheaval, fell in line behind a man of such evident personal immorality, we might ask how white working-class Americans could turn to Trump as their political savior and believe his lies and false promises. It would be hard to find a less likely candidate: a rich East Coast real estate developer who deals in lies and corruption, whose business ventures fail repeatedly, and who has a history of stiffing blue-collar workers in his employ. One might expect that the white working class would neither like nor trust the superrich. Yet as the law professor Joan Williams points out in her book *White Working Class,* the presence of the ultrarich reinforces these workers' fantasies about getting ahead in America. These blue-collar individuals focus their disdain instead on members of the professional class, who are often thoughtless or condescending toward them. Unlike the ultrawealthy, professionals are people they interact with in their daily lives.[32]

To working-class Americans, professionals are the liberal elites whom they find smug and patronizing. To those without a college degree, the status of a highly educated professional seems unattainable. Becoming rich somehow seems more attainable, and Trump's wealth feeds their fantasies about wealth. His brash speaking style tells his listeners he understands them; he is the exact opposite of the political correctness they associate with the left. And his incivility is meant to show his followers that he's tough—and therefore they are, too. "Trump promises . . . a return to an earlier era, when men were men and women knew their place. It's comfort food for high-school-educated guys. . . . Today they feel like losers—or did until they met Trump."[33]

There is no question that the working class has fallen behind in the United States. The left looks at the nation's vast inequality and thinks that the answer lies with economic policies that provide for all, especially policies aimed at helping the working class—such as minimum wage increases, access to free day care and pre-K so parents can work, job training and retraining programs, stronger unions to empower workers, free community college, and tax credits for first-time home buyers. Liberals view national problems through the lens of providing and economics and are dismayed by the movement of the working class—in particular the white working class—to Trump and the Republicans. There is a certain irony in the fact that the economic policies embraced by the right—anti-labor and anti-regulation—created many of the hardships American workers are undergoing, and yet the white working class has only moved farther right. But this movement makes sense when we recognize how the white working class interprets its economic stress: as a symptom of social disorder and social disruption.

When large segments of the white working class vote Republican, it is not because they don't recognize that they are getting less than they should economically but because they do recognize it. Yet this acknowledgment is embedded in the larger canvas of their own loss of status and the collapse of the traditional American order, where being male, white, and Christian brought social status and respect. Even if they themselves had low-paying jobs and lived in small homes, they were citizens of a country where their kind were in charge. The confluence of an increasingly diverse, multicultural America and increasing economic hopelessness has created the specter of deep disorder and threat—and with it, increasing susceptibility to demagogic messages. As noted earlier, in the 2016 election, Trump voters were motivated more by anxiety around status loss than by economic insecurity.[34]

Liberals ponder the paradox of middle- and lower-income Americans voting against their own interests but don't recognize that these conservative voters are viewing the world through a different moral lens: Social Order rather than Social Justice. The people conservatives blame for the indignity of being replaced or demoted in the social hierarchy are not the wealthy at the top of the economic ladder but the "takers" far below—and the federal government and liberal elites who assist the takers with their social justice agenda. For these working-class conservatives, the takers are primarily Black and brown American citizens and immigrants. The wealthy who benefit from inequality do not threaten the social order, but Black and brown people trying to achieve equality do.

In a series of studies across twenty-eight nations, researchers found that inequality—both objective inequality and subjective perceptions of it—is associated with support for strong leaders who are willing to use undemocratic means to get things done.[35] The social psychologists who conducted the studies looked for a mechanism that could account for this relationship and found that it was the perception of social breakdown. Those who view inequality through the lens of social disorder are more likely to support undemocratic leaders. This pattern is readily apparent in Trump's base. They see inequality in the United States less as evidence of social injustice than of social disorder; and they believe efforts on the left to remedy inequality will further upset the social order. Trump is the strong leader they believe can return order to the nation—by whatever means necessary.

Republicans see the power of catering to these Social Order concerns. The party has long used racist rhetoric and strategies to stir up white status anxiety, but Trump didn't even try to conceal what he was doing. From the Obama birther controversy to the explicit racism and xenophobia he employed while in office, Trump sought to divide the nation while promising a return to the proper "social order." This is how his followers heard "Make America Great Again": it was not exactly "make America white again," though that was part of it, but "restore the old social order." Now out of office, he continues to feed his followers' resentments and egos by demonizing outsiders and promising that his reinstatement is just around the corner.

Trump didn't deliver on his economic promises to the white working class, but this didn't matter to his followers. Journalist Fintan O'Toole described Trumpism's allure as "necromantic": "It promised to make a buried world rise again: coal mines would reopen in West Virginia, lost car plants would return to Detroit. Good, secure, unionized muscle jobs would come back. The unquestionable privilege of being white and male and native would be restored. Trump did not manage to do any of this, of course."[36] But he made his followers believe they were entitled to the status they had lost. They loved him because he validated them in a way that liberals did not.

Authoritarian Followers

Political scientists have begun to describe Trump voters as authoritarians. Matthew MacWilliams, for example, found that authoritarianism was a stronger predictor of support for Trump than income, education, gender, religion, or race. And in their book *Authoritarianism and Polarization in American Politics,* published in 2009, Marc Hetherington and Jonathan Weiler essentially predicted the strong association between authoritarianism and support for Trump. They argued that the polarization in America could generally be explained by a surprisingly large group of authoritarian voters who increasingly sorted themselves into the Republican Party, the party of law and order.[37] In this research, the term *authoritarian* describes a personality profile rather than an opinion about governance.

Particularly noteworthy about this work is the way in which authoritarianism has been measured, and thus the assumed nature of the authoritarian personality. To assess it, political scientists have relied on a measure developed by Stanley Feldman several decades ago. Feldman asked his research subjects four questions about the desirable qualities in children:

1. Please tell me which one you think is more important for a child to have: independence or respect for elders?
2. Please tell me which one you think is more important for a child to have: obedience or self-reliance?
3. Please tell me which one you think is more important for a child to have: to be considerate or to be well-behaved?
4. Please tell me which one you think is more important for a child to have: curiosity or good manners?

He defined authoritarians as those who prefer respectful, obedient, well-behaved, well-mannered children. Feldman no doubt wanted to create a brief measure that was not directly associated with political preferences, and in 1992 the American National Election Studies survey began to include these four items in its questionnaire.[38]

But does the measure actually assess authoritarianism? The items clearly tap respondents' preference for order, authority, and conformity. These are key elements of the Social Order morality that underlies conservatism. Conservatives value respect for authority, conformity, and obedience, as well as behavioral constraint in accord with group standards, all of which speaks to favoring respectful, obedient, well-behaved, and well-mannered children. As I noted in chapter 4, research on parenting and children's political orientation has found that "traditional parenting" focuses on obedience and respect for authority and is associated with children's conservatism in late adolescence.[39]

Given that Social Order underlies conservatism, we would expect a strong positive association between the four-item measure and support for Trump; those who value order and conformity are likely to be conservatives and therefore likely to vote for the Republican candidate—in this case Trump—whether or not they are authoritarians. Political scientists' use of the four-item measure risks lumping too many conservatives into its authoritarian category. And in fact the four-item measure labels a very large percentage of the population as authoritarian. For example, in a poll conducted by *Vox* in 2016 using these four items, 44 percent of white respondents nationwide were found to be authoritarian. The researchers called this finding "actually not unusual. . . . [It] lines up with previous national surveys that found that the authoritarian disposition is far from rare."[40] These previous surveys assessed authoritarianism using the same four-item measure. So *Vox* confirmed only that the same question got the same answer.

Some skepticism is warranted. Psychologists regard authoritarianism as aberrant rather than common or mainstream. The psychologist Robert Altemeyer, building on early studies of fascism by Theodor Adorno, Else Frenkel-Brunswik, and others, describes three components of authoritarianism: authoritarian submission, conventionalism, and authoritarian aggression.[41] Authoritarians are highly submissive in their deference to authority, highly conventional in their adherence to social norms and traditions, and, importantly, have aggressive tendencies toward outgroups and so-called deviants whom authorities target.

Jonathan Weiler has more recently remarked of his earlier work on authoritarianism with Marc Hetherington that their use of the term was likely overinclusive. "The term 'authoritarian,'" he said, "connotes a fringe perspective," but the people he and Hetherington described as authoritarian were "far from fringe."[42]

We might therefore think of authoritarians as conservatives with aggressive tendencies and a need to submit to a strong leader, who also feel very threatened.[43] From a psychological perspective, in contrast to the recent political science view, Trump's base would likely qualify as authoritarians. It would not be an apt label for Trump voters more generally, a group that includes conservatives who prefer the Republican candidate in any election. Trump's authoritarian base includes the insurrectionists who stormed the Capitol building on January 6, 2021, and the white supremacists who came out of the shadows under Trump. Trump not only failed to disavow them; instead his emotional rhetoric fanned their hatred, aggression, and resentment.

The Big Lie and Voter Suppression

The Republican Party believes that it cannot win elections without the support of Trump and his base. The result is a party awash in disinformation and false accounts, indispensable tools in antidemocratic, authoritarian governance.

In late May 2021, congressional Republicans blocked the creation of a bipartisan commission to investigate the mob's attack on the Capitol. In the House, thirty-five Republicans voted for the commission, and in the Senate, six did: Bill Cassidy, Susan Collins, Lisa Murkowski, Rob Portman, Mitt Romney, and Ben Sasse. Gladys Sicknick, the mother of the deceased Capitol policeman Brian Sicknick, who suffered a stroke from the riot and died a day later, tried to meet with every GOP senator to plead for the commission and stress the importance of getting at the truth. Thirteen refused to meet with her, and she didn't change the minds of the twelve she met with. The truth could hurt the party's electoral prospects in 2022. The insurrectionists were their voters, and the investigation could implicate Republican leaders.

Trump maintained his grip on the party, and his main objective remained overturning the election results. At the Conservative Political Action Conference in late February 2020, he was cheered as if he had won the presidency, and conference sessions included "Fraudulent 2020 Elections in South Korea and the United States" and "Protecting Elections: Part 2: Other Culprits: How Judges & Media Refused to Look at the Evidence." As the right-wing media continued to push the Big Lie, questionable recounts run by Trump partisans were conducted amid talk of additional ballot reviews. Trump, who continued to claim victory, remained obsessed with the idea of being reinstated as president. Yet in Maricopa County, Arizona, site of the largest sham recount, the Republican county recorder declared that the state GOP leaders knew the claims of fraud were "laughable," adding, "We can't indulge these insane lies any longer. As a party. As a state. As a country."[44] In the House of Representatives, however, Republican representative Liz Cheney was ousted from her leadership position for calling Trump's claim a lie that was poisoning our democratic system of government. The price of admission to the Republican Party was now loyalty to the Big Lie.

In state legislatures, the Big Lie has been used to justify a massive voter suppression effort. Promoted by the right as efforts to assure election integrity, more than three hundred bills were introduced in forty-seven states, aimed at limiting the Black vote in particular, a vote that goes overwhelmingly for Democrats.[45] Election integrity as a justification for these laws is blatantly deceitful, because election fraud is extremely rare in the United States. The Heritage Foundation's own database shows that there have been only 1,328 proven instances of voter fraud in all elections between 1982 and 2021. Even if we were to find 1,328 cases of fraud in just the election of 2020, the incidence of fraud would be 0.0000838.[46]

The election integrity measures included restrictions on voting by mail and on early voting, reductions in the number of drop boxes, tighter identification requirements, penalties on election officials for failure to purge people from the election rolls, elimination of drive-through voting, greater authority for poll watchers, and more power for state officials to overturn elections through claims of fraud. These laws served to protect only the Republican Party, not election integrity or the nation.

In Georgia, where Black voters often had to stand in line for hours before they could vote in recent elections, the state Republicans made it illegal to give water to people waiting to vote. In Texas, Republicans' restrictive bill initially limited voting on Sunday to the hours of 1:00 p.m. to 9:00 p.m. Why? To attack the "souls to polls" movement, a campaign by Black churches to get out the vote during Sunday morning services.[47] These racist tactics were particularly obvious, but the suppression of the Black vote was evident in bill after bill. As President Biden commented, we were witnessing the imposition of Jim Crow measures in the twenty-first century.

Of great concern as well are the state-level Republican efforts to determine election outcomes after votes are cast. These include laws that would replace leaders of county election boards with partisan officials as well as processes that make it easier to prosecute election officials and limit their independence. These changes allow legislatures to overturn the results of elections and will seriously weaken our voting system. Although Republicans believed that they could not win without Trump and therefore embraced him as their leader, the barrage of new laws shows their awareness that they cannot win with him either—unless they suppress the vote of a key Democratic demographic and control election outcomes. The Republican Party has not only become the Trump party but increasingly the anti-democracy party as well.

In 1963, when Nelson Rockefeller was running for the GOP nomination for president, he warned Republicans that if they embraced Barry Goldwater, a strong opponent of civil rights legislation, they would be pursuing a destructive, short-sighted, racist strategy. George W. Lee, a Black Republican and civil rights activist, warned at the same time that unless things changed, "the Republican Party will be taken over lock, stock, and barrel by the Ku Kluxers, the John Birchers and other extreme rightwing reactionaries."[48] But the party chose Goldwater, and we are now witnessing bald-faced efforts to suppress the Black vote.

The Anti-Democratic Republican Party

The Trump party is anathema to traditional Republicans, who have lost the party they knew. Some, such as Senators Jeff Flake and Rob Portman, have expressed their dissatisfaction by leaving the political arena. Others, particularly commentators such as Max Boot, David Frum, Jennifer Rubin, and Peter Wehner, have expressed their revulsion in newspaper and magazine columns and online. They have spoken out, but many others have not.

In the seats of power in Washington, most elected representatives know that Trump lost the election—the most fair and secure election in U.S. history—and yet with few exceptions they allow the Big Lie to go unchallenged. By their silence they have become complicit in Trump's anti-democratic ploys. Not only do passive bystanders make it easier for perpetrators to continue their wrongdoing, but their passivity alters the bystanders themselves, by making them more accepting of wrongdoing over time.[49]

Mitch McConnell, the Senate minority leader, initially tried to excuse his vote to acquit in the second impeachment trial with some damning words for Trump, but he immediately turned around and said that he would "absolutely" support Trump if he becomes the party's nominee in 2024. McConnell also voted against the January 6 commission. He has said nothing about state restrictions on voting but has explicitly asserted that he is "100 percent focused" on stopping the Biden legislative agenda. A well-functioning democracy requires input, debate, and give-and-take from all sides. But a well-functioning democracy is not McConnell's concern; putting Republicans back in power is his sole objective.[50]

Although hardball tactics are distressing, they are not the most dangerous threats to our democracy today. Gerrymandering has made seats so safe that supporters of QAnon, who not only rally behind Trump but believe (or claim to believe) that liberals are Satan-worshiping pedophiles, have won election as Republican representatives in Congress. Gerrymandering itself is anti-democratic. In 2018 in Wisconsin, for example, Democrats won every statewide election, yet Republicans nevertheless were able to get majorities in both chambers of the state legislature. In North Carolina, the overall House vote went 50 percent for Democrats and 50 percent for Republicans, but Republicans nonetheless got 70 percent of the House seats. By concentrating conservative voters, gerrymandering has moved the Republican Party further to the right. A decade ago, the Tea Party presaged this marked shift to the right, in a Republican primary in Virginia, when the far-right candidate David Brat defeated Eric Cantor, the Republican majority leader in the House. That upset was a wake-up call for the party, a warning that radical right newcomers could now unseat more established conservatives. But it wasn't until Trump took over the party that it truly became authoritarian. Here was a man who ran on law and order but placed himself above the law.

To run for office in the Republican Party in the early 2020s you have to embrace a proven falsehood—or at least appear to. The danger of a party that requires candidates to question the results of a free and fair election should not be underestimated. Multiple studies, including international investigations, have found two very disturbing patterns. First, the United States has become markedly less democratic in recent years, and second, compared with other conservative parties around the world, the Republican Party has become an outlier in its embrace of authoritarianism.

V-Dem consults with more than 3,500 international experts to assess democracies throughout the world. In a report published in 2021, V-Dem focused on autocratization, which it argues follows a similar pattern everywhere: "Ruling governments first attack the media and civil society, and polarize societies by disrespecting opponents and spreading false information, then undermine elections."[51] The report concluded that democracy in the United States declined substantially from 2010 to 2020, and it cited as key contributors Trump's repeated attacks on the media and opposition politicians, as well as the loss of checks and balances on executive power from a weakened legislature. Public political speech, particularly respect for opponents by leaders, also declined significantly in the United States.

Freedom House, a democracy watchdog group that provides annual global rankings of political rights, found similar results. Out of a possible total of 100 points, the United States dropped from 94 in

2010 to 83 in 2020, putting America on a par with Romania and Panama, behind Mongolia and Argentina, and far behind such countries as Great Britain and Costa Rica. The nation's decline as a functioning democracy accelerated under Trump and was fueled in particular by the unequal treatment of minorities, particularly in the domains of voting and criminal justice, as well as by the increased polarization in the country and the powerful influence of money in politics. The report also singles out gerrymandering, and its contribution to polarization and extremism, as "radicalizing" and "corrosive" to our politics.[52]

Further evidence makes it hard for the Republican Party to escape responsibility for this striking decline of democracy. The Global Party Survey, which involves about two thousand experts on political parties, compares political parties on their commitment to basic democratic principles.[53] The survey's report from 2020 states that when compared with the mainstream conservative parties of the OECD (comprising thirty-eight relatively wealthy countries), the U.S. Republican Party is far to the right of other mainstream conservative parties. The Democratic Party, meanwhile, remains a mainstream liberal party. The Republican Party has drifted from such mainstream counterparts as Britain's Conservative Party and Australia's Liberal Party and is now closest to such anti-democratic radical right parties as Turkey's Justice and Development Party, founded by Recep Tayyip Erdoğan, and Poland's Law and Justice Party, a right-wing nationalist-conservative party. On minority rights it ranks worse than Hungary's right-wing Fidesz Party. The current Republican Party is one of the most anti-democratic political parties in the economically developed world.

The threat to American democracy was spelled out in 2021 in a public Statement of Concern signed by more than one hundred scholars of democracy. Many of the experts—including Francis Fukuyama, Jacob Hacker, Steven Levitsky, Pippa Norris, and Daniel Ziblatt—

have spent years studying the decline of democracies. The statement reviews the changes in battleground states that are "dangerously politicizing" U.S. elections, from restricting ballot access to giving the Republican-controlled legislatures the ability to override election outcomes on "unproven allegations," to fines and criminal sentences to scare away poll workers. The scholars warn that these new laws could be used to reverse electoral outcomes, a Republican effort that was unsuccessful in 2020. In arguing for a federal voting rights law, they write:

> Democracy rests on certain elemental institutional and normative conditions. Elections must be neutrally and fairly administered. They must be free of manipulation. Every citizen who is qualified must have an equal right to vote, unhindered by obstruction. And when they lose elections, political parties and their candidates and supporters must be willing to accept defeat and acknowledge the legitimacy of the outcome. The refusal of prominent Republicans to accept the outcome of the 2020 election, and the anti-democratic laws adopted (or approaching adoption) in Arizona, Arkansas, Florida, Georgia, Iowa, Montana and Texas—and under serious consideration in other Republican-controlled states—violate these principles. More profoundly, these actions call into question whether the United States will remain a democracy. As scholars of democracy, we condemn these actions in the strongest possible terms as a betrayal of our precious democratic heritage.[54]

The Republican Party now mirrors its authoritarian leader. In spreading disinformation, restricting voting, and denying equal treatment to minorities, the party has become anti-democratic.

The Republican Party also mirrors Trump's immorality. Collective moralities underlie political liberalism and conservatism, but it does not follow that the parties reflecting these left-right political orientations are necessarily moral themselves. The morality of a political party is determined by its conduct.

A commitment to the nation as a whole, and to the nation's laws and democratic norms, is evident in the best of our political leaders, on both the left and the right. Trump has made it all too evident that the character of our leaders matters, and absent these commitments, a nation's political health is jeopardized. The Trump Republican Party has placed our country at risk of authoritarianism. It is immoral to restrict the voting rights of Americans in order to win elections, to perpetuate a lie in order to divide the nation, or to threaten our democracy in order to retain power.

11

Moving Forward

We view the world through our own political lenses, and we are certain that our views are the right ones. I extend a sincere mea culpa for my biases. Social psychologists caution us about the bias blind spot and our naive realism, the belief that others' views that differ from our own are biased or irrational, whereas we are accurate and unbiased. In explaining the bias blind spot, Emily Pronin and colleagues note that we judge others based on what they say and do but that in judging ourselves we look inward. We don't see biased motives, because they operate unconsciously; instead we see our good intentions and conclude that we have an unbiased, accurate view of the world.[1] Yet we feel certain of the other side's bad intentions.

Liberals regard conservatives' positions as selfish and intolerant; conservatives regard liberals' positions as naive and reckless. Conservatives believe that liberals do not respect time-tested traditions and contribute to social disorder. Liberals believe that conservatives disregard human dignity and defend social injustice. We are political sectarians, and hostility toward the other reigns on both sides.[2] Our differences are played out through the positions of political parties, where conflicting views on abortion, guns, entitlements, climate, and many other issues are glaringly apparent. These differences are magnified by the absence of an exchange of ideas, because we now have media silos on the left and right that function more like echo chambers than meeting places for our diverse perspectives.

Today's Republican Party has taken conservatism to a greater extreme than either its counterparts elsewhere or major American parties of the past, and the right-wing media has created an all-too-friendly environment for it. The party's extremism is a threat to the nation. People across the political spectrum should be invested in the reestablishment of a Republican Party that is not disdainful of democracy. Liberals and anti-Trump conservatives will need to find ways to work together to preserve our democracy.

As Speaker Nancy Pelosi has said, "The country needs a strong Republican Party," and columnist E. J. Dionne has noted how in the past the left "respected conservatism as a coherent and morally serious worldview. We saw it as a set of ideas advanced by thinkers such as Edmund Burke and Robert Nisbet, dedicated to preserving what is good in our institutions and traditions. Even when we emphatically disagreed, we could understand why they might be skeptical of the unintended costs of some of the reforms we might put forward."[3]

Liberals and conservatives will continue to populate our political world. Liberalism and conservatism reflect the balance inherent in the two forms of morality: proscriptive and prescriptive. To be moral and valued group members, we avoid harming others in the community and we also help them, echoing parents' efforts to protect and provide for their children. If we look beyond politics and focus on the larger society or nation, it is clear that protect and provide motives together enable a society to thrive. Nations benefit when they retain what is best in their traditions and institutions and advance the general welfare of group members. Could conservatism and liberalism, then, serve as counterweights to each other?

This suggestion might seem absurd in the current political atmosphere, but from the perspective of group flexibility in the face of challenges, the two binding moralities prepare a society to address distinct problems (such as threats and resource distribution) in different ways (through coordination or cooperation). Their progress-versus-preservation orientations may also be adaptive. Liberalism and conservatism have been described as an engine and a brake, with liberals advancing policies that move society forward and conservatives applying the brakes if things move too fast or get out of control. In his mission statement for the *National Review,* William Buckley wrote that "the conservative's role is 'to stand athwart history yelling STOP, at a time when no one else is inclined to do so.'" A healthy society is able to counter conservative complacency and temper liberal fervor.

Researchers studying tightness, which is associated with Social Order and conservatism, have found that a moderate amount is best for a country. Countries that are excessively lax or restrictive do worse on many measures than those that are moderately tight in adherence to social norms. Moderate nations have better social, health, and economic outcomes, including greater happiness, longer life expectancy, lower suicide rates, and higher GDP per capita. Tightness scores roughly reflect Social Order and not Social Justice. Yet if we look closely at the nations that fare best, they are not only moderate on tightness but typically have strong social safety nets, indicating a Social Justice orientation as well. Western European countries fare particularly well in these studies.[4]

In considering liberalism and conservatism as adaptive counterweights, it is also instructive to revisit some research on parenting. Political scientists interested in authoritarianism have relied on the four questions about strict parenting discussed in the previous chapter. In chapter 4 we looked at the relations between strict parenting and conservatism and between egalitarian parenting and liberalism. Yet if our goal is to find the most successful parenting strategy in terms of children's outcomes, what would we recommend?

In the early 1960s, the developmental psychologist Diana Baumrind interviewed and observed scores of children and their parents in an effort to classify parenting styles. Her work yielded two dimensions that are typically used to describe distinct ways of parenting. One dimension is demandingness, meaning the degree of parental control and boundary-setting; the other is responsiveness, or the degree to which parents are attuned to and supportive of their children's needs.[5] Baumrind and subsequent researchers have found that children do best—socially, emotionally, and behaviorally—when parents combine the control and limits of demandingness with the nurturance and support of responsiveness. These children fare far better than children raised by parents who are controlling and demanding but not nurturant (labeled "authoritarian" parenting) and those raised by parents who are responsive and supportive but don't set limits (labeled "permissive parenting"). Both are necessary for children's best outcomes—parents who attend to their children's needs and also confront them when they disobey. Baumrind called this optimal style "authoritative parenting."[6]

Granted that although it may be a stretch to relate this work to political orientations, the findings may nevertheless be revealing. In its focus on restrictions and limits, demandingness reflects proscriptive regulation; and in its emphasis on support and nurturance, responsiveness reflects prescriptive regulation. Conservatives may choose to emphasize parental demandingness, and liberals may instead emphasize parental responsiveness, but the combination is best for children. Regarding broader social regulation, conservatives focus on order and control in society, based in proscriptive morality, and liberals focus on the welfare and needs of its members, based in prescriptive morality. Perhaps the two orientations together are needed to produce the best outcomes for society.

This might be true in the best of all possible worlds, but we are certainly not there today. Even in our world, however, an acknowledgment of the distinct moral perspectives on the left and right can help us better understand the roots of our differences. Our current toxic politics is not sustainable. If we are to act in the best interests of the nation, we will somehow have to get past the deep distrust that divides us. Recognizing the moral bases of *both* the left and right is a start. At the very least, in an effort to move forward together, addressing the nation's gross wealth inequality would be a viable and worthwhile way for Democrats and Republicans to work together for the good of the nation. Although on its face inequality is an economic issue that is directly related to Social Justice, it is also a social issue related to Social Order. The inequality evident in the loss of jobs and income across the nation, and the impossibility, for so many Americans, of accumulating wealth, foreshadow social disorder, including increased rates of suicide, drug abuse, and family breakdown. Conservatives, who value Social Order, should recognize the reduction of inequality as a path to greater societal stability; Social Justice can engender Social Order. The extent of our inequality is a stain on our nation. Efforts to remove it would satisfy both conservatives' Social Order motive and liberals' Social Justice motive.

Both liberals and conservatives should also be alarmed about the declining state of Americans' quality of life and well-being. A global survey of 163 countries found that while the rest of the world improved, the United States and only two other countries (Brazil and Hungary) were worse off in 2020 than in 2011.[7] America's deteriorating status was most evident in indices of personal safety, personal rights, and inclusiveness—domains that reflect concerns on both sides of the political spectrum.

We will always have liberals and conservatives in the United States, and they will always have disagreements over the best policies to pursue. The nation needs political parties committed to governing, which requires negotiation and compromise, as difficult as this may be. We particularly need parties devoted to decency and democracy and to living with a flawed society even as they never stop trying to improve it. As Alexis de Tocqueville wrote in 1835, "The greatness of America lies not in being more enlightened than any other nation, but rather in her ability to repair her faults."

Notes

Chapter 1. Two Faces of Morality

1. James 1890, 549–59. Early echoes are found in Thorndike's Law of Effect (1911) and Tolman's drive theory (1932). A number of psychologists working on motivation have recently emphasized this dual system of regulation, including Higgins (1997, 1998), who posits a promotion orientation focused on positive end-states and a prevention orientation focused on negative end-states. See also Carver 2006; Carver and Scheier 1998; Gable, Reis, and Elliot 2003; and Gray 1990.

2. See Elliot and Church 1997 on need for achievement versus fear of failure, and Gable and Strachman 2008 on desire for affiliation versus fear of rejection in interpersonal relationships.

3. Davidson et al. 1990; Miller et al. 2013; Sutton and Davidson 1997.

4. Schneirla 1959.

5. Janoff-Bulman, Sheikh, and Hepp 2009. See also Janoff-Bulman and Carnes 2013a, 2013b. These labels were chosen because "proscribe" typically means to disallow or forbid, which involves avoidance, whereas "prescribe" denotes authorization and moving toward something, suggesting approach.

6. Kochanska 2002; Kochanska, Coy, and Murray 2001. The researchers referred to the toy cleanup as a "do" task and the toy prohibition as a "don't" task. Compliance with the "do" request was 14 percent at fourteen months and 30 percent at forty-five months, whereas compliance with the "don't" request was 40 percent at fourteen months and 85 percent at forty-five months, drastically different from the "do" request. At any given age assessment, compliance in one context did not predict compliance in the other.

7. See, e.g., Goodwin, Piazza, and Rozin 2014 and Leach, Ellemers, and Barreto 2007.

8. De Waal 1996; Haidt 2007, 2008; Janoff-Bulman, Sheikh, and Hepp 2009; Krebs 2008.

9. Batson 1991; Bowles 2006; Boyd 2006; de Waal 2008; Keltner 2009; Nowak and Highfield 2011; Sober and Wilson 1998.

10. See Hamilton 1964 on kin selection; Trivers 1971 on reciprocal altruism; and Alexander 1987 on indirect reciprocity.

11. Fehr and Gachter 2002, 137.

12. Wilson 2012. Wilson noted that there is "authentic altruism," and it contributes to the survival and strength of groups. See also Sober and Wilson 1998 on group cooperation and multilevel selection. Richerson and Boyd 2005 also argue that group selection shaped human nature, but they rely largely on gene-culture coevolution.

13. De Waal 2005.

14. Hamlin, Wynn, and Bloom 2007, 2010. See also Hamlin 2013 and Hamlin and Wynn 2011.

15. Tomasello and Vaish 2013, 242–43.

16. Janoff-Bulman, Sheikh, and Hepp 2009 presents seven studies differentiating between the two forms of morality.

17. For reviews of the negativity bias, see Baumeister et al. 2001 and Rozin and Royzman 2001. For loss aversion, see Kahneman and Tversky 1979 and Tverksy and Kahneman 1992.

18. Janoff-Bulman, Sheikh, and Hepp 2009, Studies 3 and 4. The fourteen "good" and fourteen "bad" ways of behaving included equal numbers of verbs and adjectives in each list. The lists were created from the most common responses provided for "should" and "should nots" in separate research.

19. Kant 2002.

20. Janoff-Bulman, Sheikh, and Hepp 2009, Studies 5, 6, and 7. Ascriptions of blame are greater in the proscriptive system than prescriptive system. The omission bias in psychology—the finding that greater blame is attributed for harmful acts (commissions) than omissions (see, e.g., Baron and Ritov 2004, and Spranca, Minsk and Baron 1991)—is likely due to proscriptive-prescriptive differences. Commissions are typically proscriptive, involving harming and doing the wrong thing. Omissions are typically prescriptive, involving not helping and not doing the right thing.

21. Knobe 2003.

22. Sheikh and Janoff-Bulman 2010. A still important basis for distinguishing between shame and guilt is the focus on self versus behavior posited by Tangney and colleagues (Tangney and Dearing 2002; Tangney, Stuewig, and Mashek 2007). Here shame is based in a negative evaluation of the global self, and guilt is based in a negative evaluation of a specific behavior. These differences are the same as Janoff-

Bulman's earlier distinction between characterological and behavioral self-blame (Janoff-Bulman 1979).

23. Janoff-Bulman, Sheikh, and Hepp 2009, Study 2. For abstract-concrete linguistic differences associated with approach and avoidance, see Semin et al. 2005.

24. Kant 2002; Aristotle 1941.

25. Sullivan 1992. Interestingly, Kennedy 1976 makes a connection "in the rhetoric of private law, between individualism and a preference for rules, and between altruism and a preference for standards" (1776).

26. In the case of estate executors and financial advisers, fiduciary responsibility is legally mandated.

27. Quoted in Currie 1986, 864. See also Berlin 1969 on two concepts of liberty.

28. Unger 1996; Singer 2009.

Chapter 2. Mapping Morality

1. Janoff-Bulman and Carnes 2013a, 2013b, 2018. Work on this model was done in collaboration with former graduate student Nate Carnes. For a test of the six-cell model of moral motives, see Janoff-Bulman and Carnes 2016. We used confirmatory factor analysis (CFA) to test model fit. Six latent factors (Self-Restraint, Industriousness, Not Harming, Helping/Fairness, Social Order, and Social Justice) represented eighteen parceled indicators. We loaded the three indicators corresponding to each construct on their respective factors and standardized the factor variances. The model also included eighteen indicator error variances and fifteen factor covariances. Model fit was excellent, and standardized parameter estimates revealed that every indicator loaded strongly on its corresponding latent factor.

2. Cultural innovations, including traditions and rituals, the rule of law, religion, governmental institutions, penal systems, forms of tribalism, and religion, create unique societies that emphasize different moral motives with different levels of effectiveness.

3. See Dahlsgaard, Peterson, and Seligman 2005 on the search for universal virtues.

4. This disapproval moves us to activating behaviors (prescriptive morality) and not restraint (proscriptive morality). We don't actually restrain laziness and sloth, which in themselves involve inaction.

5. Temperance is also one of the seven heavenly virtues and is evidence of the importance of moderation in Catholic teachings.

6. Walker and Pitts 1998.

7. For an excellent discussion of the trolley problems and related research, see Greene 2013. The dorsolateral prefrontal cortex is the same part of the brain activated in the Stroop task, which involves naming colors when the presented word interferes (e.g., the word *red* written in green). In addition to findings based on brain activation (e.g., electroencephalograms), research by Mendez, Anderson, and Shapira 2006 based on patients with a degenerative neurological disorder (i.e., frontotemporal dementia) has supported the importance of emotions in reacting to the footbridge scenario. This disorder affects the ventromedial prefrontal cortex, so these patients manifest "emotional numbing." When confronted with the footbridge dilemma, the majority of these patients approve of pushing the man off the footbridge. Alzheimer's patients, in contrast, show the standard response of strong disapproval.

8. Greene 2013.

9. See also research by Cushman et al. 2012 showing people's strong aversion to violent acts. For example, using a false leg in the laboratory, they had people engage in a violent act such as smashing the leg with a hammer. Participants knew that no one was being harmed, but they nevertheless had strong physiological reactions.

10. Cosmides 1989; Cosmides and Tooby 1992. Cosmides and Tooby use a basic cognitive task to make their point. Specifically, on the Wason selection task we are asked to choose among four cards that each have a letter on one side and a number on the other. We see the number side on two cards and the letter side on the other two (e.g., B, W, 2, 7) and are told, "If there is a B on one side, then there is a 2 on the other." We are asked to choose which cards must be turned over to determine whether the rule has been followed. The correct response is B and 7, but only about 10 percent of the population gets this right (most choose B and 2). Yet Cosmides and Tooby point out that when this same problem is presented in terms of people's social engagement (e.g., "If you are drinking alcohol then you must be over eighteen"), with ages and drinks noted on the cards, we are quite good at the task, because we are on the lookout for cheating.

11. See de Waal 1996, 2009, for additional examples. Goodall 1990 also provides many examples. She writes, "In some zoos, chimpanzees are kept on man-made islands, surrounded by water-filled moats. . . . Chimpanzees cannot swim and, unless they are rescued, will drown if they fall into deep water. Despite this, individuals have sometimes made heroic efforts to save companions from drowning—and were sometimes successful. One adult male lost his life as he tried to rescue a small infant whose incompetent mother had allowed it to fall into the water" (213).

12. Warneken and Tomasello 2006.

13. I return to empathy and helping (including the limits of empathy) in chapter 5 when discussing questions of inclusivity and exclusivity. For reviews of the positive relation between empathy and helping, see Batson 1998 and Eisenberg and Miller 1987. Keltner 2012 notes that his lab's work on the vagus nerve provides additional evidence of the inherent nature of human altruism, or at least our biological preparedness for altruism, and suggests that we are wired for compassion.

14. Blackburn 2001.

15. Tomasello and Vaish 2013, 232.

16. Benedict 1934.

17. Gelfand et al. 2011; see also Gelfand 2018. In the multicountry study, the two tightest countries are Pakistan and Malaysia, and the two loosest countries are Ukraine and Estonia. The United States is eleventh of thirty-three on the scale from loose to tight. In the supplementary materials following the article, the authors report strong positive correlations between tightness scores and conservatism, hierarchy, loyalty, and disapproval of deviant behaviors. Tightness is also strongly associated (correlation of 0.61) with preference for political systems with strong leaders and agreement with the item that reads: "The most important responsibility of government is to maintain order of society."

18. Blanton and Christie 2003.

19. See, e.g., Rawls 1971 and Tyler 2000 on the fundamental association between justice and respect. Co-membership in the human community is the minimal respect that is due another person. This is essentially the universal bestowal discussed by Immanuel Kant and other moral philosophers. In our own work we have distinguished between two types of respect. What we have labeled contingent respect is about ingroup status, or one's standing in a group, and is based on appraisals of valued dimensions across group members. Categorical respect, in contrast, is based on group membership and is accorded equally to all members of the group (Janoff-Bulman and Werther 2008).

20. Quoted in Hannah-Jones 2020. Hannah-Jones also writes that the words most remembered from Martin Luther King's "I Have a Dream" speech are about being judged by the content of your character and not the color of your skin; what is generally forgotten are his words that Blacks have come to cash "a check which has come back marked 'insufficient funds.'"

21. Hannah-Jones 2020.

22. See article 27 of the Universal Declaration of Human Rights.

23. Research on moral dilemmas has found that compared to conservatives, lib-

erals are sensitive to the consequences of actions that are for the greater good and are more accepting of norm violations if they are for the greater good. See Luke and Gawronski 2021.

24. Janoff-Bulman 2009; Janoff-Bulman and Carnes 2013a, 2016. See also Carnes and Janoff-Bulman 2016 and Carnes, Lickel, and Janoff-Bulman 2015.

25. O'Sullivan 1976, 11–12.

26. See Janoff-Bulman and Carnes 2016. See also Carnes, Lickel, and Janoff-Bulman 2015 regarding the lack of association between these self-regulation cells of MMM and political orientation.

27. Janoff-Bulman and Carnes 2016 and Carnes, Lickel, and Janoff-Bulman 2015. The two group moralities are assessed without any reference to politics. The negative correlation between the two is relatively small, typically around –0.2 in our research. Importantly, compared with the other columns of MMM, the two are not positively correlated but function more as independent dimensions. Social Order and Social Justice nevertheless have very robust associations with conservatism and liberalism respectively in our work (typically around 0.5 and 0.6). As noted above, in developing scales we specifically used items that measured aspects of the two collective moralities without reference to politics. For example, Social Order items included "It is harmful to society when people choose radically new lifestyles and ways of living" and "The best societies are usually the least permissive societies," and Social Justice items included "It is important for those who are better off to help provide resources for the most vulnerable members of society" and "Increased economic equality is ultimately beneficial to everyone in society."

28. The tight alignment of political party, ideology, and group morality in recent decades is addressed in chapter 6.

Chapter 3. What the Reigning Theory Gets Wrong

1. See, e.g., Haidt 2022.

2. Graham et al. 2011; Haidt 2007, 2008; Haidt and Graham 2007; Haidt and Kesebir 2010. In all of these papers the five foundations are referred to as Harm/Care, Fairness/Reciprocity, Ingroup/Loyalty, Authority/Respect, and Purity/Sanctity. Haidt renamed the foundations in his book *The Righteous Mind* (2012) and labeled them Harm/Care, Fairness/Cheating, Loyalty/Betrayal, Authority/Subversion, and Sanctity/Degradation. This was a change in name only, not content, and the questionnaire used to assess the five foundations remained unchanged. The primary labels of Care, Fairness, Loyalty and Authority are the same, and Purity was now

called Sanctity. In his book Haidt presented a "provisional" sixth foundation, which he labeled Liberty/Oppression, "which makes people notice and resent any sign of attempted domination" (2012, 185). The empirical findings for MFT, as presented in published papers, rely on the five foundations. Liberty/Oppression has not caught on, and MFT continues to be regarded as a five-foundation model.

3. Haidt and Joseph 2004.

4. They published their first empirical paper based on the questionnaire, known as the Moral Foundations Questionnaire (MFQ), in 2007; see Haidt and Graham 2007.

5. Graham, Haidt, and Nosek 2009; Graham et al. 2011; Haidt and Graham 2007. When Haidt includes his provisional foundation, Liberty/Oppression, he argues that liberals rely on only three foundations, and conservatives rely on all six, suggesting it is an individualizing foundation that is embraced by both liberals and conservatives.

6. Haidt 2012, 185.

7. Carnes, Lickel, and Janoff-Bulman 2015. See also Frederico et al. 2013, who found that endorsement of MFT's binding foundations was associated with social conformity.

Interestingly, Haidt and colleagues regard sanctity (purity) as a binding group morality, but sanctity could be seen as a proscriptive morality more broadly, in terms of inhibition or avoidance of "dangerous" stimuli, and could be represented in all three proscriptive cells of MMM (i.e., self, other, and group targets of moral concerns). Thus, purity regarding one's own body (e.g., matters related to sexuality, drinking, or drugs) concerns the self, the desire to avoid contagion associated with another would involve the interpersonal context, and the motivation to maintain group purity through the regulation of deviance (via avoidance and punishment) implicates group-based morality. In many ways, given the distinct origins of the sanctity foundation of morality in contagion concerns and physical disgust, it can be regarded as a broad-based proscriptive form of morality that coexists with the other proscriptive moral motives.

8. Rai and Fiske 2011 seem to recognize that there are proscriptive and prescriptive bases of group-based morality, because they note that "eliminating threats of contamination" as well as "providing aid" enable ingroups to maintain their integrity (57). In positing a single moral motive (i.e., Unity) to represent both, they importantly emphasize the broad binding function of any group-based morality but do not make further distinctions.

9. The questions about the Care foundation include both helping (e.g., caring for the weak and vulnerable) and not harming (e.g., not killing), the two interpersonal cells of MMM.

10. Graham et al. 2011.

11. See, e.g., the excellent work of Alice Eagly and Wendy Wood (Eagly 1987; Wood and Eagly 2010).

12. Graham 2013. In addition to pointing out the differences in support for Helping (both liberals and conservatives) versus Social Justice (only liberals), to address Graham's suggestion we explicitly tested how well a five-factor model, with just one factor representing Helping and Social Justice, fit with our data compared to the six-cell model of MMM. The five-factor model was actually a poor fit to the data, and specifically a significantly worse fit than the six-factor model, suggesting that Social Justice and Helping are distinct moral constructs (see Janoff-Bulman and Carnes 2016).

13. Haidt and Kesebir 2010, 822.

14. There are six items in the MFT Fairness scale. Respondents judge the relevance of the following three items to Fairness: "Whether or not some people were treated differently from others"; "Whether or not someone acted unfairly"; and "Whether or not someone was denied his or her rights." They also indicate the extent of their agreement with the following three items: "When the government makes laws, the number one principle should be ensuring that everyone is treated fairly"; "Justice is the most important requirement for a society"; and "I think it's morally wrong that rich children inherit a lot of money while poor children inherit nothing."

15. Particularly informative here is the past work of Philip Brickman and colleagues (Brickman, Folger, Goode, and Schul 1981), who distinguished between microjustice and macrojustice. Microjustice is individuating and involves known attributes of the other, whereas macrojustice is deindividuating and involves a priori constraints on the form of a distribution in the direction of equality. See also related work by Wenzel 2004 on differentiating and nondifferentiating entitlement judgments and Feather 2003 on deservingness based on an individual's efforts and entitlement based in laws and social norms external to the person. Proportional outcomes have typically been studied under the rubric of equity judgments by social psychologists and have been distinguished from equality (see, e.g., Walster, Walster, and Berscheid 1978). Importantly, fairness outcomes are equal when inputs are equal.

16. Separate samples provided descriptions of Fairness and Social Justice. When

yet another group described instances of Justice (rather than Social Justice) the responses focused overwhelmingly on criminal and retributive justice, involving discussions of crimes, punishments, jail time, and/or police. Once the term *social* was added, the meaning of justice shifted to questions of equal treatment and equality of outcomes. It is worth noting that in considering distributional outcomes we use the phrase "*social* justice" but not "*social* fairness," likely reflecting our implicit recognition that the latter is not based on a shared group or social category.

17. See Turner et al. 1987 on Self-Categorization Theory. We are likely to have multiple social identities, and the salience of any particular social identity is determined by the social context. In a house of worship the focus is likely to be one's religious identity; in thinking about tomorrow's scheduled soccer game, the team identity is apt to be most salient.

18. The work of Brett Litz and colleagues on "moral injury" is very relevant here. See Litz et al. 2009.

19. It seems worth mentioning that there may also be reason to question the morality of wealthy companies that offer these unpaid internships. They are in essence employing young workers without paying them.

20. Our Fairness scale was adapted from the Preference for the Merit Principle Scale (Davey et al. 1999), because the items reflect proportionality. This series of studies on Fairness and Social Justice was conducted in collaboration with former graduate student Prerana (Ria) Bharadwaj.

21. Ironically, Rawls's name for his philosophy is "justice as fairness." Despite differences in the use of terms, he has demonstrated that the morality of Social Justice (a la MMM) would be the basis of our chosen society were we unaware of the individual attributes that would otherwise be used in Fairness considerations.

22. Haidt 2012, 185.

23. Libertarians and other political distinctions, such as "economic conservatives," which I suggest is a misnomer, are addressed more fully in chapter 6.

Chapter 4. Threat and Coordination
Versus Hope and Cooperation

1. Zakaria 2008.

2. Cooper 2008.

3. See Bonanno and Jost 2006 regarding the impact of 9/11. See also experimental studies by Landau et al. 2004 and Napier et al. 2018.

4. Gelfand 2018; Gelfand et al. 2011.

5. Thomas et al. 2014.

6. See Cartwright, Gillett, and Van Vugt 2013; Thomas et al. 2013; and Van Vugt, Hogan, and Kaiser 2008.

7. Magee and Galinsky 2008, 357.

8. Thomas et al. 2013. A second type of cooperation game, less well known than the prisoner's dilemma, is the public goods game. Here multiple players are given tokens or money and can privately choose how much to contribute to the public pot. The total in the pot is multiplied by a factor between 1 and the number of players, and the resulting total is divided among all the participants. Given that players can keep their money and not contribute, they can easily "free ride," and this might be the "rational" choice, but if everyone free rides, there are no resources to distribute. This resembles the tragedy of the commons, whereby if all the farmers selfishly allow their animals to graze on the common land, the grass will soon be depleted and all will suffer.

9. Van Lange 1999. See also Van Lange et al. 2013, as well as Pletzer et al. 2018, who found that prosocials are not only more cooperative but believe that other people will be cooperative, too.

10. These policies supporting greater equality affected Blacks as well as whites. There were sharp improvements in the economic well-being of Blacks from the 1940s to the mid-1970s, followed by a decline in their economic fortunes after this period. See Maloney 1994 and Margo 1995.

11. Van der Toorn, Napier, and Dovidio 2014.

12. Smeltz et al. 2020.

13. See Dodd et al. 2012; Hibbing, Smith, and Alford 2013, 2014; McLean et al. 2014; Oxley et al. 2008; Pyszczynski et al. 2006; Shook and Fazio 2009; and Vigil 2010. For a review, see Jost and Amodio 2012.

14. Lavine et al. 1999.

15. Shook and Fazio 2009.

16. Altemeyer 1998. See also Jost, Glaser, et al. 2003 and Jost, Napier, et al. 2007, who found that conservatives score higher than liberals on a dispositional measure of death anxiety. In their research they also ruled out a competing hypothesis that the need to manage threat is associated with ideological extremity rather than conservatism.

17. See, e.g., Feinberg et al. 2014; Inbar, Pizarro, and Bloom 2009; Inbar et al. 2012; Terrizzi, Shook, and Ventis 2010.

18. Jost 2006; Jost, Glaser, et al. 2003; Jost, Napier, et al. 2007.

19. Barbaranelli et al. 2007; Gerber et al. 2010; Jost 2006; Jost, Nosek, and Gosling 2008; Lavine et al. 1999; McCrae 1996; Rentfrow et al. 2009; Shook and Fazio 2009.

20. Luke and Gawronski 2021.

21. Carney et al. 2008; see also Jost, Nosek, and Gosling 2008.

22. Hibbing, Smith, and Alford 2013, 2014. See also Hatemi et al. 2014.

23. Block and Block 2006, 734; Fraley et al. 2012. Fraley and colleagues' large sample was drawn from the National Institute of Child Health and Human Development Study of Early Childhood and Youth Development.

24. See Lakoff 2002 and Feinberg et al. 2020. Feinberg and colleagues also found that Strict Father was positively associated with Social Order (and negatively with Social Justice), and Nurturant Parent was positively associated with Social Justice (and negatively with Social Order).

25. Fraley et al. 2012.

26. Janoff-Bulman, Carnes, and Sheikh 2014; McAdams et al. 2008. See also Lakoff 2002. In our research we found that both strict mothers and strict fathers were associated with conservatism in grown children.

27. Alwin, Cohen, and Newcomb 1991; Sears and Levy 2003.

28. Similar arguments could be made about vaccinations, but I am focusing on masks, which were recommended before the availability of vaccinations and from the first were an easy way to maximize the likelihood of avoiding the virus and minimizing its spread.

29. Democratic governors of hard-hit blue states emphasized masks and social distancing from the start. There were clearly some responsible Republican governors who also did not ignore science: Governor Larry Hogan of Maryland and Governor Charlie Baker of Massachusetts were two in particular, but both were moderate Republicans who were often critical of Trump.

30. Woodward 2020. Trump told Woodward that he didn't want the public to know how dangerous the virus was because he didn't want to create a panic. Given Trump's attempts to sow chaos and division, this excuse surely doesn't ring true. Even if it were true, however, he could have softened the news and presented the dangers over time—which he clearly never did.

31. Interestingly, although Trump did not wear a mask in the White House, all staff members were required to wear a mask in the building.

32. The right's pleas about liberty arose whether or not they were subject to state mandates, which differed widely, and current laws abound when it comes to public

safety, including most laws of the road (e.g., speeding, stoplights) and seat belts in particular. The masks themselves do little to minimize freedom. And yet wearing them became anathema for many on the right who revere strength and power.

33. Vozzella 2020.

34. Walker 2020.

35. Dhaval et al. 2020.

36. Dawsey, Leonnig, and Knowles 2020.

37. See Aistrup 1996.

38. Herbert 2005.

39. See Jost, Federico, and Napier 2009.

Chapter 5. Reactions to Outsiders

1. Will 2008.

2. Margolis and Sances 2013. The difference between conservative and liberal giving disappeared when controlled for differences in religiosity and income.

3. Margolis and Sances 2013 1.

4. Hiltzik 2014. Regarding charitable donations more generally, neuroscience research has found that donating to charity activates parts of the brain that are associated with pleasure and reward. See Harbaugh and Burghart 2007 and Moll et al. 2006.

5. See, e.g., Hiltzik 2014, who reports on a study by Indiana University researchers from 2007.

6. Farmer, Kidwell, and Hardesty 2020. The researchers also tested whether the other moralities in MMM (moderation, industriousness, not harming, and helping) significantly mediated the relation between political ideology and charitable giving, and they did not. Only Social Order and Social Justice were significant mediators.

7. See Uslaner 2002 on "particularized" versus "generalized" trust; see also Kramer 2010. One might suppose that trust of close family and friends would generalize to the broader social world. Attachment theory would suggest similarity or continuity across these domains, from parental attachment and trust to more generalized trust of others. Yet there is scant evidence that this is the case. Cross-cultural work has found that in Japan and China there is strong trust within the family but low trust of other members of society more generally (Fukuyama 1995; Yamagishi and Yamagishi 1994). In fact, a growing body of research has found lower levels of

general trust in these collectivist societies, despite very strong family bonds (see, e.g., Buchan, Croson, and Dawes 2002; Kuwabara et al. 2007).

8. For Durkheim the shift from mechanical to organic solidarity represented a change from simple societies to denser, more complex societies that required a division of labor. Nevertheless, the two types of solidarity describe two paths to binding groups—common identity and interdependence—that could be applied to any collectives.

9. Brewer, Hong, and Li 2004; Haslam, Rothschild, and Ernst 2000. Empirical work has found that both essence and agency can account for group "entitativity." Emphasizing category membership increases the extent to which a collection of people is perceived as a group and so does emphasizing the extent to which people in the group interact (Rutchick, Hamilton, and Sack 2008).

10. Sparkman, Eidelman, and Till 2019; van der Toorn, Napier, and Dovidio 2014; see also Janoff-Bulman and Carnes 2013.

11. Singer 1981; Opotow 1990. The "scope of justice" is a phrase used by Opotow. Relatedly, Walzer 1983 claims that membership in some human community is the primary good that we distribute to one another. See Bar-Tal 1990; Janoff-Bulman and Werther 2008; and Staub 1989 for more on mistreatment outside the scope of justice; and see Schwartz 2007 on universalism and inclusion.

The outer circle of Singer's circle of moral concern includes all animals as well as all humans. Singer maintains that our natural, premodern moral circle is focused on kin and tribe, and expansion outward is based on rational thought. Recent work on the Moral Expansiveness Scale reflects a similar interest in the size of our moral circle (Crimston et al. 2016).

12. See Brewer 1979, 1999, for reviews.

13. Hamlin et al. 2013; Kinzler, Dupoux, and Spelke 2007.

14. Choi and Bowles 2007.

15. Graham et al. 2017, 63.

16. Hasson et al. 2018.

17. Bloom 2016; Pinker 2011. But see also Zaki 2019, who claims that empathy gives force to moral behavior, is not a limited resource, and can be used to expand the moral circle.

18. Warren and Kerwin 2017. For the immigration statistics, see Budiman 2020.

19. *United States v. Texas* 2016.

20. Budiman 2020; Lopez, Bialik, and Radford 2018.

21. Smeltz et al. 2020. See fig. D: Top 7 Critical Threats.

22. Markel and Stern 2002. For a review of research on immigration and disgust sensitivity, see Aaroe, Petersen, and Arceneaux 2017.

23. Ostfeld 2017; Hainmueller and Hopkins 2014, 2015. Hainmueller and Hopkins call the preference for educated, high status, English-speaking immigrants the "hidden American immigration consensus."

24. Brooks, Manza, and Cohen 2016; see also Hainmueller and Hopkins 2014.

25. The lead researcher for these studies was a graduate student, Rachel Steele, and I was involved in the early stages. The studies are now under review for publication. For moral typecasting, see Gray and Wegner 2009, who argued that a moral lens leads us to see people as agents (harm doers) or patients (victims of harm), perceptions that are generally mutually exclusive.

26. In Study 2, scale items were developed to represent the agent and victim themes that emerged in open-ended responses in Study 1. Support for punishing was measured with four items: force illegal immigrants to return to their country of origin, require illegal immigrants to serve time in prison, require illegal immigrants to pay a large fine, and fire illegal immigrants from their jobs (i.e., not allow them to have a job). Support for helping undocumented immigrants was measured with four items: allow illegal immigrants to collect welfare, give illegal immigrants the right to vote, permit children of illegal immigrants to receive scholarships or funding to U.S. colleges, and provide free medical care to illegal immigrants. The emotion findings in this research were consistent with Gray and Wegner's work on moral typecasting.

27. See, e.g., National Academies of Sciences, Engineering, and Medicine 2015 and Doleac 2017.

28. National Academy of Sciences, Engineering, and Medicine 2017.

29. Hainmueller and Hopkins 2014, 241.

30. For a thorough review and discussion, see Lowrey 2019.

31. Colby and Ortman 2015.

32. Craig and Richeson 2014b; Major, Blodorn, and Major-Blascovich 2018. In Major, Blodorn, and Major-Blascovich, party affiliation also significantly predicted (in the expected direction) participants' position on all dependent measures (e.g., immigration, support for Trump), but there was no party x condition (high versus low identification) interaction.

33. Abramowitz 2018; Pew Research Center 2020.

34. See, e.g., Mutz 2018; Cox, Lienesch, and Jones 2017.

35. Sidanius and Pratto 2001. Regarding social dominance and racial and ethnic prejudice, see also Pratto et al. 1994.

In 2001 John Duckitt proposed two distinct paths to prejudice based on SDO (social dominance orientation) and RWA (right wing authoritarianism), specifically "the competitively driven dominance-power-superiority motivation and threat-driven social control and group defense motivation. These motivational goals are aroused by two main kinds of situational characteristics of intergroup relationships: social and intergroup threat and inequalities in or competition over power and dominance" (41). Interestingly, conservatives appear to view outsiders as threatening *both* social conformity and their own dominance in the social hierarchy.

36. For an excellent examination of the American race-based hierarchy, specifically the racial caste system in America, see Wilkerson 2020.

37. Abramowitz 2012, 67.

38. Chernow 2005, 336. Similarly, Henry J. Cookingham, a delegate to the New York State constitutional convention in 1894, noted, "I say without fear of contradiction that the average citizen in the rural district is superior in intelligence, superior in morality, superior in self-government, to the average citizen in the great cities" (Grier 2018).

39. Badger 2016. There is increasing tension between red states and their blue cities, creating political clashes such as the battle in 2016–17 in North Carolina. The Republican general assembly not only chose to overturn a Charlotte ordinance that banned discrimination against LGBT people but passed a state law (HB2) that barred cities in North Carolina from passing nondiscrimination regulations and at the same time banned local minimum wage laws. The result was a national outcry that included boycotts by sports teams, musicians, and businesses. The cities suffered most. Charlotte's chamber of commerce estimated it lost almost $285 million and 1,300 jobs in the first two months. Soon the NBA pulled its 2017 All-Star Game from the city. Asheville reported that it lost millions from conferences that were canceled. HB2 was repealed in 2017, although some features of the initial bill remained. In particular, regulation of bathroom access was left to the legislature, and local governments were prohibited from passing their own nondiscrimination ordinances until 2020.

40. Kron 2012.

41. With the help of gerrymandering, the politics of large population centers has not translated into control of state legislatures, and thus the politics and policies of many states continue to reflect the right of rural American rather than the left of

urban America. Regarding the presidential election of 2020, see Rucker and Coast 2020.

42. Wilkinson 2019.

43. Bishop, 2008; Motyl et al. 2014.

44. Kron 2012.

45. Nunning 2017.

46. Sacchetti and Guskin 2017. According to the 2011–15 census, foreign-born residents constituted 2.3 percent of the population in rural counties and close to 15 percent of urban counties. New York, Los Angeles, and Miami were home to the largest populations of immigrants, and in 2016 most immigrants (28.3 million, or 65 percent of the nation's total) lived in just twenty major U.S. cities. Most of the country's undocumented immigrants also lived in these twenty urban areas (Lopez, Bialik, and Radford 2018). According to Davidson 2017, "The cities with the highest proportion of foreign-born residents, like New York, Miami, San Diego, and Houston, are also among the most economically muscular; those with the smallest are often depressed. That's circular, of course: Immigrants go to Miami rather than Birmingham, Alabama, because that's where the jobs are. And those influxes keep the population at a healthy churn, allowing cities to diversify their economies. In 2013 immigrants made up 43% of New York's workforces and generated a third of its output."

47. Hochschild 2017, 147.

48. Pettigrew and Tropp 2006. Research by Putnam (2007) raised questions about the beneficial role of contact, because he found that more diversity in a community was associated with less trust, both between groups and within one's own ethnic group. People seemed simply to engage less with their community. Yet we know that cities, with their diverse populations, are our most liberal localities. Putnam's findings of the negative effects of diversity on trust have been countered in several annual reviews (see Portes and Vickstrom 2011 and van der Meer and Tolsma 2014). Ramos et al. 2019 is important here; the authors' research was based on religious diversity, but as they note, racial and ethnic diversity are highly associated with different religious affiliations. Based on data from more than one hundred countries and over twenty years, the researchers found that over time greater heterogeneity is associated with greater trust and quality of life. Although people initially react negatively to increased diversity, with time—and increased contact—these reactions reverse and become positive. Importantly, intergroup contact eliminates any early negative effects, as proposed by the contact hypothesis.

49. Pettigrew and Tropp 2008.

50. Bai, Ramos, and Fiske 2020. The researchers looked at stereotypes regarding both competence and warmth, and they explored country-level data, state-level data, online individual responses, and responses from a longitudinal study of college students at American universities.

51. Zebrowitz, White, and Wieneke 2008. In the study with Black faces, the stimuli were presented subliminally so the participants did not know they had been exposed to the faces. The mere exposure effect still held. The frequent, neutral contacts may serve as counter-stereotypes to the negative stereotypes that are pervasive in the United States. Research has shown the positive impact of counter-stereotypes on the reduction of implicit prejudice (see, e.g., Dasgupta and Rivera 2008). In this research the counter-stereotypic examples are positive rather than neutral, but benign contacts are not negative and, if frequent, could conceivably have the same effect.

52. Davidson 2017.

53. Rock and Janoff-Bulman 2010 found that conservatives are less inclusive when categorizing, which is what we would expect if they are more sensitive to group boundaries. The stimuli in this research did not involve words associated with politics or social groups.

54. This joining of different people and perspectives suggests an unexpected affinity to Habermas's notion of the public sphere, represented by seventeenth- and eighteenth-century coffeehouses and salons in Europe. Here common concerns were discussed, and, at least aspirationally, the settings were inclusive and the status of participants was equal or ignored. Habermas argued that these played a central role in the development of the liberal Enlightenment. We might think of the city itself, at its best, as a grand public sphere where diverse opinions are debated, and common concerns are discussed. Habermas would no doubt be disappointed to see our coffeehouses today, where it seems few people go to interact but are instead glued to their computers, but the diversity of the city beyond the walls of the coffeehouse provides opportunities to interact with dissimilar others. See Pinsker 2018, discussing the role of cafés in the transition of Jewish culture from clan to cosmopolitanism.

55. Systemic racism is made all the more evident by the finding that many Blacks in the United States also show an implicit bias against Blacks. Typically between 60 percent and 70 percent of whites show pro-white implicit bias, and about 30 percent of Blacks show pro-white implicit bias. See Project Implicit 2011 (which continues to collect online data) under Frequently Asked Questions: "Do Black par-

ticipants show a preference for Black people over White people on the race attitude IAT?" See also Morin 2015.

56. Regarding the low correlations between implicit association test (IAT) scores and behavior, see Gawronski 2019 and Perugini, Richetin, and Zogmeister 2010. Implicit prejudice can nevertheless be impactful; doctor-patient interactions and health outcomes have been found to be associated with doctors' implicit biases (for a review, see Hall et al. 2015).

57. Dasgupta 2013, 247.

58. Daalder 2018.

Chapter 6. Party Politics and Policy Preferences

1. According to county findings reported by Ripley, Rekha, and He 2019, educated, white urbanites were most politically prejudiced, but the authors also noted that a 2014 Pew survey found that Republicans dislike Democrats more than vice versa. As to bias more generally, some recent social psychological research suggests that both groups are equally biased (Ditto et al. 2019); other social psychologists argue that conservatives are more biased (Baron and Jost 2019). Regardless, work on attributions tells us that suspicion underlies our perception of outgroups, and we overattribute hostile or deceptive intentions to outgroup members (Kramer 1999).

2. Erikson and Tedin 2003, 64.

3. Noel 2013, 20. See also the classic paper by Converse (1964) arguing that ideologies are "configurations of ideas and attitudes in which the elements are bound together by some form of constraint or functional interdependence" (207). For Converse, constraint refers to our success in predicting further attitudes from our knowledge of an individual's single specified attitude.

4. Noel 2013; in 1850, for example, there were 648 opinions representing 68 pundits and 84 issues. In 1990, this rose to 1,379 opinions, 173 pundits, and 170 issues.

5. Ellis and Stimson 2012; Nash 1996. See also Grossman and Hopkins 2016 and Noel 2013.

6. See Jost, Nosek, and Gosling 2008, table 4.

7. Bawn et al. 2012.

8. Abramowitz 2018.

9. Skitka, Bauman, and Sargis 2005; Skitka and Houston 2001; Skitka and Mullen 2002.

10. Parker and Janoff-Bulman 2013. In three studies we demonstrated the joint

NOTES TO PAGES 114-121

impact of ingroup positivity and outgroup negativity for morality-based groups. We studied responses of liberals and conservatives, as well as the responses of those supporting and opposing legal abortion. For the non-morality-based groups we used avid sports fans. In Massachusetts it wasn't difficult to recruit participants who strongly approved of the Red Sox and strongly disapproved of the Yankees, their traditional rivals. The primacy of the ingroup was apparent only for the sports fans, and not for the morality-based groups, where negativity toward the opposition played an equally powerful role in members' identification with their own group.

11. Quoted in Cobb 2021. According to the Brennan Center, by early February 2021, 165 restrictive bills were introduced, prefiled, or carried over, compared to 35 such bills by early February 2020.

12. Egan 2013. Egan notes that Bill Clinton's focus on crime and George W. Bush's focus on education produced a brief change in each party's issue ownership— but these changes were quite brief and reverted back to the other party's issue ownership. Egan claims that long-term issue ownership rarely changes because the fundamental priorities of the party really don't change.

13. For example, Grossman and Hopkins 2016 write, "We share the common assumption that ideology is a unidimensional attribute ranging from the liberal left to the conservative right" (25). Noel 2013 also regards ideology as unidimensional. Others have argued that more than one dimension is needed to fully represent the structure of most people's political attitudes (see, e.g., Conover and Feldman 2004 and Kerlinger 1984). As Jost, Frederico, and Napier 2009 note, "Exploratory and confirmatory factor analyses suggest that evaluations of 'liberal' and 'conservative' attitude objects often load onto different latent variables and that these variables are at least somewhat independent of one another. However, it should be noted that measures of liberalism and conservatism are seldom if ever truly uncorrelated" (312). Although more than one dimension may best underlie political ideologies, as I argue here using two distinct forms of morality, liberals and conservatives nevertheless typically hold opposing policy preferences.

14. The distinction between economic and social issues is apparent in past work on political issues and attitudes. For reviews, see Feldman 2013 and Jost, Frederico, and Napier 2009.

15. McMahon 2005.

16. *Washington Post* 2019.

17. Walzer 1983.

18. Ditto and Liu 2016, 118.

19. Egan 2013.

20. Cohen 2003. For a discussion of the powerful role of political identity in the current state of polarization, see Klein 2020.

21. For a review of cognitive consistency in the moral domain, see Ditto and Liu 2016.

22. See Festinger 1957 on cognitive dissonance; Kunda 1990 on motivated reasoning; and Tetlock 2002 on intuitive judgments.

23. Kahan et al. 2012. Essentially the same partisan-based differences in perception were found when the same protest was described as a demonstration against the military's "don't ask, don't tell" policy in front of a military recruitment center. For the classic Dartmouth-Princeton study, see Hastorf and Cantril 1954.

In their work Kahan and colleagues make the distinction between hierarchical individualists and egalitarian communitarians. They differ in who should be making decisions for a society, with the former relying on status authorities and the latter supporting collective action. See Kahan et al. 2012.

24. Antonio and Brulle 2011 make an interesting point that the dominant policy perspective of a given period has a tendency to affect subsequent political policies. They write, "Hegemonic rule by one of the two regimes has tended to move overall political discourse in its direction and shape accordingly public beliefs about what is politically possible and what is not. Governing in the wake of the Johnsonian Great Society, for example, Republican 'conservative' Richard Nixon, supported a minimum annual income, employed price controls, and presided over creation of the Environmental Protection Agency (EPA). By contrast, in the aftermath of the Reagan Revolution, Democratic 'liberal' Bill Clinton, supported welfare reform, cut the deficit and presided over financial deregulation" (195).

25. To distinguish this group from conservatives, the latter group is sometimes referred to as social conservatives, but they are the true conservatives. This group represents the "three-legged" conservative ideology that characterizes modern conservativism, which includes economic freedom and social traditionalism (as well as hawkish foreign policy).

26. See, e.g., Pearson 1995. Etzioni 2003 argues for a more open form of community. He writes, "Early communitarians might be charged with being, in effect, social conservatives, if not authoritarians. However, many contemporary communitarians, especially those who define themselves as responsive communitarians, fully realize and often stress that they do not seek to return to traditional communities, with their authoritarian power structure, rigid stratification, and discriminatory prac-

tices against minorities and women. Responsive communitarians seek to build communities based on open participation, dialogue, and truly shared values" (228).

27. Libertarians and communitarians constitute far smaller groups than the major categories of liberals and conservatives (Drutman 2019; Jost, Frederico, and Napier 2009). As the latter authors note, "Neither of these groups are large. . . . Although the social and economic dimensions of political ideology may be distinct in conceptual and factor-analytic terms, it is rare for them to be completely orthogonal" (313). That is, it is rare for them to be completely independent or unrelated.

Chapter 7. What Conservatives Are Protecting

1. Jamieson 2013.

2. Wintemute 2013.

3. Grinshteyn and Hemenway 2016.

4. For a review, see Buttrick 2020.

5. *New York Times* 1997.

6. See, e.g., Hemenway and Solnick 2015.

7. Quoted in Stolberg 2021b.

8. Rand Corporation 2020.

9. OpenSecrets 2019.

10. American Psychological Association, Kentucky Psychological Association, et al. 2015, 4–5.

11. Pinsof and Haselton 2016. For the county-level sociological study, see McVeigh and Diaz 2009.

12. Pew Research Center 2019.

13. Given the negative connotations of terms associated with the opposite of "pro-life" and "pro-choice," I will use the terms encouraged by the Associated Press: "abortion rights" and "anti-abortion."

14. Guttmacher Institute 2019; Jones and Jerman 2017. Other facts include: white women accounted for 39 percent of abortions in 2014, Black women for 28 percent and Hispanic women for 25 percent, with other races and ethnicities making up 9 percent. In 2014, 17 percent of the women identified as mainline Protestant, 13 percent as evangelical Protestant and 24 percent as Catholic; fully 38 percent reported no religious affiliation and 8 percent reported some other affiliation. Although the overall number of abortions declined, medication abortions increased from 5 percent of all abortions in 2001 to 39 percent in 2017.

15. *Roe v. Wade,* 410 U.S. 113 (1973). In *Planned Parenthood v. Casey* (1992), the

Court rejected *Roe*'s trimester framework in favor of viability, which could be at twenty-three or twenty-four weeks, or even earlier, given medical advances. The Court also replaced the "strict scrutiny" test with the weaker "undue burden" standard for evaluating state restrictions on abortion. In *Whole Woman's Health v. Hellerstedt*, a landmark case from 2016, the Supreme Court decided 5–3 that restrictions Texas placed on the delivery of abortion services placed an *undue burden* on women. Texas had required that abortion providers have admitting privileges to a hospital within thirty miles and abortion facilities meet the standards of ambulatory surgical centers. The Court ruled that these requirements were not about safety but rather an attempt to limit access to abortion.

16. Ginsburg 1992.

17. Nash 2019; Nash and Cross 2021a.

18. Iati and Paul 2019. For the differences between an embryo and fetus, see Stoppler 2020.

19. Here the right is using a strategy based on hyperbolic compliance with laws in order to disrupt policies they oppose. Law professors Jessica Bulman-Pozen and David Pozen (2015) identified this form of dissent and disruption and labeled it "uncivil obedience."

20. Jones et al. 2022.

21. Bruder 2022.

22. Belluck 2013.

23. In his opinion Alito cites Matthew Hale, a seventeenth-century English jurist, more than a dozen times. According to Deanna Pan (2022), Hale was "particularly misogynistic" even among his contemporaries: "Hale is notorious in the law for laying the legal foundation clearing husbands from criminal liability for raping their wives, and for sentencing two women accused of witchcraft to death, a case that served as a model for the infamous Salem witch trials 30 years later."

24. Nash and Cross 2021b.

25. Bruder 2022.

26. Bui, Miller, and Sanger-Katz 2020.

27. Paul Weyrich, co-founder of the Moral Majority with Jerry Falwell Sr., had tried to organize white evangelicals as a political bloc since the Barry Goldwater campaign. According to Dartmouth historian Randall Balmer (2014), the evangelicals became interested only after the IRS denied an evangelical college a tax exemption on the basis of racial discrimination. Weyrich believed that abortion would be a more appealing issue for evangelicals than racial discrimination, and the new vot-

ing bloc was established. White evangelicals remain the largest religious group in the Republican Party.

28. Before this time, Catholics and evangelical Christians were generally at odds. In the 1960 election, for example, it was very clear that evangelicals and Catholics were not on the same team, as evangelicals worked very hard to defeat John F. Kennedy.

29. Balmer 2006.

30. Perhaps the passage in the Bible that is most telling about when human life begins is Genesis 2:7, in which the first human being becomes a "living being" (*nefesh hayah*, a living breath) when it started to breathe after God blew into its nostrils. From this perspective life begins when we start to breathe and ends when we stop breathing (Lowery 2012).

31. The difference between the Catholic clergy and the laity should be noted. A Pew Research Center poll in 2019 found that 68 percent of Catholics do not want *Roe* overturned. In contrast, 35 percent of white evangelicals do not want *Roe* overturned. These findings are reported in Fahmy 2020.

32. Beaty 2020.

33. Beaty 2020.

34. Barna Group 2017.

35. Glick and Fiske 2001.

36. Becker and Wright 2011.

37. Chu and Posner 2013. Because abortion restrictions were included among the thirteen indices of health, it was important to use only indices of economic security and leadership in assessing women's status. Relying on these measures alone, the same ten states where women were most unequal to men were still the states with the greatest restrictions on abortion.

38. Pollitt 2014. It is also worth noting that in the late 1970s the Equal Rights Amendment was close to being ratified by the requisite thirty-eight states when conservative Phyllis Schlafly mobilized women on the right by arguing that the ERA would disadvantage housewives, threaten child custody and alimony following divorce, and cause women to be drafted.

39. Reagan 1998, 8.

40. Reagan 1998, 11.

41. Cunha 2019.

42. Kristof 2020, which discusses both Duford and Sister Traupman. Both explained their choice of Biden over Trump in the 2020 presidential election.

43. Krider 2020.

44. Population Institute 2017.

45. Shorto 2006.

46. Pollitt 2014, 148.

47. Nelson and Cwiak 2011; Jensen and Creinin 2019.

48. Shorto 2006.

49. Santelli et al. 2017, 273. See also Stanger-Hall and Hall 2011. Using national data and information about states' laws and policies regarding sex education, these researchers showed that "increasing emphasis on abstinence education is positively correlated with teenage pregnancy and birth rates. This trend remains significant after accounting for socioeconomic status, teen educational attainment, ethnic composition of the teen population, and availability of Medicaid waivers for family planning services in each state. These data show clearly that abstinence-only education as a state policy is ineffective in preventing teenage pregnancy and may actually be contributing to the high teenage pregnancy rates in the U.S."

50. Weeden and Kurzban 2014.

51. BBC News 2012. The religious exemption that Sandra Fluke was addressing has been a successful route used by the right to restrict contraceptive access. Under the Affordable Care Act of 2010, federal law requires insurance coverage for the full range of contraceptives used by women. Conservatives want a sweeping exemption for any employer who has religious or moral objections to including contraception in the health plans they sponsor. Current federal policy already accommodates these religious objections, because these employers can avoid arranging for, discussing, or paying for such coverage while their employees or dependents receive coverage from the same insurance company. Not surprisingly, conservatives celebrated the Supreme Court *Hobby Lobby* decision of 2015, which allowed the craft store chain and other closely held corporations to be exempt from coverage of contraception for their female employees under the Affordable Care Act. By 2019, fully twenty-one states allowed some employers and insurers to refuse to comply with the federal contraceptive mandate, and the Trump administration tried to make it easier for any employer to do so.

52. Quoted in Bazelon 2007.

53. See, e.g., American Psychological Association 2008; Cohen 2013; Steinberg et al. 2018; and Stotland 1992. Lazzarini 2008 writes, "The purported increased risks of psychological distress, depression, and suicide that physicians are required to warn women about are not supported by the bulk of the scientific literature. By requiring

physicians to deliver such misinformation and discouraging them from providing alternative accurate information, the statute forces physicians to violate their obligation to solicit truly informed consent" (2191).

54. National Cancer Institute 2003; Committee on Gynecologic Practice 2009.

55. See Frank et al. 1993. This study of 10,767 women found that women who had at least two abortions had the same future fertility prospects as those who had two full-term pregnancies.

56. Raymond and Grimes 2012; American College of Obstetricians and Gynecologists and American Medical Association 2013.

57. Siegel 2005, 77, 81.

Chapter 8. What Liberals Are Providing

1. According to a recent Pew Research Center survey (see Drake 2013), a majority of Americans (55 percent) have actually received benefits from one or more of the six best-known government entitlement programs—Social Security, Medicare, Medicaid, unemployment insurance, Temporary Assistance for Needy Families (welfare), and Supplemental Nutrition Assistance Program (food stamps). Entitlement programs are essentially rights granted by federal law and include contributory and non-contributory programs. Social Security, Medicare, and unemployment insurance are contributory programs available to all Americans, but to get benefits the recipients must have worked and contributed to the programs by paying taxes. Medicaid, welfare, and food stamps, are non-contributory, and receipt of benefits is based on the low income of recipients, which is determined by the federal poverty level. Additionally, to get food stamps, recipients without children must work after three months (this is waived in areas with high unemployment) and must work eighty hours a month or participate in job training. Some states, including Alaska, California, and Nevada, have opted out of the work requirement. There are also additional requirements for welfare benefits: recipients must get a job within two years, cannot get more money if they have another child, and in some states can receive benefits for five years or less. According to research by the Center on Budget and Policy Priorities (2021), in 2019, only 23 of every 100 families living in poverty received welfare benefits (Temporary Assistance for Needy Families, the primary source of cash for families with children); and in fourteen states, only 10 of every 100 families living in poverty received benefits.

2. Ghilardu 2018.

3. Light 2013; Reagan 1961.

4. Roy 2012.

5. Quoted in Madison 2011a.

6. Uberoi, Finegold, and Gee 2016.

7. These states had considerably lower uninsured rates than those that did not adopt the expansion, and according to a U.S. Census Report in 2018, of the seventeen states with uninsured rates greater than 9 percent, fully fourteen of these had not expanded Medicaid eligibility. None of the five states with uninsured rates over 12 percent had expanded Medicaid coverage. See Berchick, Barnett, and Upton 2019, fig. 8: Uninsured Rate by State 2018.

8. Elmendorf 2011. To help defray costs, ACA included an excise tax on health insurers based on market share and also instituted an additional Medicare tax of 0.9 percent applied to those with high incomes; the threshold amounts for the tax were $250,000 for a married couple filing jointly, $125,000 for married taxpayers filing separately, and $200,000 for all others.

9. Cohn 2010.

10. The individual mandate was initially a conservative idea, dating back to 1989 when the Heritage Foundation proposed it as an alternative to a single-payer system. It was espoused not because of any interest in redistribution, but because it was regarded as market-based and a way to avoid a free-rider problem in health care. Yet as an aspect of Obamacare, conservatives regarded the individual mandate as anathema. This opposition no doubt largely reflected the plan crafted by Republicans to repeatedly block Obama's initiatives to prevent his reelection in 2012. The plan was developed at a private dinner of fifteen Republicans that included House members Eric Cantor, Jeb Hensarling, Pete Hoekstra, Dan Lungren, Kevin McCarthy, Paul Ryan, and Pete Sessions; Senate members Tom Coburn, Bob Corker, Jim DeMint, John Ensign, and Jon Kyl; and former House speaker Newt Gingrich and Republican strategist Frank Luntz. See Draper 2012.

11. Cunha 2019.

12. The Supreme Court's decision viewed the individual mandate as constitutional when regarded as a tax, and not under the Commerce Clause.

13. There have also been a number of court cases revolving around the cost-sharing reductions subsidies included in ACA. These are subsidies paid to insurance companies to reduce deductibles and co-payments for enrollees with incomes up to 250 percent of the federal poverty level. President Trump ended these subsidies in October 2017, an act consistent with his open opposition to Obamacare. A year earlier the Congressional Budget Office predicted that ending the payments would

result in a 15–20 percent increase in costs of health care and would increase the federal budget over the next decade by $200 billion.

14. The settled legal concept of severability seemed readily to apply to the case. Severability requires that the court ask what Congress would have wanted. In this case, Congress had already eliminated the penalty for failing to purchase health insurance, thereby essentially severing the individual mandate from the rest of the act. Congress therefore let Obamacare stand without the individual mandate.

15. Stolberg 2021a.

16. Quoted in Benen 2017.

17. Notably, article 25 of the Universal Declaration of Human Rights states: "Everyone has the right to a standard of living adequate for the health and well-being of himself and of his family, including food, clothing, housing and medical care and necessary social services, and the right to security in the event of unemployment, sickness, disability, widowhood, old age or other lack of livelihood in circumstances beyond his control."

18. See Weiner, Osborne, and Rudolph 2011 for a review of this research; see also the review by Sahar 2014 and the research by Skitka et al. 2002 on the greater likelihood of liberal (versus conservative) aid when causes are presented as controllable.

19. See Jost, Banaji, and Nosek 2004 for a review of research on system justification. Relatedly, conservatives are more likely than liberals to regard homosexuality as a choice, and liberals are more likely to embrace genetic explanations (see Haider-Markel and Joslyn 2008 and Whitehead and Baker 2012).

20. Rank 2021. Liberals are more likely to take into account situational constraints when making attributions for others' behaviors.

21. The same pattern applies to the social domain for the left; in the absence of a group-based *protect* morality (Social Order), the left relies on an individualized morality that proscribes harming others (Not Harming). Liberalism is based in providing for the group, and when it comes to protecting, their focus is on the individual.

22. Chetty et al. 2018.

23. Atkin 2018.

24. Duflo and Banerjee 2019. See also Shapiro et al. 2016.

25. Long and Van Dam 2020.

26. Gilens 1999. Both then and now, the clear majority of welfare recipients are white.

27. Borrelli 2019. Borrelli also notes, "That said, Reagan's speeches are lessons in

NOTES TO PAGES 177-182

opportunism, distortion and at the very least, blinkered self-awareness—the former president's own father, an alcoholic who had trouble holding jobs, found his steadiest work as a welfare administrator in Dixon, Ill." Regarding the "welfare queen," see also Levin 2019.

28. Knowles, Lowery, and Schaumberg 2010.

29. See Kristof and WuDunn 2020a for a good discussion of this blaming of Black culture.

30. Quoted in Baum 2016, 22.

31. Alexander 2011, 5.

32. See Alexander 2011 for a review.

33. Alexander 2011, 180. Alexander notes that the United States imprisons a larger percentage of Blacks than South Africa did at the height of apartheid. In Washington, D.C., approximately three out of four young Black men can expect to serve time in prison.

34. Wilson 1996.

35. Kristof and WuDunn 2020b. See also Kristof and WuDunn 2020a and Wilson 1996.

36. MacGillis 2015.

37. Hochschild 2017, 151. Hochschild also discusses these people's support for big business despite the lack of alignment between the interests of big and small businesses. She writes, "Ironically, the economic sector that stands to suffer the most from big monopolies is small business. . . . It might not be too much to say that the embrace of the 1 percent by the mom-and-pop store owners is a bit like the natural seed-using small farmers' embrace of Monsanto, the corner grocery store's embrace of Walmart, the local bookstore owner's embrace of Amazon. Under the same banner of the 'free market,' the big are free to dominate the small. . . . But it is very hard to criticize an ally, and the right sees the free market as its ally against the powerful alliance of the federal government and the takers" (150–51).

38. See, e.g., Slovic et al. 2004 and Weber 2006. See also Trope and Liberman 2003, who show that distant events are represented abstractly and more recent events are represented concretely.

39. "Climate Change: How Do We Know?" *Global Climate Change: Vital Signs of the Planet,* produced by the Earth Science Communications Team at NASA's Jet Propulsion Laboratory, California Institute of Technology, climate.nasa.gov /evidence.

40. Kenney and Hefferon 2019.

41. Antonio and Brulle 2011.

42. Manzi and Wehner 2015.

43. Consistent with the left's provide orientation, also included in the initial bill was money for better schools, child care, and caregiving for the disabled and elderly, including increased access to home-based care and building more care centers. The $1 trillion that ultimately passed focused almost exclusively on hard infrastructure, particularly transportation, broadband, and utilities. "Social infrastructure" spending would have to wait.

Chapter 9. Social Justice and the Bane of Inequality

1. Telford 2019; see also the census data at U.S. Census Bureau 2019.

2. Bump 2020.

3. Bailey 2021.

4. Serious conservatives have a genuine interest in free speech, but for many conservatives an emphasis on cancel culture is a prized strategy to divide the left and unite the right. The hypocritical nature of their attack should be apparent, given the countless restrictive efforts on the right to "cancel" the teaching of factual U.S. history and to suppress the voting rights of Americans (addressed in chapter 10).

5. McWhorter 2011.

6. McWhorter 2021.

7. Bruni 2021.

8. For a review of competitive victimhood, see Young and Sullivan 2016.

9. Craig and Richeson 2014a; Vollhardt 2015.

10. See work on the "common group identity model" by Dovidio and Gaertner (Dovidio, Gaertner, and Saguy 2000; Gaertner and Dovidio 2000; Gaertner et al. 1999). Benefits of both identities includes broad generalization of positive attitudes and behaviors.

11. Although bemoaning identity politics on the left, many on the right have nevertheless embraced an identity politics of their own, focused on native-born white Christians as the "real Americans."

12. Quoted in Reilly 2016. Clinton later expressed regret for having made these comments.

13. Federal Reserve Bank of St. Louis 2018.

14. Federal Reserve Bank of St. Louis 2018.

15. Kraus et al. 2019. These researchers did not include political orientation in their analyses.

NOTES TO PAGES 194-201

16. McIntosh et al. 2020.

17. Collins et al. 2016.

18. See Percheski and Gibson-Davis 2020. Their findings are based on the Survey of Consumer Finances (2004–16). See also Coates 2014.

19. Coates 2014.

20. Hannah-Jones 2020.

21. Coates 2014.

22. Hannah-Jones 2020.

23. Peterson-Withorn 2021.

24. Friedman 1980, 247.

25. Hacker and Pierson 2011, 4.

26. Telford 2019; see also Batty et al. 2019.

27. Mishel and Wolfe 2019. When based on compensation that included stock options granted rather than realized (cashed in), CEO compensation actually grew by 1,007.5 percent.

28. Duflo and Banerjee 2019.

29. See, e.g., Suls and Miller 1977.

30. Saez and Zucman 2019.

31. I return to these educational inequalities below when discussing social mobility. For the World Inequality Report 2018, see Alvaredo et al. 2018. The report relies on work and data collected by more than one hundred economists over five continents.

32. Schwartz 2020.

33. Piketty 2014. Based on his research on economic history, Piketty claims that the decades between 1914 and 1973 were an anomaly because the rate of economic growth was greater than the rate of return on capital. Since then the return on capital has returned to pre-1914 levels and is greater than the rate of economic growth. He believes that the pattern of the years 1914–73 is unlikely to be repeated.

34. Some on the left find Piketty too pessimistic. For example, Dean Baker, senior economist at the Center for Economic and Policy Research, recommends additional remedies, including taxes on finance and financial transactions, a higher minimum wage, and labor laws that would allow workers the right to organize (i.e., stronger unions) (Baker 2014).

35. Drutman, Williamson, and Wong 2019. Regarding the composition of the research team, an article in *Forbes* notes that "the mostly conservative American En-

terprise Institute and Cato were also on board with professors from Stanford and Georgetown Universities when conducting this study" (Rapoza 2019).

36. Page, Bartels, and Seawright 2013. Most of the study participants fell into or near the top 1 percent of the U.S. population wealth-wise. The sample's average wealth was $14,006,338 and median wealth was $7,500,000. According to Page, Bartels, and Seawright, "The wealthy are much more favorable toward cutting social welfare programs, especially Social Security and health care. They are considerably less supportive of several jobs and income programs, including an above poverty-level minimum wage, a 'decent' standard of living for the unemployed, increasing the Earned Income Tax Credit, and having the federal government 'see to'—or actually provide—jobs for those who cannot find them in the private sector. Judging by our evidence, wealthy Americans are much less willing than others to provide broad educational opportunities, by 'spend[ing] whatever is necessary to ensure that all children have really good public schools they can go to' or 'mak[ing] sure that everyone who wants to go to college can do so.' They are less willing to pay more taxes in order to provide health coverage for everyone, and they are much less supportive of tax-financed national health insurance. The wealthy tend to favor lower estate tax rates and to be less eager to increase income taxes on high income people" (67).

37. Drutman, Williamson, and Wong 2019 (see n. 29).

38. Drutman, Williamson, and Wong 2019.

39. Madison 2011b.

40. Office of the Press Secretary, the White House 2012.

41. Legitimizing myths are widely accepted cultural ideologies that provide a justification for society's social practices, in particular its social hierarchies. Social psychologists view racism, sexism, and negative stereotypes of non-dominant groups as legitimizing myths that serve to enforce dominant-subordinate positions in the social hierarchy. See, e.g., Sidanius and Pratto 2001.

42. See Jost, Banaji, and Nosek 2004 on system justification theory, which posits that people are motivated to see the current social system as legitimate, even when the system actually works against their own interests.

43. Swanson 2018.

44. OECD 2018.

45. Leatherby 2016.

46. Quoted in Pazzanese 2016.

47. Markovits 2019; Sandel 2020.

48. The Educational Opportunity Monitoring Project 2018.

49. Shai and Gilovich 2015; see also Kraus and Tan 2015.

50. Shariff, Wiwad, and Aknin 2016.

51. Page, Bartels, and Seawright 2013; for the association between wealth and political activity, see Schlozman, Verba, and Brady 2012.

52. Confessore, Cohen, and Yourish 2015.

53. *The Code of Capitalism* (2019), by law professor Katharina Pistor, makes a compelling case for the central role of the legal code in creating wealth and inequality.

54. Ross, Amabile, and Steinmetz 1977.

55. Like the observers, contestants also viewed the contestants and questioners differently; they rated themselves as well below average in general knowledge and the questioners as well above average. The questioners, who knew they were coming up with very tough questions, rated both themselves and the contestants as average. There were actually two separate studies. Study 1 did not include observers, and Study 2 was a replication with the very important addition of the observer group.

56. For social psychologists, this tendency to underestimate the impact of social roles on behavior is often regarded as illustrative of a broader phenomenon referred to as the "fundamental attribution error" (Ross 1977; Nisbett and Ross 1980), whereby we underestimate the power of situations and overestimate the contribution of internal, dispositional factors in our understanding of behavior.

57. Cote, House, and Willer 2015.

58. See van Kleef et al. 2008. See also Vohs, Mead, and Goode 2006, who found that reminders of money made people less helpful, more likely to want to work alone, and more physically distant from a new acquaintance.

59. See, e.g., Blader, Shirako, and Chen 2016; Fiske 1993; Galinsky, Magee, Inesi, and Gruenfeld 2006; and Keltner, Gruenfeld, and Anderson 2003.

60. See, e.g., Twenge, Campbell, and Carter 2014.

61. For benefits of societal equality, see, e.g., Deaton 2003; Kesebir 2012; Oishi, Kesebir, and Diener 2011; and Wilkinson and Pickett 2009. For problems associated with inequality, see, e.g., Hsieh and Pugh 1993; Kawachi et al. 1997; Stiglitz 2012; and Uslaner 2002.

Chapter 10. Social Order and Authoritarianism

1. Office of Public Affairs, U.S. Department of Justice, 2019.

2. Deneen 2018, 187. George Will (2020) warns against a wholesale attack on

individualism, writing that "fascism fancied itself as modernity armed—science trans-lated into machines, especially airplanes, and pure energy restlessly seeking things to smash. Actually, it was a recoil against Enlightenment individualism: the idea that good societies allow reasoning, rights-bearing people to define for themselves the worthy life. Individualism, fascists insisted, produces a human dust of deracinated people (Nietzsche's 'the sand of humanity'), whose loneliness and purposelessness could be cured by gusts of charismatic leadership blowing them into vibrant national-cum-tribal collectivities."

3. The Commonwealth Fund 2020.

4. The major American psychological and medical societies presented an over-view of research on marriage in their *Obergefell* amicus brief; American Psychologi-cal Association, Kentucky Psychological Association, et al. 2015, 13–16, 19–22. See also the review of marriage and child well-being in Brown 2010.

5. Deneen 2018, 39.

6. Edsall 2019.

7. Finkel et al. 2014, 35. Finkel's numbers are from marriages up to the mid-1990s, but findings from more recent studies show the same differences. Specifically, according to researchers at the National Center for Health Statistics, 78 percent of college-educated women who married for the first time between 2006 and 2010 could expect their marriages to last at least twenty years, compared to only 40 percent of those with a high school education or less (see Wang 2015). In the United States, education and political orientation are strongly related, with more education associ-ated with greater likelihood of being liberal (see Pew Research Center 2016).

8. Finkel 2019.

9. Brickman 1987.

10. Brooks 2018.

11. Edsall 2019.

12. Putnam 2017.

13. Kristof and WuDunn 2020a.

14. Barr 2020.

15. Fahmy 2018.

16. Boot 2020. The research was conducted with Max Boot's research associate, Sherry Cho.

17. Pew Research Center 2019.

18. For a review of this research, see Galen 2012.

19. Tsai et al. 2014; Tsai, Lucas, and Kawachi 2015. Social integration in these

NOTES TO PAGES 222-231

studies was assessed with a seven-item index that included marital status, social network size, frequency of contact, and participation in religious or other social groups. See also Putnam 2000, 2020. Regarding suicide, there are strong echoes here of Durkheim's anomic suicide, which is based in a lack of social integration.

20. See Flavin and Radcliff 2009; Kim 2016; Stack 2018.

21. Blanchflower and Oswald 2020.

22. Kristof and WuDunn 2020a.

23. Margulies 2021.

24. Kessler, Rizzo, and Kelly 2021. "When The Washington Post Fact Checker team first started cataloguing President Donald Trump's false or misleading claims, we recorded 492 suspect claims in the first 100 days of his presidency. On Nov. 2 alone, the day before the 2020 vote, Trump made 503 false or misleading claims as he barnstormed across the country in a desperate effort to win reelection. This astonishing jump in falsehoods is the story of Trump's tumultuous reign. By the end of his term, Trump had accumulated 30,573 untruths during his presidency—averaging about 21 erroneous claims a day."

25. V-Dem Institute 2021b. V-Dem is a team of more than fifty social scientists across six continents who work with more than 3,500 country experts and a global International Advisory Board.

26. Muller 2021.

27. Although often attributed to Joseph Goebbels, the "Big Lie" was actually coined by Hitler in *Mein Kampf* to describe his belief about the behavior of Jews, whom he accused of lying to discredit German activities during World War I. Nevertheless, Goebbels and the Nazi propaganda machine did use the propaganda technique of repeated lies to get support for rabid antisemitism and the Final Solution.

28. *Economist*/YouGov 2021.

29. Arendt 1994, 361.

30. Luban 2021, 20.

31. See Factbase 2020 for a transcript of Maria Bartiromo's interview with Donald Trump on Fox News.

32. Williams 2017.

33. Williams 2016.

34. See, e.g., Mutz 2018. See also Cox, Lienesch, and Jones 2017 and Green 2017.

35. Sprong et al. 2019. See also Kakkar and Sivanathan 2017. Based on data from sixty-nine counties over two decades, Kakkar and Sivanathan found that peo-

ple prefer dominant leaders under conditions of economic uncertainty (e.g., high poverty rate, high unemployment). They noted the rise of populist authoritarian leaders across the globe, leaders who are "overbearing in their narrative, aggressive in their behavior, and often exhibit questionable moral character" (6734).

36. O'Toole 2020, 6.

37. MacWilliams 2016; Hetheringon and Weiler 2009. See also Taub 2016.

38. The survey, conducted coincident to U.S. federal elections every two years, asks about voting behavior and political opinions; American National Election Studies, https://electionstudies.org/.

39. As noted in chapter 4, Fraley et al. 2012 explored the relationship between mothers' approach to parenting when their child was one month old and the political orientation of the children eighteen years later. The parenting scale used in the research was the thirty-item Parental Modernity Inventory (Schaefer and Edgerton 1985), which actually produces two composite scores defined as "traditional parenting" and "progressive parenting." To highlight the differences in attitudes toward authority, Fraley and colleagues changed the composite names to "authoritarian" and "egalitarian" parenting. Importantly, the "traditional parenting" items focus on essentially the same attributes as those assessed in Feldman's four-item authoritarian scale, specifically obedience and respect for authority (e.g., "Children should always obey their parents"), and in this research the scores were positively associated with the children's political conservatism eighteen years later.

40. Taub 2016. Fully 44 percent of the white respondents scored high or very high on the measure.

41. Altemeyer 1996. Altemeyer referred to the authoritarian personality as right-wing authoritarianism (RWA) and developed the twenty-two-item RWA scale.

42. Quoted in Worthen 2018.

43. See Stenner 2005, who posits that authoritarians have latent tendencies that get triggered by disorienting social change or physical threats. See also Feldman and Stenner 1997.

44. Dawsey and Helderman 2021.

45. Wehle 2021.

46. See the Heritage Foundation's database, www.heritage.org/voterfraud. These numbers are based on the database as of June 22, 2022. The 0.0000838 percent is based on a total vote of 158,376,519 voters in the presidential election of 2020: 81,268,924 for Biden, 74,216,154 for Trump, and 2,891,441 for others.

47. Democrats walked out of the legislature, denying the Republicans a vote on

the initial restrictive bill. Even the *Wall Street Journal* editorial board criticized the obvious attack on the "souls to polls" campaign, after which some Texas GOP legislators shamelessly claimed it was actually a typo and should have read "11:00" instead of "1:00."

48. Quoted in Cobb 2021. Cobb notes that the remark is from a forthcoming book by Marsha Barrett titled *The Politics of Moderation: Nelson Rockefeller's Failed Fight to Save the Party of Lincoln.*

49. See, e.g., Staub 2015.

50. See Fishkin and Pozen 2018 on the asymmetry in the political parties' use of uncompromising, hardball tactics more generally, with the Republicans relying on them more than the Democrats.

51. V-Dem Institute 2021a, 18.

52. Repucci 2021.

53. Norris 2020. The Global Party Survey, which draws on 1,861 election and party experts, is directed by Pippa Norris at Harvard University.

54. Statement of Concern 2021.

Chapter 11. Moving Forward

1. Pronin, Lin, and Ross 2002; Ross and Ward 1996.

2. See Finkel et al. 2020 on "political sectarianism."

3. Dionne 2020; see Lemon 2020 for Pelosi's comments, made as she bemoaned the current state of the Republican Party hijacked by Trump.

4. Gelfand et al. 2011; Harrington, Boski, and Gelfand 2015. See also Janoff-Bulman and Carnes 2016, Study 3, for similar findings based on economic figures from the World Bank and happiness measures from the United Nations.

5. Baumrind 1967, 1991; see also Macoby and Martin 1983. Sometimes the demandingness dimension is referred to as high and low control, and the responsiveness dimension as warm and cold, or alternatively accepting and unaccepting.

6. For a review, see Larzelere, Morris, and Harrist 2013. Parenting that is low on both demandingness and responsiveness is labeled "neglectful."

7. Green, Harmacek, and Krylova 2020. The index is based on fifty measures of well-being, including health, education, shelter, environmental quality, personal freedom, and nutrition. It does not include economic indices. The data predated the Covid-19 pandemic. Overall the United States ranked twenty-eighth, down from nineteenth in 2011.

References

Aaroe, Lene, Michael Bang Petersen, and Kevin Arceneaux. 2017. "The Be-
havioral Immune System Shapes Political Intuitions: Why and How
Individual Differences in Disgust Sensitivity Underlie Opposition to
Immigration." *American Political Science Review* 111: 277–94.

Abramowitz, Alan I. 2012. *The Polarized Public: Why American Government
Is So Dysfunctional.* New York: Pearson.

———. 2018. *The Great Alignment.* New Haven: Yale University Press.

Aistrup, Joseph A. 1996. *The Southern Strategy Revisited: Republican Top-Down
Advancement in the South.* Lexington: University Press of Kentucky.

Alexander, Michelle. 2011. *The New Jim Crow: Mass Incarceration in the Age
of Colorblindness.* New York: New Press.

Alexander, Richard. 1987. *The Biology of Moral Systems.* Hawthorne, N.Y.:
Aldine de Gruyter.

Allport, Gordon W. 1954. *The Nature of Prejudice.* Cambridge, Mass.:
Addison-Wesley.

Altemeyer, Bob. 1996. *The Authoritarian Specter.* Cambridge, Mass.: Harvard University Press.

———. 1998. "The Other 'Authoritarian Personality.'" In *Advances in Experimental Social Psychology,* edited by Mark Zanna, 47–92. San Diego,
Calif.: Academic Press.

Alvaredo, Facundo, Lucas Chancel, Thomas Piketty, Emmanuel Saez, and
Gabriel Zucman. 2018. "World Inequality Report 2018: Executive
Summary." https://wir2018.wid.world/files/download/wir2018-summary
-english.pdf.

Alwin, Duane F., Ronald Cohen, and Theodore M. Newcomb. 1991. *Politi-*

cal Attitudes over the Life Span: The Bennington Women After Fifty Years. Madison: University of Wisconsin Press.

American College of Obstetricians and Gynecologists and American Medical Association. 2013. "Brief of Amici Curiae in *Planned Parenthood of Greater Texas Surgical Health Services et al. v. Attorney General Gregory Abbot et al.*"

American Psychological Association. 2008. "APA Task Force Finds Single Abortion Not a Threat to Women's Mental Health." https://www.apa .org/news/press/releases/2008/08/single-abortion.

American Psychological Association, Kentucky Psychological Association, Ohio Psychological Association, American Psychiatric Association, American Academy of Pediatrics, American Association for Marriage and Family Therapy, Michigan Association for Marriage and Family Therapy, et al. 2015. "Amici Curiae in Support of Petitioners." https://www .apa.org/about/offices/ogc/amicus/obergefell-supreme-court.pdf.

Antonio, Robert J., and Robert J. Brulle. 2011. "The Unbearable Lightness of Politics: Climate Change Denial and Political Polarization." *Sociological Quarterly* 52: 195–202.

Arendt, Hannah. 1994. *The Origins of Totalitarianism.* New York: Harvest Books.

Aristotle. 1941. "Nicomachean Ethics" [350 BCE]. In *The Basic Works of Aristotle,* edited by Richard McKeon, 927–1112. New York: Random House.

Atkin, Emily. 2018. "The Republican Threat to Food Stamps in 2018." *New Republic,* January 4. https://newrepublic.com/article/146448/republican -threat-food-stamps-2018.

Badger, Emily. 2016. "As American as Apple Pie? The Rural Vote's Disproportionate Slice of Power." *New York Times,* November 20. https://www .nytimes.com/2016/11/21/upshot/as-american-as-apple-pie-the-rural -votes-disproportionate-slice-of-power.html.

Bai, Xuechunzi, Miguel R. Ramos, and Susan T. Fiske. 2020. "As Diversity Increases, People Paradoxically Perceive Social Groups as More Similar. *PNAS* 117: 12741–49.

Bailey, Holly. 2021. "A Ballot Initiative on Overhauling Police After George Floyd's Death Is Tearing Minneapolis Apart." *Washington Post,* October

22. https://www.washingtonpost.com/nation/2021/10/22/minneapolis
-police-reform-ballot-initiative/.

Baker, Dean. 2014. "Economic Policy in a Post-Piketty World." *Truthout,*
April 21. https://truthout.org/articles/economic-policy-in-a-post-piketty
-world/.

Balmer, Randall Herbert. 2006. *Thy Kingdom Come.* New York: Basic Books.

———. 2014. "The Real Origins of the Religious Right." *Political Magazine,*
May 27. https://www.politico.com/magazine/story/2014/05/religious
-right-real-origins-107133.

Barbaranelli, Claudio, Gian Vittorio Caprara, Michele Vecchione, and
Chris R. Fraley. 2007. "Voters' Personality Traits in Presidential Election." *Personality and Individual Differences* 42: 1199–208.

Barna Group. 2017. "What Americans Think About Women in Power."
March 8. https://www.barna.com/research/americans-think-women
-power/.

Baron, Jonathan, and John T. Jost. 2019. "False Equivalence: Are Liberals
and Conservatives in the United States Equally Biased?" *Perspectives on
Psychological Science* 14: 292–303.

Baron, Jonathan, and Ilana Ritov. 2004. "Omission Bias, Individual Differences, and Normality." *Organizational Behavior and Human Decision
Processes* 94: 74–85.

Barr, William P. 2020. Remarks at the 2020 National Religious Broadcasters Convention Nashville, Tenn., February 26. https://www.justice.gov
/opa/speech/attorney-general-william-p-barr-delivers-remarks-2020
-national-religious-broadcasters.

Bar-Tal, Daniel. 1990. "Causes and Consequences of Delegitimization: Models of Conflict and Ethnocentrism." *Journal of Social Issues* 46: 65–81.

Batson, C. Daniel. 1991. *The Altruism Question: Toward a Social-Psychologi-
cal Answer.* Mahwah, N.J.: Lawrence Erlbaum Associates.

———. 1998. "Altruism and Prosocial Behavior." In *The Handbook of Social
Psychology,* edited by Daniel T. Gilbert, Susan T. Fiske, and Gardner
Lindzey, 262–316. New York: McGraw-Hill.

Batty, Michael, Jesse Bricker, Joseph Briggs, Elizabeth Holmquist, Susan
McIntosh, Kevin Moore, Eric Nielsen, et al. 2019. "Introducing the

Distributional Financial Accounts of the United States." Finance and Economics Discussion Series 2019-017. Washington, D.C.: Board of Governors of the Federal Reserve System. https://www.federalreserve .gov/econres/feds/files/2019017pap.pdf.

Baum, Dan. 2016. "Legalize It All." *Harper's Magazine,* April. https://archive .harpers.org/2016/04/pdf/HarpersMagazine-2016-04-0085915.pdf.

Baumeister, Roy F., Ellen Brataslavsky, Catrin Finkenauer, and Kathleen D. Vohs. 2001. "Bad Is Stronger Than Good." *Review of General Psychology* 5: 323–70.

Baumrind, Diana. 1967. "Child Care Practices Anteceding Three Patterns of Preschool Behavior." *Genetic Psychology Monographs* 75: 43–88.

———. 1991. "The Influence of Parenting Style on Adolescent Competence and Substance Use." *Journal of Early Adolescence* 11: 56–95.

Bawn, Kathleen, Martin Cohen, David Karol, Seth Maskt, Hans Noel, and John Zaller. 2012. "A Theory of Parties: Groups, Policy Demanders and Nominations in American Politics." *Perspectives on Politics* 10: 571–97.

Bazelon, Emily. 2007. "Is There a Post-Abortion Syndrome?" *New York Times Magazine,* January 21. 2007. https://www.nytimes.com/2007/01 /21/magazine/21abortion.t.html.

BBC News. 2012. "Limbaugh Slut Slur Student Sandra Fluke Gets Obama Call." March 2. https://www.bbc.com/news/world-us-canada-17241803.

Beaty, Katelyn. 2020. "Why Only Amy Coney Barrett Gets to Have It All." *New York Times,* October 13. https://www.nytimes.com/2020/10/13 /opinion/amy-coney-barrett-motherhood.html.

Becker, Julia C., and Stephen Wright. 2011. "Yet Another Dark Side of Chivalry: Benevolent Sexism Undermines and Hostile Sexism Motivates Collective Action for Social Change." *Journal of Personality and Social Psychology* 101: 62–77.

Belluck, Pam. 2013. "Pregnancy Centers Gain Influence in Anti-Abortion Arena." *New York Times,* January 4. https://www.nytimes.com/2013/01 /05/health/pregnancy-centers-gain-influence-in-anti-abortion-fight .html.

Benedict, Ruth. 1934. *Patterns of Culture.* New York: Houghton Mifflin.

Benen, Steve. 2017. "GOP Senator: Health Care Coverage Is 'a Privilege,' Not a Right." MSNBC, October 2. http://www.msnbc.com/rachel -maddow-show/gop-senator-health-care-coverage-privilege-not-right.

Berchick, Edward R., Jessica C. Barnett, and Rachel D. Upton. 2019. *Health Insurance Coverage in the United States: 2018.* U.S. Census Bureau. Washington, D.C.: U.S. Government Printing Office.

Berlin, Isaiah. 1969. "Two Concepts of Liberty." In *Four Essays on Liberty,* 118–72. London: Oxford University Press.

Bishop, Bill. 2008. *The Big Sort.* New York: Houghton Mifflin Harcourt.

Blackburn, Simon. 2001. *Ethics: A Very Short Introduction.* Oxford: Oxford University Press.

Blader, Steven L., Aiwa Shirako, and Ya-Ru Chen. 2016. "Looking Out from the Top: Differential Effects of Status and Power on Perspective-Taking." *Personality and Social Psychological Bulletin* 42: 723–37.

Blanchflower, David G., and Andrew J. Oswald. 2020. "Trends in Extreme Distress in the United States, 1993–2019." *American Journal of Public Health* 110: 1538–44.

Blanton, Hart, and Charlene Christie. 2003. "Deviance Regulation: A Theory of Action and Identity." *Review of General Psychology* 7: 115–49.

Block, Jack, and Jeanne H. Block. 2006. "Nursery School Personality and Political Orientation Two Decades Later." *Journal of Research in Personality* 40: 734–49.

Bloom, Paul. 2016. *Against Empathy: The Case for Rational Compassion.* New York: Ecco.

Bonanno, George A., and John T. Jost. 2006. "Conservative Shift Among High-Exposure Survivors of the September 11th Terrorist Attacks." *Basic and Applied Social Psychology* 28: 311–23.

Boot, Max. 2020. "William Barr's America vs. Reality in 2020." *Washington Post,* February 19. https://www.washingtonpost.com/opinions/2020/02 /19/william-barrs-america-vs-reality-2020/.

Borrelli, Christopher. 2019. "Reagan Used Her, the Country Hated Her; Decades Later the Welfare Queen Refuses to Go Away." *Chicago Tribune,* June 10. https://www.chicagotribune.com/entertainment/ct-ent -welfare-queen-josh-levin-0610-story.html.

Bowles, Samuel. 2006. "Group Competition, Reproductive Leveling, and the Evolution of Human Altruism." *Science* 314: 1569–72.

Boyd, Robert. 2006. "The Puzzle of Human Sociality." *Science* 314: 1555–56.

Brewer, Marilynn B. 1979. "In-Group Bias in the Minimal Intergroup Situation: A Cognitive-Motivational Analysis." *Psychological Bulletin* 86: 307–24.

———. 1999. "The Psychology of Prejudice: Ingroup Love and Outgroup Hate?" *Journal of Social Issues* 55: 429–44.

Brewer, Marilynn B., Ying-Yi Hong, and Qiong Li. 2004. "Dynamic Entitativity: Perceiving Groups as Actors." In *The Psychology of Group Perception: Perceived Variability, Entitativity, and Essentialism,* edited by Vincent Yzerbyt, Charles M. Judd, and Olivier Corneille, 25–38. Hove, U.K.: Psychology Press.

Brickman, Philip. 1987. *Commitment, Conflict, and Caring.* Englewood Cliffs, N.J.: Prentice-Hall.

Brickman, Philip, Robert Folger, Erica E. Goode, and Yaacov Schul. 1981. "Microjustice and Macrojustice." In *The Justice Motive in Social Behavior,* edited by Melvin J. Lerner and Sally C. Lerner, 173–202. New York: Plenum.

Brooks, Arthur C. 2006. *Who Really Cares: The Surprising Truth About Compassionate Conservatism.* New York: Basic Books.

Brooks, Clem, Jeff Manza, and Emma D. Cohen. 2016, "Political Ideology and Immigrant Acceptance." *Socius: Sociological Research for a Dynamic World* 2: 1–12.

Brooks, David. 2018. "How Democracies Perish." *New York Times,* January 11. https://www.nytimes.com/2018/01/11/opinion/how-democracies-perish.html.

Brown, Susan. 2010. "Marriage and Child Well-Being: Research and Policy Perspectives. *Journal of Marriage and the Family* 72: 1059–77.

Bruder, Jessica. 2022. "The Abortion Underground: Inside the Covert Network of Activists Preparing for a Post-*Roe* Future." *Atlantic,* May 22–32.

Bruni, Frank. 2021. "Ted Cruz, I'm Sorry." *New York Times,* June 17. https://

www.nytimes.com/2021/06/17/opinion/frank-bruni-final-times-column .html.

Buchan, Nancy R., Rachel Croson, and Robyn M. Dawes. 2002. "Swift Neighbors and Persistent Strangers: A Cross-Cultural Investigation of Trust and Reciprocity in Social Exchange." *American Journal of Sociology* 108: 168–206.

Budiman, Abby. 2020. "Key Findings About U.S. Immigrants." Pew Research Center, August 20. https://www.pewresearch.org/fact-tank/2020 /08/20/key-findings-about-u-s-immigrants/.

Bui, Quoctrung, Claire Cain Miller, and Margot Sanger-Katz. 2020. "If Roe Ends, a 'Tremendous Inequality' in Access." *New York Times,* October 19, 2020.

Bulman-Pozen, Jessica, and David E. Pozen. 2015. "Uncivil Obedience." *Columbia Law Review* 115: 809–72.

Bump, Philip. 2020. "Over the Past 60 Years, More Spending on Police Hasn't Necessarily Meant Less Crime." *Washington Post,* June 7. https:// www.washingtonpost.com/politics/2020/06/07/over-past-60-years -more-spending-police-hasnt-necessarily-meant-less-crime/.

Buttrick, Nicholas. 2020. "Protective Gun Ownership as a Coping Mechanism." *Perspectives on Psychological Science* 15: 835–55.

Carnes, Nate C., and Ronnie Janoff-Bulman. 2016. "Restraining Self-Interest or Enabling Altruism: Morality and Politics." In *Social Psychology of Political Polarization,* edited by Piercarlo Valdesolo and Jesse Graham, 123–42. New York: Routledge.

Carnes, Nate C., Brian Lickel, and Ronnie Janoff-Bulman. 2015. "Shared Perceptions: Morality Is Embedded in Social Contexts." *Personality and Social Psychology Bulletin* 41: 351–62.

Carney, Dana R., John T. Jost, Samuel D. Gosling, and Jeffrey Potter. 2008. "The Secret Lives of Liberals and Conservatives: Personality Profiles, Interaction Styles, and the Things They Leave Behind." *Political Psychology* 29: 807–40.

Carter, Dan T. 1999. *From George Wallace to Newt Gingrich: Race in the Conservative Counterrevolution, 1963–1994.* Baton Rouge, La.: LSU Press.

Cartwright, Edward, Joris Gillet, and Mark Van Vugt. 2013. "Leadership by Example in the Weak-Link Game." *Economic Inquiry* 51: 2028–43.

Carver, Charles. 2006. "Approach, Avoidance, and the Self-Regulation of Affect and Action." *Motivation and Emotion* 30: 105–10.

Carver, Charles S., and Michael F. Scheier. 1998. *On the Self-Regulation of Behavior.* New York: Cambridge University Press.

Center on Budget and Policy Priorities. 2021. "Chart Book: Temporary Assistance for Needy Families (TANF) at 25." August 5. https://www.cbpp.org/research/family-income-support/temporary-assistance-for-needy-families-tanf-at-25#part01.

Chernow, Ron. 2005. *Alexander Hamilton.* New York: Penguin Books.

Chetty, Raj, John Friedman, Nathaniel Hendren, Maggie R. Jones, and Sonya R. Porter. 2018. "The Opportunity Atlas: Mapping the Childhood Roots of Social Mobility." NBER Working Paper No. 25147. https://opportunityinsights.org/wp-content/uploads/2018/10/atlas_paper.pdf.

Choi, Jung-Kyoo, and Samuel Bowles. 2007. "The Coevolution of Parochial Altruism and War." *Science* 318: 636–40.

Chu, Anna, and Charles Posner. 2013. "Explore the Data: The State of Women in America." Center for American Progress, September 25. https://www.americanprogress.org/issues/women/news/2013/09/25/75076/explore-the-data-the-state-of-women-in-america/.

Coates, Ta-Nehesi. 2014. "The Case for Reparations." *Atlantic,* June. https://www.theatlantic.com/magazine/archive/2014/06/the-case-for-reparations/361631.

Cobb, Jelani. 2021. "What Is Happening to the Republicans?" *New Yorker,* March 15. https://www.newyorker.com/magazine/2021/03/15/what-is-happening-to-the-republicans.

Cohen, Geoffrey L. 2003. "Party over Policy: The Dominating Impact of Group Influence on Political Beliefs." *Journal of Personality and Social Psychology* 85: 808–22.

Cohen, Susan A. 2013. "Still True: Abortion Does Not Increase Women's Risk of Mental Health Problems." *Guttmacher Policy Review,* June 25. https://www.guttmacher.org/gpr/2013/06/still-true-abortion-does-not-increase-womens-risk-mental-health-problems.

Cohn, Jonathan. 2010. "Common Sense: Why Americans Should Support an Individual Mandate." *New Republic,* April 9. https://newrepublic.com /article/74332/why-americans-should-support-individual-mandate.

Colby, Sandra L., and Jennifer M. Ortman. 2015. "Projections of the Size and Composition of the U.S. Population: 2014–2060. *United States Census Bureau Current Population Reports.* https://www.census.gov/content /dam/Census/library/publications/2015/demo/p25-1143.pdf.

Collins, Chuck, Dedrick Asante-Muhammed, Josh Hoxie, and Emanuel Nieves. 2016. "The Ever-Growing Gap: Failing to Address the Status Quo Will Drive the Racial Wealth Divide for Centuries to Come." Institute for Policy Studies, August 8. https://ips-dc.org/report-ever -growing-gap/.

Committee on Gynecologic Practice. 2009. "ACOG Committee Opinion No. 434: Induced Abortion and Breast Cancer Risk." *Obstetrics and Gynecology* 113: 1417–18.

The Commonwealth Fund. 2020. "New International Report on Health Care: U.S. Suicide Rate Highest Among Wealthy Nations." January 30. https://www.commonwealthfund.org/press-release/2020/new-inter national-report-health-care-us-suicide-rate-highest-among-wealthy.

Confessore, Nicholas, Sara Cohen, and Karen Yourish. 2015. "Just 158 Families Have Provided Nearly Half of the Early Money for Efforts to Capture the White House." *New York Times,* October 10. https://www.ny times.com/interactive/2015/10/11/us/politics/2016-presidential-election -super-pac-donors.html.

Conover, Pamela Johnston, and Stanley Feldman. 2004. "The Origins and Meaning of Liberal/Conservative Self-Identifications." In *Political Psychology: Key Readings,* edited by John T. Jost and Jim Sidanius, 200–216. New York: Psychology Press.

Converse, Philip E. 1964. "The Nature of Belief Systems in Mass Publics." In *Ideology and Discontent,* edited by David E. Apter, 206–61. New York: Free Press.

Cooper, Michael. 2008. "No. 1 Faux Pas in Washington? Candor, Perhaps." *New York Times,* June 25. https://www.nytimes.com/2008/06/25/us/politics /25memo.html.

Cosmides, Leda. 1989. "The Logic of Social Exchange: Has Natural Selection Shaped How Humans Reason? Studies with the Wason Selection Task." *Cognition* 31: 187–276.

Cosmides, Leda, and John Tooby. 1992. "Cognitive Adaptations for Social Exchange." In *The Adapted Mind: Evolutionary Psychology and the Generation of Culture,* edited by Jerome H. Barkow, Leda Cosmides, and John Tooby, 163–228. Oxford: Oxford University Press.

Cote, Stephanie, Julian House, and Robb Willer. 2015. "High Economic Inequality Leads Higher-Income Individuals to Be Less Generous." *PNAS* 112: 15838–43.

Cox, Daniel, Rachel Lienesch, and Robert P. Jones. 2017. "Beyond Economics: Fears of Cultural Displacement Pushed the White Working Class to Trump." *PRRI/The Atlantic Report,* May 9. https://www.prri.org/research /white-working-class-attitudes-economy-trade-immigration-election -donald-trump/.

Craig, Maureen A., and Jennifer A. Richeson. 2014a. "Discrimination Divides Across Identity Dimensions: Perceived Racism Reduces Support for Gay Rights and Increases Anti-Gay Bias." *Journal of Experimental Social Psychology* 55: 169–74.

———. 2014b. "On the Precipice of a 'Majority-Minority' Nation: Perceived Status Threat from the Racial Demographic Shift Affects White Americans' Political Ideology." *Psychological Science* 25: 1189–97.

Crimston, Charlie R., Paul G. Bain, Matthew J. Hornsey, and Brock Bastian. 2016. "Moral Expansiveness: Variability in the Extension of the Moral World." *Journal of Personality and Social Psychology* 111: 636–53.

Cunha, Darlena. 2019. "How Florida Republicans Are Talking About Impeachment." *New York Times,* October 21. https://www.nytimes.com /2019/10/21/opinion/florida-republicans-impeachment.html.

Currie, David P. 1986. "Positive and Negative Constitutional Rights." *University of Chicago Law Review* 53: 864–90.

Cushman, Fiery, Kurt Gray, Allison Gaffey, and Wendy Berry Mendes. 2012. "Simulating Murder: The Aversion to Harmful Action." *Emotion* 12: 2–7.

Daalder, Ivo. 2018. "The Battle for Liberal Democracy Will Be Waged in

Cities." *Financial Times,* June 6. https://www.ft.com/content/f6422018
-68a5-11e8-b6eb-4acfcfbo8c11.

Dahlsgaard, Katherine, Christopher Peterson, and Martin E. P. Seligman.
2005. "Shared Virtue: The Convergence of Valued Human Strengths
Across Culture and History." *Review of General Psychology* 9: 203–13.

Dasgupta, Nilanjana. 2013. "Implicit Attitudes and Beliefs Adapt to Situa-
tions: A Decade of Research on the Malleability of Implicit Prejudice,
Stereotypes, and the Self-Concept." In *Advances in Experimental Social
Psychology,* vol. 47, edited by Patricia Devine and Ashley Plant, 233–79.
Amsterdam: Elsevier.

Dasgupta, Nilanjana, and Luis M. Rivera. 2008. "When Social Context Matters: The Influence of Long-Term Contact and Short-Term Exposure to
Admired Outgroup Members on Implicit Attitudes and Behavioral Intentions." *Social Cognition* 26: 54–66.

Davey, Liane M., D. Ramona Bobocel, Leanne S. Son Hing, and Mark P.
Zanna. 1999. "Preference for the Merit Principle Scale: An Individual
Difference Measure of Distributive Justice Preferences." *Social Justice
Research* 12: 223–40.

Davidai, Shai, and Thomas Gilovich. 2015. "Building a More Mobile
America—One Income Quintile at a Time." *Perspectives on Psychological Science* 10: 60–71.

Davidson, Justin. 2017. "Cities vs. Trump." *New York Magazine,* April. https://
nymag.com/intelligencer/2017/04/the-urban-rural-divide-matters
-more-than-red-vs-blue-state.html.

Davidson, Richard J., Paul P. Ekman, Clifford D. Saron, Joseph A. Senulis,
and Wallace V. Friesen. 1990. "Approach Withdrawal and Cerebral
Asymmetry: Emotional Expression and Brain Physiology: I." *Journal
of Personality and Social Psychology* 58: 330–41.

Dawsey, Josh, and Rosalind S. Helderman. 2021. "Trump Has Grown Increasingly Consumed with Ballot Audits as He Pushes Falsehood That
Election Was Stolen." *Washington Post,* June 2. https://www.washington
post.com/politics/trump-2020-election-audits/2021/06/02/95fd3004
-c2ec-11eb-8c34-f8095f2dc445_story.html.

Dawsey, Josh, Carol D. Leonnig, and Hannah Knowles. 2020. "Secret Service Agents, Doctors Aghast at Trump's Drive Outside Hospital." *Washington Post,* October 4. https://www.washingtonpost.com/politics/2020/10/04/trump-hospital-drive-criticism/.

Deaton, Angus. 2003. "Health, Inequality, and Economic Development." *Journal of Economic Literature* 41: 113–58.

Deneen, Patrick J. 2018. *Why Liberalism Failed.* New Haven: Yale University Press.

de Waal, Frans B. M. 1996. *Good Natured: The Origins of Right and Wrong in Humans and Other Animals.* Cambridge, Mass.: Harvard University Press.

———. 2005. *Our Inner Ape.* New York: Riverhead Books.

———. 2008. "Putting the Altruism Back into Altruism: The Evolution of Empathy." *Annual Review of Psychology* 59: 279–300.

———. 2009. *Primates and Philosophers: How Morality Evolved.* Princeton, N.J.: Princeton University Press.

Dhaval, Dave, Andrew Friedson, Drew McNichols, and Joseph J. Sabia. 2020. "The Contagion Externality of a Superspreading Event: The Sturgis Motorcycle Rally and COVID-19." Center for Health Economics and Policy Studies, San Diego State University, September 5. https://cheps.sdsu.edu/docs/Contagion_Externality_Sturgis_Motorcycle_Rally_9-5-20_Dave_et_al.pdf.

Dionne, Eugene J., Jr. 2020. "Biden Reaches Out; the GOP Slaps Him in the Face." *Washington Post,* November 22. https://www.washingtonpost.com/opinions/biden-reaches-out-the-gop-slaps-him-in-the-face/2020/11/20/5111029e-2b76-11eb-92b7-6ef17b3fe3b4_story.html.

Ditto, Peter H., and Brittany S. Liu. 2016. "Moral Coherence and Political Conflict." In *Social Psychology of Political Polarization,* edited by Piercarlo Valdesolo and Jesse Graham, 102–22. New York: Routledge.

Ditto, Peter, Brittany S. Liu, Cory Clark, Sean Wojcik, Eric E. Chen, Rebecca Hofstein Grady, Jared Celniker, et al. 2019. "At Least Bias Is Bipartisan: A Meta-Analytic Comparison of Partisan Bias in Liberals and Conservatives." *Perspectives on Psychological Science* 14: 273–91.

Dodd, Michael, Amanda Friesen, Carly M. Jacobs, and John R. Hibbing.

2012. "The Political Left Rolls with the Good and the Political Right Confronts the Bad: Connecting Physiology and Cognition to Preferences." *Philosophical Transactions of the Royal Society B Biological Sciences* 367: 640–49.

Doleac, Jennifer. 2017. "Are Immigrants More Likely to Commit Crimes?" *Econofact,* February 14. https://econofact.org/are-immigrants-more-likely-to-commit-crimes.

Dovidio, John F., Samuel L. Gaertner, and Tamar Saguy. 2009. "Commonality and the Complexity of 'We': Social Attitudes and Social Change." *Personality and Social Psychology Review* 13: 3–20.

Drake, Bruce. 2013. "A Majority of Americans Have Received Benefits from Federal Entitlement Programs." Pew Research Center, May. https://www.pewresearch.org/fact-tank/2013/05/08/a-majority-of-americans-have-received-benefits-from-federal-entitlement-programs/.

Draper, Robert. 2012. *Do Not Ask What Good We Do.* New York: Free Press.

Drutman, Lee. 2019. "Political Divisions in 2016 and Beyond." Democracy Fund Voter Study Group, June. https://www.voterstudygroup.org/publication/political-divisions-in-2016-and-beyond.

Drutman, Lee, Vanessa Williamson, and Felicia Wong. 2019. "On the Money: How Americans' Economic Views Define—and Defy—Party Lines." Democracy Fund Voter Study Group. https://www.voterstudygroup.org/publication/on-the-money.

Duckitt, John. 2001. "A Dual-Process Cognitive-Motivational Theory of Ideology and Prejudice." In *Advances in Experimental Social Psychology,* edited by Mark P. Zanna, 41–113. New York: Academic Press.

Duflo, Esther, and Abhijit Banerjee. 2019. "Economic Incentives Don't Always Do What We Want Them To." *New York Times,* October 26. https://www.nytimes.com/2019/10/26/opinion/sunday/duflo-banerjee-economic-incentives.html.

Durkheim, Émile. 1964. *The Division of Labor in Society* [1893]. New York: Free Press.

Eagly, Alice H. 1987. *Sex Differences in Social Behavior: A Social-Role Interpretation.* Hillsdale, N.J.: Lawrence Erlbaum.

Economist/YouGov Poll. 2021. "Percent Who Say Joe Biden Legitimately Won the Election." April 17–20. https://docs.cdn.yougov.com/e89wuts0a9/econTabReport.pdf.

Edsall, Thomas B. 2019. "Liberals Do Not Want to Destroy the Family." *New York Times,* November 27. https://www.nytimes.com/2019/11/27/opinion/barr-liberals-family.html.

The Educational Opportunity Monitoring Project. 2018. "Racial and Ethnic Achievement Gaps." Center for Education Policy Analysis, Stanford University. https://cepa.stanford.edu/educational-opportunity-monitoring-project/achievement-gaps/race/.

Egan, Patrick J. 2013. *Partisan Priorities: How Issue Ownership Drives and Distorts American Politics.* New York: Cambridge University Press.

Eisenberg, Nancy, and Paul A. Miller. 1987. "The Relation of Empathy to Prosocial and Related Behaviors." *Psychological Bulletin* 101: 91–119.

Elliot, Andrew J., and Marcy A. Church. 1997. "A Hierarchical Model of Approach and Avoidance Achievement Motivation." *Journal of Personality and Social Psychology* 72: 218–32.

Ellis, Christoper, and James A. Stimson. 2012. *Ideology in America.* Cambridge: Cambridge University Press.

Elmendorf, Douglas W. 2011. "CBO's Analysis of the Major Health Care Legislation Enacted in March 2010." Congressional Budget Office, March 30. https://www.cbo.gov/sites/default/files/112th-congress-2011-2012/reports/03-30-healthcarelegislation.pdf.

Erikson, Robert S., and Kent L. Tedin. 2003. *American Public Opinion: Its Origins, Content, and Impact.* New York: Longman.

Etzioni, Amitai, 2003. "Communitarianism." In *Encyclopedia of Community: From the Village to the Virtual World,* edited by Karen Christensen and David Levinson, 224–28. Thousand Oaks, Calif.: Sage.

Factbase 2020. "Maria Bartiromo Interviews Donald Trump on Fox News." November 29, 2020." https://factba.se/transcript/donald-trump-interview-fox-news-sunday-morning-futures-maria-bartiromo-november-29-2020.

Fahmy, Dalia. 2018. "Americans Are Far More Religious Than Adults in Other Wealthy Nations." Pew Research Center Survey, July 31. https://

www.pewresearch.org/fact-tank/2018/07/31/americans-are-far-more
-religious-than-adults-in-other-wealthy-nations/.

———. 2020. "With Religion-Related Rulings on the Horizon, U.S. Christians See the Supreme Court Favorably." Pew Research Center, March 3.
https://www.pewresearch.org/fact-tank/2020/03/03/with-religion-related
-rulings-on-the-horizon-u-s-christians-see-supreme-court-favorably/.

Farmer, Adam, Blair Kidwell, and David M. Hardesty. 2020. "Helping a
Few a Lot or Many a Little: Political Ideology and Charitable Giving."
Journal of Consumer Psychology 30: 64–630.

Feather, Norman T. 2003. "Distinguishing Between Deservingness and Entitlement: Earned Outcomes Versus Lawful Outcomes." *European Journal of Social Psychology* 33: 367–85.

Federal Reserve Bank of St. Louis. 2018. "The Bigger They Are, the Harder
They Fall: The Decline of the White Working Class." *Demographics of
Wealth,* 2018 Series, Essay No. 3. https://www.stlouisfed.org/household
-financial-stability/the-demographics-of-wealth/decline-of-white
-working-class.

Fehr, Ernst, and Simon Gachter, S. 2002. "Altruistic Punishment in Humans." *Nature* 415: 137–40.

Feinberg, Matthew, Olga Antonenko, Robb Willer, E. J. Horberg, and Ol-
iver P. John. 2014. "Gut Check: Reappraisal of Disgust Helps Explain
Liberal-Conservative Differences on Issues of Purity." *Emotion* 14: 513–21.

Feinberg, Matthew, Elisabeth Wehling, Joanne M. Chung, Laura R. Saslow,
and Ingrid Melvaer Paulin. 2020. "Measuring Moral Politics: How
Strict and Nurturant Family Values Explain Conservatism, Liberalism,
and the Political Middle." *Journal of Personality and Social Psychology*
118: 777–804.

Feldman, Stanley. 2013. "Political Ideology." In *The Oxford Handbook of Political Psychology,* edited by Leonie Huddy, David O. Sears, and Jack S.
Levy, 591–626. Oxford: Oxford University Press.

Feldman, Stanley, and Karen Stenner. 1997. "Perceived Threat and Authoritarianism." *Political Psychology* 18: 741–70.

Festinger, Leon. 1957. *A Theory of Cognitive Dissonance.* Palo Alto, Calif.:
Stanford University Press.

Finkel, Eli. 2019. "Educated Americans Paved the Way for Divorce—Then Embraced Marriage." *Atlantic,* January 8. https://www.theatlantic.com /family/archive/2019/01/education-divide-marriage/579688/.

Finkel, Eli J., Christopher A. Bail, Mina Cikara, Peter H. Ditto, Shanto Iyengar, Samara Klar, Lilliana Mason, et al. 2020. "Political Sectarianism in America." *Science* 370: 533–36.

Finkel, Eli, Chin Ming Hui, Kathleen L. Carswell, and Grace M. Larso. 2014. "The Suffocation of Marriage: Climbing Mount Maslow Without Enough Oxygen." *Psychological Inquiry* 25: 1–41.

Fishkin, Joseph, and David Pozen. 2018. "Asymmetric Constitutional Hardball." *Columbia Law Review* 118: 915–82.

Fiske, Susan T. 1993. "Controlling Other People: The Impact of Power on Stereotyping." *American Psychologist* 48: 621–28.

Flavin, Patrick, and Benjamin Radcliff. 2009. "Public Policies and Suicide Rates in the American States." *Social Indicators Research* 90: 195–209.

Florida, Richard. 2013. "What Is It Exactly That Makes Big Cities Vote Democratic?" *Bloomberg CityLab,* February 19. https://www.bloomberg .com/news/articles/2013-02-19/what-is-it-exactly-that-makes-big-cities -vote-democratic.

Fraley, R. Chris, Brian N. Griffin, Jay Belsky, and Glenn I. Roisman. 2012. "Developmental Antecedents of Political Ideology: A Longitudinal Investigation from Birth to Age 18 Years." *Psychological Science* 23: 1425–31.

Frank, Peter I., Roseanne McNamee, Philip C. Hannaford, Clifford R. Kay, and Sybil Hirsch. 1993. "The Effect of Induced Abortion on Subsequent Fertility." *British Journal of Obstetrics and Gynaecology* 100: 575–80.

Frederico, Christopher M., Christopher R. Weber, Damla Ergun, and Corrie Hunt. 2013. "Mapping the Connections Between Politics and Morality: The Multiple Sociopolitical Orientations Involved in Moral Intuition." *Political Psychology* 34: 589–610.

Friedman, Milton. 1980. *Free to Choose.* San Diego, Calif.: Harcourt.

Fukuyama, Francis. 1995. *Trust: The Social Virtues and the Creation of Prosperity.* New York: Free Press.

Gable, Shelly L., Harry T. Reis, and Andrew J. Elliot. 2003. "Evidence for

Bivariate Systems: An Empirical Test of Appetition and Aversion Across Domains." *Journal of Research in Personality* 37: 349–72.

Gable, Shelly L., and Amy Strachman. 2008. "Approaching Social Rewards and Avoiding Social Punishments: Appetitive and Aversive Social Motivation." In *Handbook of Motivation Science,* edited by James Y. Shah and Wendi L. Gardner, 561–75. New York: Guilford.

Gaertner, Samuel L., and John F. Dovidio. 2000. *Reducing Intergroup Bias: The Common Ingroup Identity Model.* Washington, D.C.: Psychology Press.

Gaertner, Samuel L., John F. Dovidio, Jason A. Nier, Christine M. Ward, and Brenda S. Banker. 1999. "Across Cultural Divides: The Value of a Superordinate Identity." In *Cultural Divides: Understanding and Overcoming Group Conflict,* edited by Deborah A. Prentice and Dale T. Miller, 173–212. New York: Russell Sage Foundation.

Galen, Luke W. 2012. "Does Religious Belief Promote Prosociality? A Critical Examination." *Psychological Bulletin* 138: 876–906.

Galinsky, Adam D., Joe C. Magee, M. Ena Inesi, and Deborah H. Gruenfeld. 2006. "Power and Perspectives Not Taken." *Psychological Science* 17: 1068–74.

Gawronski, Bertram. 2019. "Six Lessons for a Cogent Science of Implicit Bias and Its Criticism." *Perspectives on Psychological Science* 14: 574–95.

Gelfand, Michele J. 2018. *Rule Makers, Rule Breakers: How Tight and Loose Cultures Wire Our World.* New York: Scribner.

Gelfand, Michele J., Jana L. Raver, Lisa Nishii, Lisa M. Leslie, Janetta Lun, Beng Chong Lim, Lili Duan, et al. 2011. "Differences Between Tight and Loose Cultures: A 33-Nation Study." *Science* 332: 1100–1104.

Gerber, Alan S., Gregory A. Huber, David Doherty, Conor M. Dowling, and Shang E. Ha. 2010. "Personality and Political Attitudes: Relationships Across Issue Domains and Political Contexts." *American Political Science Review* 104: 111–33.

Ghilardu, Teresa. 2018. "Republicans' Public Opposition to Social Security and Medicare." *Forbes,* November 2. https://www.forbes.com/sites/teresaghilarducci/2018/11/02/republican-public-opposition-to-social-security-and-medicare/.

Gilens, Martin. 1999. "The News Media and the Racialization of Poverty." In *Why Americans Hate Welfare: Race, Media, and the Politics of Antipoverty Policy,* 102–32. Chicago: University of Chicago Press.

Ginsburg, Ruth Bader. 1992. "Speaking in a Judicial Voice." *NYU Law Review* 67: 1185–209.

Glick, Peter, and Susan T. Fiske. 2001. "An Ambivalent Alliance: Hostile and Benevolent Sexism as Complementary Justifications for Gender Inequality." *American Psychologist* 56: 109–18.

Goodall, Jane. 1990. *Through a Window: My Thirty Years with the Chimpanzees of Gombe.* Boston: Houghton Mifflin.

Goodwin, Geoffrey P., Jared Piazza, and Paul Rozin. 2014. "Moral Character Predominates in Person Perception and Evaluation." *Journal of Personality and Social Psychology* 106: 148–68.

Graham, David A. 2017. "Red State, Blue City." *Atlantic,* March. https://www.theatlantic.com/magazine/archive/2017/03/red-state-blue-city/513857/.

Graham, Jesse. 2013. "Mapping the Moral Maps from Alternate Taxonomies to Competing Predictions." *Personality and Social Psychology Review* 17: 237–41.

Graham, Jesse, Jonathan Haidt, and Brian A. Nosek. 2009. "Liberals and Conservatives Use Different Sets of Moral Foundations." *Journal of Personality and Social Psychology* 96: 1029–46.

Graham, Jesse, Brian A. Nosek, Jonathan Haidt, Ravi Iyer, Spassena Koleva, and Peter H. Ditto. 2011. "Mapping the Moral Domain." *Journal of Personality and Social Psychology* 101: 366–85.

Graham, Jesse, Adam Waytz, Peter Meindl, Ravi Iyer, and Liane Young. 2017. "Centripetal and Centrifugal Forces in the Moral Circle: Competing Constraints on Moral Learning." *Cognition* 167: 58–65.

Gray, Jeffrey A. 1990. "Brain Systems That Mediate Both Emotion and Cognition." *Cognition and Emotion* 4: 269–88.

Gray, Kurt, and Daniel M. Wegner. 2009. "Moral Typecasting: Divergent Perceptions of Moral Agents and Moral Patients." *Journal of Personality and Social Psychology* 96: 505–20.

Green, Emma. 2017. "It Was Cultural Anxiety That Drove White, Working-Class Voters to Trump." *Atlantic,* May 9. https://www.theatlantic.com

/politics/archive/2017/05/white-working-class-trump-cultural-anxiety
/525771/.

Green, Michael, Jaromir Harmacek, and Petra Krylova. 2020. "2020 Social Progress Index Executive Summary." https://www.socialprogress.org/static /37348b3ecb088518a945fa4c83d9b9f4/2020-social-progress-index-executive -summary.pdf.

Greene, Joshua. 2013. *Moral Tribes: Emotion, Reason, and the Gap Between Us and Them.* New York: Penguin Press.

Grier, Peter. 2018. "The Deep Roots of America's Rural-Urban Political Divide." *Christian Science Monitor,* December 26. https://www.csmonitor .com/USA/Politics/2018/1226/The-deep-roots-of-America-s-rural -urban-political-divide.

Grinshteyn, Erin, and David Hemenway. 2016. "Violent Death Compared with Other High-Income OECD Countries, 2010." *American Journal of Medicine* 129: 266–73.

Grossman, Matt, and David A. Hopkins. 2016. *Asymmetric Politics: Ideological Republicans and Group Interest Democrats.* New York: Oxford University Press.

Guttmacher Institute. 2019. "Induced Abortion in the United States, September 2019 Fact Sheet." https://www.guttmacher.org/fact-sheet/induced -abortion-united-states.

Hacker, Jacob S., and Paul Pierson. 2011. *Winner-Take-All Politics: How Washington Made the Rich Richer—and Turned Its Back on the Middle Class.* New York: Simon and Schuster.

Haider-Markel, Donald, and Mark Joslyn. 2009. "Beliefs About the Origins of Homosexuality and Support for Gay Rights: An Empirical Test of Attribution Theory." *Public Opinion Quarterly* 72: 291–310.

Haidt, Jonathan. 2007. "The New Synthesis in Moral Psychology." *Science* 316: 998–1002.

———. 2008. "Morality." *Perspectives on Psychological Science* 3: 5–72.

———. 2012. *The Righteous Mind: Why Good People Are Divided by Politics and Religion.* New York: Pantheon.

———. 2022. "After Babel: How Social Media Dissolved the Mortar of Society and Made America Stupid." *Atlantic,* May, 54–66.

Haidt, Jonathan, and Jesse Graham. 2007. "When Morality Opposes Justice: Conservatives Have Moral Intuitions That Liberals May Not Recognize." *Social Justice Research* 20: 98–116.

Haidt, Jonathan, and Craig Joseph. 2004. "Intuitive Ethics: How Innately Prepared Intuitions Generate Culturally Variable Virtues." *Daedalus* 133: 55–66.

Haidt, Jonathan, and Selin Kesebir. 2010. "Morality." In *The Handbook of Social Psychology,* edited by Daniel T. Gilbert, Susan T. Fiske, and Gardner Lindzey, 797–832. Hoboken, N.J.: John Wiley.

Hainmueller, Jens, and Daniel J. Hopkins. 2014. "Public Attitudes Toward Immigration." *Annual Review of Political Science* 17: 225–49.

———. 2015. "The Hidden American Immigration Consensus: A Conjoint Analysis of Attitudes Toward Immigrants." *American Journal of Political Science* 59: 529–48.

Hall, William J., Mimi V. Chapman, Kent M. Lee, Yesenia M. Merino, Tainayah W. Thomas, B. Keith Payne, Eugenia Eng, et al. 2015. "Implicit Racial/Ethnic Bias Among Health Care Professionals and Its Influence on Health Care Outcomes: A Systematic Review." *American Journal of Public Health* 105: e60–e76.

Hamilton, William Donald. 1964. "The Genetical Evolution of Social Behavior I and II." *Journal of Theoretical Biology* 7: 1–52.

Hamlin, J. Kiley. 2013. "Moral Judgment and Action in Preverbal Infants and Toddlers: Evidence for an Innate Moral Core." *Current Directions in Psychological Science* 22: 186–193.

Hamlin, J. Kiley, Neha Mahajan, Zoe Liberman, and Karen Wynn. 2013. "Not Like Me = Bad: Infants Prefer Those Who Harm Dissimilar Others." *Psychological Science* 24: 589–94.

Hamlin, J. Kiley, and Karen Wynn. 2011. "Young Infants Prefer Prosocial to Antisocial Others." *Cognitive Development* 26: 30–39.

Hamlin, J. Kiley, Karen Wynn, and Paul Bloom. 2007. "Social Evaluation by Preverbal Infants." *Nature* 450: 557–59.

———. 2010. "3-Month-Olds Show a Negativity Bias in Social Evaluation." *Developmental Science* 13: 923–39.

Hannah-Jones, Nikole. 2020. "What Is Owed." *New York Times,* June 30.

https://www.nytimes.com/interactive/2020/06/24/magazine/reparations
-slavery.html.

Harbaugh, William T., Ulrich Mayr, and Daniel Burghart. 2007. "Neural
Responses to Taxation and Voluntary Giving Reveal Motives for Charitable Donations." *Science* 316: 1622–25.

Harrington, Jesse R., Pawel Boski, and Michele J. Gelfand. 2015. "Culture
and National Well-Being: Should Societies Emphasize Freedom or Constraint?" *PLoS ONE* 10: e0127173.

Haslam, Nick, Louis Rothschild, and Donald Ernst. 2000. "Essentialist
Beliefs About Social Categories." *British Journal of Social Psychology* 39:
113–27.

Hasson, Yossi, Maya Tamir, Kea S. Brahms, J. Christopher Cohrs, and Eran
Halperin. 2018. "Are Liberals and Conservatives Equally Motivated to
Feel Empathy Toward Others?" *Personality and Social Psychology Bulle-
tin* 44: 1449–59.

Hastorf, Albert H., and Hadley Cantril. 1954. "They Saw a Game; a Case
Study." *Journal of Abnormal and Social Psychology* 49: 129–34.

Hatemi, Peter K., Sarah E. Medland, Robert Klemmensen, Sven Oskarrson,
Levente Littvay, Chris Dawes, Brad Verhulst, et al. 2014. "Genetic In-
fluences on Political Ideologies: Twin Analyses of 19 Measures of Political Ideologies from Five Democracies and Genome-Wide Findings from
Three Populations." *Behavioral Genetics* 44: 282–94.

Hemenway, David, and Sara J. Solnick. 2015. "The Epidemiology of Self-
Defense Gun Use: Evidence from the National Crime Victimization
Surveys, 2007–2011." *Preventive Medicine* 29: 22–27.

Herbert, Bob. 2005. "Impossible, Ridiculous, Repugnant." *New York Times,*
October 6. https://www.nytimes.com/2005/10/06/opinion/impossible
-ridiculous-repugnant.html.

Hetherington, Marc J., and Jonathan D. Weiler. 2009. *Authoritarianism
and Polarization in American Politics.* New York: Cambridge University
Press.

Hibbing, John, Kevin B. Smith, and John R. Alford. 2013. *Predisposed: Liberals, Conservatives, and the Biology of Political Differences.* New York:
Routledge.

————. 2014. "Differences in Negativity Bias Underlie Variations in Political Ideology." *Behavioral and Brain Sciences* 37: 297–307.

Higgins, E. Tory. 1997. "Beyond Pleasure and Pain." *American Psychologist* 52: 1280–300.

————. 1998. "Promotion and Prevention: Regulatory Focus as a Motivational Principle." In *Advances in Experimental Social Psychology,* edited by Mark Zanna, 1–46. New York: Academic Press.

Hiltzik, Michael. 2014. "Who's More Charitable—Conservatives or Liberals?" *Los Angeles Times,* March 31. https://www.latimes.com/business /hiltzik/la-fi-mh-conservatives-or-liberals-20140331-story.html.

Hochschild, Arlie R. 2017. *Strangers in Their Own Land: Anger and Mourning on the American Right.* New York: New Press.

Hsieh, Ching-Chi, and M. D. Pugh. 1993. "Poverty, Income Inequality, and Violent Crime: A Meta-Analysis of Recent Aggregate Data Studies." *Criminal Justice Review* 18: 182–202.

Iati, Marisa, and Deanna Paul. 2019. "Everything You Need to Know About the Abortion Ban News." *Washington Post,* May 17. https://www.washing tonpost.com/health/2019/05/17/havent-been-following-abortion-ban -news-heres-everything-you-need-know/.

Inbar, Yoel, David A. Pizarro, and Paul Bloom. 2009. "Conservatives Are More Easily Disgusted Than Liberals." *Cognition and Emotion* 23: 714–25.

Inbar, Yoel, David A. Pizarro, Ravi Iyer, and Jonathan Haidt. 2012. "Disgust Sensitivity, Political Conservatism, and Voting." *Social Psychological and Personality Science* 3: 537–44.

James, William. 1890. *The Principles of Psychology.* New York: Henry Holt.

Jamieson, Christine. 2013. "Gun Violence Research: History of the Federal Funding Freeze." *Psychological Science Agenda.* American Psychological Association. https://www.apa.org/science/about/psa/2013/02/gun-violence.

Janoff-Bulman, Ronnie. 1979. "Characterological Versus Behavioral Self-Blame: Inquiries into Depression and Rape." *Journal of Personality and Social Psychology* 37: 1798–1809.

————. 1992. *Shattered Assumptions: Towards a New Psychology of Trauma.* New York: Free Press.

———. 2009. "To Provide or Protect: Motivational Bases of Political Liberalism and Conservatism." *Psychological Inquiry* 20: 120–28.

Janoff-Bulman, Ronnie, and Nate C. Carnes. 2013a. "Surveying the Moral Landscape: Moral Motives and Group-Based Moralities." *Personality and Social Psychology Review* 17: 219–36.

———. 2013b. "Moral Context Matters: A Reply to Graham." *Personality and Social Psychology Review* 17: 242–47.

———. 2016. "Social Justice and Social Order: Binding Moralities Across the Political Spectrum." *PLoS ONE* 11: e015249.

———. 2018. "Model of Moral Motives: A Map of the Moral Domain." In *The Atlas of Moral Psychology,* edited by Jesse Graham and Kurt Gray, 223–30. New York: Guilford.

Janoff-Bulman, Ronnie, Nate C. Carnes, and Sana Sheikh. 2014. "Parenting and Politics: Exploring Early Moral Bases of Political Orientation." *Journal of Social and Political Psychology* 2: 43–60.

Janoff-Bulman, Ronnie, Sana Sheikh, and Sebastian Hepp, S. 2009. "Proscriptive Versus Prescriptive Morality: Two Faces of Moral Regulation." *Journal of Personality and Social Psychology* 96: 521–37.

Janoff-Bulman, Ronnie, and Amelie Werther. 2008. "The Social Psychology of Respect: Implications for Delegitimization and Reconciliation." In *The Social Psychology of Intergroup Reconciliation,* edited by Arie Nadler, Thomas E. Malloy, and Jeffrey Fisher, 145–70. New York: Oxford University Press.

Jensen, Jeffrey T., and Mitchell D. Creinin. 2019. *Speroff and Darney's Clinical Guide to Contraception.* Philadelphia: Wolters Kluwer.

Jones, Rachel K., and Jenna Jerman. 2017. "Population Group Abortion Rates and Lifetime Incidence of Abortion: United States, 2008–2014." *American Journal of Public Health* 107: 1904–9.

Jones, Rachel K., Elizabeth Nash, Lauren Cross, Jesse Philbin, and Marielle Kirstein. 2022. "Medication Abortion Now Accounts for More Than Half of All US Abortions." Guttmacher Institute, Policy Analysis, February. https://www.guttmacher.org/article/2022/02/medication-abortion-now-accounts-more-half-all-us-abortions.

Jost, John T. 2006. "The End of the End of Ideology." *American Psychologist* 61: 651–70.

Jost, John T., and David M. Amodio. 2012. "Political Ideology as Motivated Social Cognition: Behavioral and Neuroscientific Evidence." *Motivation and Emotion* 36: 55–64.

Jost, John T., Mahzarin R. Banaji, and Brian A. Nosek. 2004. "A Decade of System Justification Theory: Accumulated Evidence of Conscious and Unconscious Bolstering of the Status Quo." *Political Psychology* 25: 881–919.

Jost, John T., Christopher Frederico, and Jaime Napier. 2009. "Political Ideology: Its Structure, Functions, and Elective Affinities." *Annual Review of Psychology* 60: 307–37.

Jost, John T., Jack Glaser, Arie W. Kruglanski, and Frank J. Sulloway. 2003. "Political Conservatism as Motivated Social Cognition." *Psychological Bulletin* 129: 339–75.

Jost, John T., Jaime Napier, Hulda Thorisdottir, Samuel T. Gosling, Tibor P. Palfai, and Brian Ostafin. 2007. "Are Needs to Manage Uncertainty and Threat Associated with Political Conservatism or Ideological Extremity?" *Personality and Social Psychology Bulletin* 33: 989–1007.

Jost, John T., Brian A. Nosek, and Samuel Gosling. 2008. "Ideology: Its Resurgence in Social, Personality, and Political Psychology." *Perspectives on Psychological Science* 3: 126–36.

Kahan, Dan M., David A. Hoffman, Donald Braman, Danieli Evans, and Jeffrey J. Rachlinski. 2012. "They Saw a Protest: Cognitive Illiberalism and the Speech-Conduct Distinction." *Stanford Law Review* 64: 851–906.

Kahan, Dan M., Ellen Peters, Maggie Wittlin, Paul Slovic, Lisa Larrimore Ouellette, Donal Braman, and Gregory N. Mandel. 2012. "The Polarizing Impact of Science Literacy and Numeracy on Perceived Climate Change." *Nature Climate Change* 2: 732–35.

Kahneman, Daniel, and Amos Tversky. 1979. "Prospect Theory: An Analysis of Decision Under Risk." *Econometrica* 47: 263–91.

Kakkar, Hemant, and Niro Sivanathan. 2017. "When the Appeal of a Dominant Leader Is Greater Than a Prestige Leader." *PNAS* 114: 6734–39.

Kant, Immanuel. 2002. *Groundwork of the Metaphysics of Morals* [1785]. Translated by Alan Wood. New Haven: Yale University Press.

Kawachi, Ichiro, Bruce P. Kennedy, Kimberly Lochner, and Deborah Prothrow-Stith. 1997. "Social Capital, Income Inequality and Morality." *American Journal of Public Health* 87: 1491–98.

Keltner, Dacher. 2009. *Born to Be Good: The Science of a Meaningful Life.* New York: W. W. Norton.

———. 2012. "The Compassionate Species." *Greater Good Magazine,* July 31. https://greatergood.berkeley.edu/article/item/the_compassionate_species.

Keltner, Dacher, Deborah H. Gruenfeld, and Cameron Anderson. 2003. "Power, Approach, and Inhibition." *Psychological Review* 110: 265–84.

Kennedy, Duncan. 1976. "Form and Substance in Private Law Adjudication." *Harvard Law Review* 89: 1685–1778.

Kenney, Brian, and Meg Hefferon. 2019. "U.S. Concern About Climate Change Is Rising, but Mainly Among Democrats." Pew Research Center, *Facttank,* August 28. https://www.pewresearch.org/fact-tank/2019/08/28/u-s-concern-about-climate-change-is-rising-but-mainly-among-democrats/.

Kerlinger, Fred N. 1984. *Liberalism and Conservatism: The Nature and Structure of Social Attitudes.* Hillsdale, N.J.: Erlbaum.

Kesebir, Selin. 2012. "The Superorganism Account of Human Sociality: How and When Human Groups Are Like Beehives." *Personality and Social Psychology Review* 16: 233–61.

Kessler, Glen, Salvador Rizzo, and Meg Kelly. 2021. "Trump's False or Misleading Claims Total 30,573 over 4 Years." *Washington Post,* January 24. https://www.washingtonpost.com/politics/2021/01/24/trumps-false-or-misleading-claims-total-30573-over-four-years/.

Kim, Daniel. 2016. "The Associations Between U.S. State and Local Social Spending, Income Inequality, and Individual All-Cause and Cause-Specific Mortality: The National Longitudinal Mortality Study." *Preventive Medicine* 84: 62–68.

Kinzler, Katherine, Emmanuel Dupoux, and Elizabeth S. Spelke. 2007. "The Native Language of Social Cognition." *PNAS* 104: 12577–80.

Klein, Ezra. 2020. *Why We're Polarized.* New York: Avid Reader Press.

Knobe, Joshua. 2003. "Intentional Action and Side Effects in Ordinary Language." *Analysis* 63: 190–93.

Knowles, Eric D., Brian S. Lowery, and Rebecca L. Schaumberg. 2010. "Racial Prejudice Predicts Opposition to Obama and His Health Care Reform Plan." *Journal of Experimental Social Psychology* 46: 420–23.

Kochanska, Grazyna. 2002. "Committed Compliance, Moral Self, and Internalization: A Mediational Model." *Developmental Psychology* 38: 339–51.

Kochanska, Grazyna, Katherine C. Coy, and Kathleen T. Murray. 2001. "The Development of Self-Regulation in the First Four Years of Life." *Child Development* 72: 1091–111.

Kramer, Roderick M. 1999. "Paranoid Cognition in Social Systems: Thinking and Acting in the Shadow of Doubt." *Personality and Social Psychology Review* 2: 251–75.

———. 2010. "Trust." In *Encyclopedia of Group Processes and Intergroup Relations,* edited by John M. Levine and Michael A. Hogg, 931–39. Thousand Oaks, Calif.: Sage.

Kraus, Michael W., Ivuoma N. Onyeador, Natalie M. Daumeyer, Julian M. Rucker, and Jennifer A. Richeson. 2019. "The Misperception of Racial Economic Inequality." *Perspectives on Psychological Science* 14: 899–921.

Kraus, Michael W., and Jacinth J. X. Tan. 2015. "Americans Overestimate Social Class Mobility." *Journal of Experimental Social Psychology* 58: 101–11.

Krebs, Dennis L. 2008. "Morality: An Evolutionary Account." *Perspectives on Psychological Science* 3: 149–72.

Krider, Stephanie Ranade. 2020. "I'm a Pro-Life Evangelical; In Supporting Trump, My Movement Sold Its Soul." *Washington Post,* October 8. https://www.washingtonpost.com/outlook/im-a-pro-life-evangelical-in-supporting-trump-my-movement-sold-its-soul/2020/10/07/04d90712-0733-11eb-859b-f9c27abe638d_story.html.

Kristof, Nicholas. 2020. "She Is Evangelical, 'Pro-Life' and Voting for Biden." *New York Times,* October 22.

Kristof, Nicholas, and Sheryl WuDunn. 2020a. *Tightrope: Americans Reaching for Hope.* New York: Alfred A. Knopf.

———. 2020b. "Who Killed the Knapp Family?" *New York Times,* January 9.

https://www.nytimes.com/2020/01/09/opinion/sunday/deaths-despair
-poverty.html.

Kron, Josh. 2012. "Red State, Blue City: How the Rural-Urban Divide Is Splitting America." *Atlantic,* November 30. https://www.theatlantic.com /politics/archive/2012/11/red-state-blue-city-how-the-urban-rural -divide-is-splitting-america/265686/.

Kunda, Ziva. 1990. "The Case for Motivated Reasoning." *Psychological Bulletin* 108: 480–98.

Kuwabara, Ko, Robb Willer, Michael W. Macy, Rie Mashima, Shigeru Terai, and Toshio Yamagishi. 2007. "Culture, Identity, and Structure in Social Exchange: A Web-Based Trust Experiment in the United States and Japan." *Social Psychology Quarterly* 70: 461–79.

Lakoff, George. 2002. *Moral Politics: How Liberals and Conservatives Think.* Chicago: University of Chicago Press.

Landau, Mark L., Sheldon Solomon, Jeff Greenberg, Florette Cohen, Tom Pyszczynski, Jamie Arndt, Claude Miller, et al. 2004. "Deliver Us from Evil: The Effects of Mortality Salience and Reminders of 9/11 on Support for President George W. Bush." *Personality and Social Psychology Bulletin* 30: 1136–50.

Larzelere, Robert E., Amanda Sheffield Morris, and Amanda W. Harrist, editors. 2013. *Authoritative Parenting: Synthesizing Nurturance and Discipline for Optimal Child Development.* Washington, D.C.: American Psychological Association.

Lavine, Howard, Diana Burgess, Mark Snyder, John Transue, John L. Sullivan, Beth Haney, and Stephen Wagner. 1999. "Threat, Authoritarianism, and Voting: An Investigation of Personality and Persuasion." *Personality and Social Psychology Bulletin* 25: 337–47.

Lazzarini, Zita. 2008. "South Dakota's Abortion Script—Threatening the Physician-Patient Relationship." *New England Journal of Medicine* 359: 2189–91.

Leach, Colin Wayne, Naomi Ellemers, and Manuela Barreto. 2007. "Group Virtue: The Importance of Morality (vs. Competence and Sociability) in the Positive Evaluation of In-Groups." *Journal of Personality and Social Psychology* 93: 234–49.

Leatherby, Lauren. 2016. "US Social Mobility Gap Continues to Widen." *Financial Times,* December 16. https://www.ft.com/content/7de9165e-c3d2-11e6-9bca-2b93a6856354.

Lemon, Jason. 2020. "Nancy Pelosi Says America 'Needs a Strong Republican Party,' Not a Hijacked 'Cult.'" *Newsweek,* September 30. https://www.newsweek.com/nancy-pelosi-says-america-needs-strong-republican-party-not-hijacked-cult-1535343.

Levin, Josh. 2019. *The Queen: The Forgotten Life Behind an American Myth.* New York: Little, Brown.

Light, John. 2013. "Déjà Vu: A Look Back at Some of the Tirades Against Social Security and Medicare." *Moyers,* October 1. https://billmoyers.com/content/deja-vu-all-over-a-look-back-at-some-of-the-tirades-against-social-security-and-medicare/5/.

Litz, Brett T., Nathan Stein, Eileen Delaney, Leslie Lebowitz, William P. Nash, Caroline Silva, C., and Shira Maguen. 2009. "Moral Injury and Moral Repair in War Veterans: A Preliminary Model and Intervention Strategy." *Clinical Psychology Review* 29: 695–706.

Long, Heather, and Andrew Van Dam. 2020. "Why Aren't More Americans Working? Fed Chair Powell Says Blame Education and Drugs, Not Welfare." *Washington Post,* February 15. https://www.washingtonpost.com/business/2020/02/15/powell-labor-force/.

Lopez, Gustavo, Kristen Bialik, and Jynnah Radford. 2018. "Key Findings About U.S. Immigrants." *Pew Research Center Report,* November 30. http://www.pewresearch.org/fact-tank/2017/05/03/key-findings-about-u-s-immigrants/.

Lord, Charles G., Lee Ross, and Mark R. Lepper. 1979. "Biased Assimilation and Attitude Polarization: The Effects of Prior Theories on Subsequently Considered Evidence." *Journal of Personality and Social Psychology* 37: 2098–2109.

Lowery, Rick. 2012. "Abortion: What the Bible Says (and Doesn't Say)." *Huffington Post,* September 14. https://www.huffpost.com/entry/abortion-what-the-bible-says-and-doesnt-say_b_1856049.

Lowrey, Annie. "Conservatives Are Wrong About What's Driving Immigra-

tion." *Atlantic*, August 1. https://www.theatlantic.com/ideas/archive/2019
/08/immigrants-arent-coming-for-our-health-care/595240/.

Luban, David. 2021. "Hannah Arendt Meets QAnon: Conspiracy, Ideology,
and the Collapse of Common Sense." Available at SSRN: https://ssrn
.com/abstract=3852241.

Luke, Dillon, and Bertram Gawronski. 2021. "Political Ideology and Moral
Dilemma Judgments: An Analysis Using the CNI Model." *Personality
and Social Psychology Bulletin* 47: 1520–31.

Maccoby, Eleanor E., and John A. Martin. 1983. "Socialization in the Context of the Family: Parent-Child Interaction." In *Handbook of Child Psychology*, edited by Paul H. Mussen and E. Mavis Hetherington, 1–101.
New York: Wiley.

MacGillis, Alec. 2015. "Who Turned My Blue State Red?" *New York Times*,
November 20. https://www.nytimes.com/2015/11/22/opinion/sunday
/who-turned-my-blue-state-red.html.

MacWilliams, Matthew. 2016. "The One Weird Trait That Predicts Whether
You're a Trump Supporter." *Politico Magazine*, January 17. https://www
.politico.com/magazine/story/2016/01/donald-trump-2016-authoritarian
-213533/.

Madison, Lucy. 2011a. "On Bus Tour Obama Embraces 'Obamacare,' Says
'I Do Care.'" *CBS News*, August 15. https://www.cbsnews.com/news/on
-bus-tour-obama-embraces-obamacare-says-i-do-care/.

———. 2011b. "There Is Nobody in This Country Who Got Rich on
His Own." *CBS News*, September 22. https://www.cbsnews.com/news
/elizabeth-warren-there-is-nobody-in-this-country-who-got-rich-on-his
-own/.

Magee, Joe C., and Adam D. Galinsky. 2008. "Social Hierarchy: The Self-
Reinforcing Nature of Power and Status." *Academy of Management Annals* 2: 351–98.

Major, Brenda, Alison Blodorn, and Gregory Major-Blascovich. 2018. "The
Threat of Increasing Diversity: Why Many White Americans Support
Trump in the 2016 Presidential Election." *Group Processes and Intergroup
Relations* 21: 931–40.

Maloney, Thomas N. 1994. "Wage Compression and Wage Inequality Between Black and White Males in the United States, 1940–1960." *Journal of Economic History* 54: 358–81.

Manzi, Jim, and Peter Wehner. 2015. "Conservatives and Climate Change." *National Affairs,* Summer. https://www.nationalaffairs.com/ublications /detail/conservatives-and-climate-change.

Margo, Robert A. 1995. "Explaining Black-White Wage Convergence, 1940– 1950." *Industrial and Labor Relations Review* 48: 470–81.

Margolis, Michele, and Michael Sances. 2013. "Who Really Gives? Partisanship and Charitable Giving in the United States." August 9. Available at SSRN: http://dx.doi.org/10.2139/ssrn.2148033.

Margulies, Joseph. 2021. *Thanks for Everything (Now Get Out): Can We Restore Neighborhoods Without Destroying Them?* New Haven: Yale University Press.

Markel, Howard, and Alexandra Minna Stern. 2002. "The Foreignness of Germs: The Persistent Association of Immigrants and Disease in American Society." *Milbank Quarterly* 80: 757–88.

Markovits, Daniel. 2019. *The Meritocracy Trap.* New York: Penguin.

McAdams, Dan P., Michelle Albaugh, Emily Farber, Jennifer Daniels, Regina Logan, and Brad Olson. 2008. "Family Metaphors and Moral Intuitions: How Conservatives and Liberals Narrate Their Lives." *Journal of Personality and Social Psychology* 95: 978–90.

McCrae, Robert R. 1996. "Social Consequences of Experiential Openness." *Psychological Bulletin* 120: 323–37.

McIntosh, Kriston, Emily Moss, Ryan Nunn, and Jay Shambaugh. 2020. "Examining the Black-White Wealth Gap." Brookings, February 27. https://www.brookings.edu/blog/up-front/2020/02/27/examining-the -black-white-wealth-gap/.

McLean, Scott P., John P. Garza, Sandra A. Wiebe, Michael D. Dodd, Kevin B. Smith, John R. Hibbing, and Kimberly Andrews Espy. 2014. "Applying the Flanker Task to Political Psychology: A Research Note." *Political Psychology* 35: 831–40.

McMahon, Kevin J. 2005. "A 'Moral Values' Election?" In *Winning the White House, 2004: Region by Region, Vote by Vote,* by Kevin J. McMahon,

David Rankin, Donald W. Beachler, and John Kenneth White, 23–46. New York: Palgrave Macmillan.

McVeigh, Rory, and Maria-Elena D. Diaz. 2009. "Voting to Ban Same-Sex Marriage: Interests, Values, and Communities." *American Sociological Review* 74: 891–915.

McWhorter, John. 2011. "Frances Fox Piven, Jim Sleeper, and Me." *New Republic,* January 25. https://newrepublic.com/article/82122/frances-fox -piven-jim-sleeper-and-me.

———. 2021. "The Neoracists." *Persuasion,* February 8. https://www.persua sion.community/p/john-mcwhorter-the-neoracists.

Mendez, Mario F., Eric Anderson, and Jill S. Shapira. 2006. "An Investigation of Moral Judgment in Frontotemporal Dementia." *Cognitive and Behavioral Neurology* 18: 193–97.

Miller, Gregory A., Laura D. Crocker, Jeffrey M. Spielberg, Zachary P. Infantolino, and Wendy Heller. 2013. "Issues in Localization of Brain Function: The Case of Lateralized Frontal Cortex in Cognition, Emotion, and Psychopathology." *Frontiers in Integrative Neuroscience.* https:// doi.org/10.3389/fnint.2013.00002.

Mishel, Lawrence, and Julia Wolfe. 2019. "CEO Compensation Has Grown 940% Since 1978." Economic Policy Institute, August 14. https://www .epi.org/publication/ceo-compensation-2018/.

Moll, Jorge, Frank Krueger, Roland Zahn, Matteo Pardini, Ricardo de Oliveira-Souza, and Jordan Grafman. 2006. "Human Fronto-Mesolimbic Networks Guide Decisions About Charitable Donation." *PNAS* 103: 15623–28.

Morin, Rich. 2015. "Exploring Racial Bias Among Biracial and Single-Race Adults: The IAT." Pew Research Center, August 19. https://www.pew research.org/social-trends/2015/08/19/exploring-racial-bias-among -biracial-and-single-race-adults-the-iat/.

Motyl, Matt, Ravi Iyer, Shigehiro Oishi, Sophie Trawalter, and Brian A. Nosek. 2014. "How Ideological Migration Geographically Segregates Groups." *Journal of Experimental Social Psychology* 51: 1–14.

Muller, Jan-Werner. 2021. *Democracy Rules.* New York: Farrar, Straus and Giroux.

Mutz, Diana C. 2018. "Status Threat, Not Economic Hardship, Explains the 2016 Presidential Vote." *PNAS* 115: E4330–E4339.

Napier, Jaime L., Julie Huang, Andrew J. Vonasch, and John A. Bargh. 2018. "Superheroes for Change: Physical Safety Promotes Socially (But Not Economically) Progressive Attitudes Among Conservatives." *European Journal of Social Psychology* 48: 187–95.

Nash, Elizabeth. 2019. "A Surge in Bans on Abortion as Early as Six Weeks, Before Most People Know They Are Pregnant." Guttmacher Institute, May 30. https://www.guttmacher.org/article/2019/03/surge-bans-abortion -early-six-weeks-most-people-know-they-are-pregnant.

Nash, Elizabeth, and Lauren Cross. 2021a. "2021 Is on Track to Become the Most Devastating Anti-Abortion State Legislative Session in Decades." Guttmacher Institute, Policy Analysis, April. https://www.guttmacher .org/article/2021/04/2021-track-become-most-devastating-antiabortion -state-legislative-session-decades.

———. 2021b. "26 States Are Certain or Likely to Ban Abortion Without Roe: Here's Which Ones and Why." Guttmacher Institute, Policy Analysis, October. https://www.guttmacher.org/article/2021/10/26-states-are -certain-or-likely-ban-abortion-without-roe-heres-which-ones-and -why.

Nash, George H. 1996. *The Conservative Intellectual Movement in America Since 1945.* Rev. ed. Wilmington, Del.: Intercollegiate Studies Institute.

National Academies of Sciences, Engineering, and Medicine. 2015. *The Integration of Immigrants into American Society.* Washington, D.C.: National Academies Press. http://doi.org/10.17226/21746.

———. 2017. *The Economic and Fiscal Consequences of Immigration.* Washington, D.C.: National Academies Press. https://www.nationalacademies .org/our-work/economic-and-fiscal-impact-of-immigration.

National Cancer Institute. 2003. "Abortion, Miscarriage, and Breast Cancer Risk." https://www.cancer.gov/types/breast/abortion-miscarriage-risk.

Nelson, A. L., and Carrie Cwiak. 2011. "Combined Oral Contraceptives (COCs)." In *Contraceptive Technology,* edited by Robert A. Hatcher, James Trussell, Anita L. Nelson, Willard Cates, Deborah Kowal, and Michael S. Policar, 249–341. New York: Ardent Media.

New York Times. 1997. "Protecting Children from Guns." September 7. https://www.nytimes.com/1997/09/07/opinion/protecting-children -from-guns.html.

Nisbett, Richard E., and Lee D. Ross. 1980. *Human Inference: Strategies and Shortcomings of Social Judgment.* New York: Prentice-Hall.

Noel, Hans. 2013. *Political Ideologies and Political Parties in America.* New York: Cambridge University Press.

Norris, Pippa. 2020. "Global Party Survey, 2019." Harvard Dataverse, V3, UNF:6:ZJDKjnJskyudaqjUu98PPw==[fileUNF]. https://doi.org/10.7910 /DVN/WMGTNS. [Also see Global Party Survey, https://www.global partysurvey.org/.]

Nowak, Martin A., and Roger Highfield. 2011. *SuperCooperators: Altruism, Evolution, and Why We Need Each Other to Succeed.* New York: Free Press.

Nunning, Loey. 2017. "6 Big Differences That Turn City Dwellers into Liberals." *Cracked,* February 18. http://www.cracked.com/blog/6-ways-big -cities-turn-you-liberal-converts-perspective/.

OECD. 2018. "A Broken Social Elevator? How to Promote Social Mobility." https://www.oecd.org/social/soc/Social-mobility-2018-Overview-Main Findings.pdf.

Office of the Press Secretary, the White House. 2012. "Remarks by the President at a Campaign Event in Roanoke, Virginia." July 13. https://obama whitehouse.archives.gov/the-press-office/2012/07/13/remarks-president -campaign-event-roanoke-virginia.

Office of Public Affairs, U.S. Department of Justice. 2019. "Attorney General William P. Barr Delivers Remarks to the Law School and the de Nicola Center for Ethics and Culture at the University of Notre Dame." October 11. https://www.justice.gov/opa/speech/attorney-general-william -p-barr-delivers-remarks-law-school-and-de-nicola-center-ethics.

Oishi, Shigehiro, Selin Kesebir, and Ed Diener. 2011. "Income Inequality and Happiness." *Psychological Science* 22: 1095–1100.

OpenSecrets. 2019. "Gun Rights vs Gun Control." https://www.opensecrets .org/news/issues/guns.

Opotow, Susan. 1990. "Moral Exclusion and Injustice: An Introduction." *Journal of Social Issues* 46: 1–20.

Ostfeld, Mara. 2017. "The Backyard Politics of Attitudes Toward Immigration." *Political Psychology* 38: 1–37.

O'Sullivan, Noel. 1976. *Conservatism.* London: Littlehampton.

O'Toole, Fintan. 2020. "Democracy's Afterlife." *New York Review of Books,* December 3. https://www.nybooks.com/articles/2020/12/03/democracys-afterlife/.

Oxley, Douglas R., Kevin B. Smith, John R. Alford, Matthew V. Hibbing, Jennifer L. Miller, Mario Scalora, Peter K. Hatemi, et al. 2008. "Political Attitudes Vary with Physiological Traits." *Science* 321: 1667–70.

Page, Benjamin I., Larry M. Bartels, and Jason Seawright. 2013. "Democracy and the Policy Preferences of Wealthy Americans." *Perspectives on Politics* 11: 51–73.

Pan, Deanna. 2022. "Who Was Matthew Hale, the 17th-Century Jurist Alito Invokes in His Draft Overturning Roe?" *Boston Globe,* May 6. https://www.bostonglobe.com/2022/05/06/metro/who-was-matthew-hale-17th-century-jurist-alito-invokes-his-draft-overturning-roe/.

Parker, Michael T., and Ronnie Janoff-Bulman. 2013. "Lessons from Morality-Based Social Identity: The Power of Outgroup 'Hate,' Not Just Ingroup 'Love.'" *Social Justice Research* 26: 81–96.

Pazzanese, Christina. 2016. "The Costs of Inequality: Increasingly It's the Rich and the Rest." *Harvard Gazette,* February 8. https://news.harvard.edu/gazette/story/2016/02/the-costs-of-inequality-increasingly-its-the-rich-and-the-rest/.

Pearson, David E. 1995. "Community and Sociology." *Society* 32: 44–50.

Pedersen, Walker S., L. Tugan Muftuler, and Christine L. Larson. 2018. "Conservatism and the Neural Circuitry of Threat: Economic Conservatism Predicts Greater Amygdala—BNST Connectivity During Periods of Threat vs Safety." *Social Cognitive and Affective Neuroscience* 13: 43–51.

Percheski, Christine, and Christina Gibson-Davis. 2020. "A Penny on the Dollar: Racial Inequalities in Wealth Among Households with Children." *Socius: Sociological Research for a Dynamic World* 6: 1–17.

Perugini, Marco, Juliette Richetin, and Christina Zogmaister. 2010. "Prediction of Behavior." In *Handbook of Implicit Social Cognition: Measurement, Theory, and Applications,* edited by Bertram Gawronski and B. Keith Payne, 255–77. New York: Guilford.

Peterson-Withorn, Chase. 2021. "How Much Money America's Billionaires Have Made During the Covid-19 Pandemic." *Forbes,* April 30. https://www.forbes.com/sites/chasewithorn/2021/04/30/american-billionaires-have-gotten-12-trillion-richer-during-the-pandemic/.

Pettigrew, Thomas F., and Linda R. Tropp. 2006. "A Meta-Analytic Test of Intergroup Contact Theory." *Journal of Personality and Social Psychology* 90: 751–83.

———. 2008. "How Does Intergroup Contact Reduce Prejudice? Meta-Analytic Tests of Three Mediators." *European Journal of Social Psychology* 38: 922–34.

Pew Research Center. 2016. "Wider Ideological Gap Between More and Less Educated Adults, U.S. Politics and Policy." April 26. https://www.pewresearch.org/politics/2016/04/26/a-wider-ideological-gap-between-more-and-less-educated-adults/.

———. 2019a. "Attitudes on Same-Sex Marriage, Fact Sheet." May 14, 2019. https://www.pewforum.org/fact-sheet/changing-attitudes-on-gay-marriage/.

———. 2019b. "U.S. Has World's Highest Rate of Children Living in Single-Parent Households." December 12. https://www.pewresearch.org/fact-tank/2019/12/12/u-s-children-more-likely-than-children-in-other-countries-to-live-with-just-one-parent/.

———. 2020. "A Changing U.S. Electorate, Widening Differences Between the Republican and Democratic Coalitions." June 2. https://www.pewresearch.org/politics/2020/06/02/in-changing-u-s-electorate-race-and-education-remain-stark-dividing-lines/.

Piketty, Thomas. 2014. *Capitalism in the Twenty-First Century.* Cambridge, Mass.: Belknap Press of Harvard University Press.

Pinker, Steven. 2011. *The Better Angels of Our Nature.* New York: Viking.

Pinsker, Shachar. 2018. *A Rich Brew: How Cafés Created Modern Jewish Culture.* New York: NYU Press.

Pinsof, David, and Martie Haselton. 2016. "The Political Divide over Same-Sex Marriage: Mating Strategies in Conflict?" *Psychological Science* 27: 435–42.

Pistor, Katharina. 2019. *The Code of Capitalism*. Princeton, N.J.: Princeton University Press.

Pletzer, Jan Luca, Daniel Balliet, Jeff Joireman, Michael D. Kuhlman, Sven C. Voelpel, and Paul A. M. Van Lange. 2018. "Social Value Orientation, Expectations, and Cooperation in Social Dilemmas: A Meta-Analysis." *European Journal of Personality* 32: 62–83.

Pollitt, Katha. 2014. *Pro: Reclaiming Abortion Rights*. New York: Picador.

Population Institute. 2017. "Senseless: The War on Birth Control." October 3. https://www.populationinstitute.org/our-news/senseless-the-war-on -birth-control/.

Portes, Alejandro, and Erik Vickstrom. 2011. "Diversity, Social Capital and Cohesion." *Annual Review of Sociology* 37: 461–69.

Pratto, Felicia, Jim Sidanius, Lisa M. Stallworth, and Bertram F. Malle. 1994. "Social Dominance Orientation: A Personality Variable Predicting Social and Political Attitudes." *Journal of Personality and Social Psychology* 67: 741–63.

Project Implicit. 2011. "Implicit Association Test." https://implicit.harvard .edu/implicit/iatdetails.html.

Pronin, Emily, Daniel Y. Lin, and Lee Ross. 2002. "The Bias Blind Spot: Perceptions of Bias in Self Versus Others." *Personality and Social Psychology Bulletin* 28: 369–81.

Putnam, Robert. 2000. *Bowling Alone: The Collapse and Revival of American Community*. New York: Simon and Schuster.

———. 2007. "*E Pluribus Unum:* Diversity and Community in the Twenty-First Century: The 2006 Johan Skytte Prize Lecture." *Scandinavian Political Studies* 30: 137–74.

———. 2017. "Hearing on the State of Social Capital in America." May 17. https://www.jec.senate.gov/public/_cache/files/222a1636-e668-4893-b082 -418a100fd93d/robert-putnam-testimony.pdf.

———. 2020. *The Upswing*. New York: Simon and Schuster.

Pyszczynski, Tom, Abdolhosein Abdollahi, Sheldon Solomon, Jeffrey Greenberg, Florette Cohen, and David Weise. 2006. "Mortality Salience, Martyrdom, and Military Might: The Great Satan Versus the Axis of Evil." *Personality and Social Psychology Bulletin* 32: 525–37.

Rai, Tage Shakti, and Alan Page Fiske. 2011. "Moral Psychology Is Relationship Regulation: Moral Motives for Unity, Hierarchy, Equality, and Proportionality." *Psychological Review* 118: 57–75.

Ramos, Miguel R., Matthew R. Bennett, Douglas S. Massey, and Miles Hewstone. 2019. "Humans Adapt to Social Diversity over Time." *PNAS* 116: 12244–49.

Rand Corporation. 2020. "Gun Policy Research Review." *Gun Policy in America.* https://www.rand.org/research/gun-policy/analysis.html.

Rank, Mark R. 2021. "Five Myths About Poverty." *Washington Post,* March 26. https://www.washingtonpost.com/outlook/five-myths/5-myths-about-poverty/2021/03/25/bf75d5f4-8cfe-11eb-a6bd-0eb91c03305a_story.html.

Rapoza, Kenneth. 2019. "How Democrats and Republicans Differ on Matters of Wealth and Equality." *Forbes,* June 24. https://www.forbes.com/sites/kenrapoza/2019/06/24/how-democrats-and-republicans-differ-on-matters-of-wealth--equality/.

Rawls, John. 1971. *A Theory of Justice.* Cambridge, Mass.: Harvard University Press.

Raymond, Elizabeth G., and David A. Grimes. 2012. "The Comparative Safety of Legal Induced Abortion and Childbirth in the United States." *Obstetrics and Gynecology* 119: 215–19.

Reagan, Leslie J. 1998. *When Abortion Was a Crime: Women, Medicine, and Law in the United States, 1867–1973.* Los Angeles: University of California Press.

Reagan, Ronald. 1961. "Ronald Reagan Speaks Out Against Socialized Medicine." Recorded ca. 1961. https://www.americanrhetoric.com/speeches/ronaldreagansocializedmedicine.htm.

Reilly, Katie. 2016. "Read Hillary Clinton's 'Basket of Deplorables' Remarks About Donald Trump Supporters." *Time,* September 10. https://time.com/4486502/hillary-clinton-basket-of-deplorables-transcript/.

Rentfrow, Peter J., John T. Jost, Samuel D. Gosling, and Jeffrey Potter. 2009. "Statewide Differences in Personality Predict Voting Patterns in 1996–

2004 U.S. Presidential Elections." In *Social and Psychological Bases of Ideology and System Justification,* edited by John T. Jost, Aaron C. Kay, and Hulda Thorisdottir, 314–47. New York: Oxford University Press.

Repucci, Sarah. 2021. "From Crisis to Reform: A Call to Strengthen America's Battered Democracy, Special Report 2021." *Freedom House.* https://freedomhouse.org/report/special-report/2021/crisis-reform-call-strengthen-americas-battered-democracy.

Richerson, Peter, and Robert Boyd. 2005. *Not by Genes Alone: How Culture Transformed Human Evolution.* Chicago: University of Chicago Press.

Ripley, Amanda, Rekha Tenjarla, and Angelica Y. He. 2019. "The Geography of Partisan Prejudice." *Atlantic,* March 4. https://www.theatlantic.com/politics/archive/2019/03/us-counties-vary-their-degree-partisan-prejudice/583072/.

Rock, Mindi, and Ronnie Janoff-Bulman. 2010. "Where Do We Draw Our Lines? Politics, Rigidity, and the Role of Self-Regulation." *Social Psychological and Personality Science* 1: 26–33.

Ross, Lee D. 1977. "The Intuitive Psychologist and His Shortcomings: Distortions in the Attribution Process." In *Advances in Experimental Social Psychology,* edited by Leonard Berkowitz, 173–220. New York: Academic Press.

Ross, Lee D., Teresa M. Amabile, and Julia L. Steinmetz. 1977. "Social Roles, Social Control, and Biases in Social-Perception Processes." *Journal of Personality and Social Psychology* 35: 485–94.

Ross, Lee, and Andrew Ward. 1996. "Naive Realism in Everyday Life: Implications for Social Conflict and Misunderstanding." In *Values and Knowledge,* edited by Edward S. Reed, Elliot Turiel, and Terrance Brown, 103–35. Hillsdale, N.J.: Erlbaum.

Roy, Avik. 2012. "Obamacare: America's Last Entitlement." *Forbes,* November 9. https://www.forbes.com/sites/theapothecary/2012/11/09/obamacare-americas-last-entitlement/.

Rozin, Paul, and Edward Royzman. 2001. "Negativity Bias, Negativity Dominance, and Contagion." *Personality and Social Psychology Review* 5: 296–320.

Rucker, Philip, and Robert Coast. 2020. "Election Reveals Deeper Divides

Between Red and Blue America." *Washington Post,* November 4. https://www.washingtonpost.com/politics/america-divided-rural-urban/2020/11/04/8ddac854-1ebf-11eb-b532-05c751cd5dc2_story.html.

Rutchick, Abraham M., David Hamilton, and Jeremy D. Sack. 2008. "Antecedents of Entitativity in Categorically and Dynamically Construed Groups." *European Journal of Psychology* 38: 905–21.

Sacchetti, Maria, and Emily Guskin. 2017. "In Rural America, Fewer Immigrants and Less Tolerance." *Washington Post,* June 17. https://www.washingtonpost.com/local/in-rural-america-fewer-immigrants-and-less-tolerance/2017/06/16/7b448454-4d1d-11e7-bc1b-fddbd8359dee_story.html.

Saez, Emmanuel, and Gabriel Zucman. 2019. *The Triumph of Injustice.* New York: W. W. Norton.

Sahar, Gail. 2014. "On the Importance of Attribution Theory in Political Psychology." *Social and Personality Psychology Compass* 8: 229–49.

Sandel, Michael. 2020. *The Tyranny of Merit.* New York: Farrar, Straus and Giroux.

Santelli, John S., Leslie M. Kantor, Stephanie A. Grilo, Ilene S. Speizer, Laura D. Lindberg, Jennifer Heitel, Amy T. Schalet, et al. 2017. "Abstinence-Only-Until-Marriage: An Updated Review of U.S. Policies and Programs and Their Impact." *Journal of Adolescent Health* 61: 273–80.

Schaefer, Earl S., and Marianna Edgerton. 1985. "Parent and Child Correlates of Parental Modernity." In *Parental Belief Systems: The Psychological Consequences for Children,* edited by Irving E. Sigel, 287–318. Hillsdale, N.J.: Lawrence Erlbaum.

Schlesinger, Arthur M., Jr. 1992. *The Disuniting of America: Reflections on a Multicultural Society.* New York: W. W. Norton.

Schlozman, Kay Lehman, Sidney Verba, and Henry E. Brady. 2012. *The Unheavenly Chorus: Unequal Political Voice and the Broken Promise of American Democracy.* Princeton, N.J.: Princeton University Press.

Schneirla, Theodore C. 1959. "An Evolutionary and Developmental Theory of Biphasic Processes Underlying Withdrawal." In *Nebraska Symposium on Motivation,* edited by Marshall R. Jones, 1–42. Lincoln: University of Nebraska Press.

Schwartz, Nelson D. 2020. "Is America on the Way to a Caste System?" *New York Times,* March 1.

Schwartz, Shalom H. 2007. "Universalism Values and the Inclusiveness of Our Moral Universe." *Journal of Cross-Cultural Psychology* 38: 711–28.

Sears, David O., and Sheri Levy. 2003. "Childhood and Adult Political Development." In *Oxford Handbook of Political Psychology,* edited by David O. Sears, Leone Huddy, and Robert Jervis, 60–109. Oxford: Oxford University Press.

Semin, Gun R., Tory Higgins, Lorena de Montes, Yvette Estourget, and Jose F. Valencia. 2005. "Linguistic Signatures of Regulatory Focus: How Abstraction Fits Promotion More Than Prevention." *Journal of Personality and Social Psychology* 89: 36–45.

Shapiro, Isaac, Robert Greenstein, Danilo Trisi, and Bryann Dasilva. 2016. "It Pays to Work: Work Incentives and the Safety Net." Center on Budget and Policy Perspectives, March 3. https://www.cbpp.org/research/federal-tax/it-pays-to-work-work-incentives-and-the-safety-net.

Shariff, Azim F., Dylan Wiwad, and Lara B. Aknin. 2016. "Income Mobility Breeds Tolerance for Income Inequality: Cross-National and Experimental Evidence." *Perspectives on Psychological Science* 11: 373–80.

Sheikh, Sana, and Ronnie Janoff-Bulman. 2010. "A Self-Regulatory Perspective on Shame and Guilt." *Personality and Social Psychology Bulletin* 36: 213–24.

Shook, Natalie, and Russell H. Fazio. 2009. "Political Ideology, Exploration of Novel Stimuli, and Attitude Formation." *Journal of Experimental Social Psychology* 45: 995–98.

Shorto, Russell. 2006. "Contra-Contraception." *New York Times Magazine,* May 7. https://www.nytimes.com/2006/05/07/magazine/07contraception.html.

Sidanius, Jim, and Felicia Pratto. 2001. *Social Dominance.* New York: Cambridge University Press.

Siegel, Reva B. 2005. "Revised Opinions in *Roe v. Wade* and *Doe v. Bolton* (Concurring)." In *What Roe v. Wade Should Have Said,* edited by Jack M. Balkin, 63–85. New York: NYU Press.

Singer, Peter. 1981. *The Expanding Circle: Ethics, Evolution, and Moral Progress.* New York: Farrar, Straus and Giroux.

———. 2009. *The Life You Can Save: Acting Now to End World Poverty.* New York: Random House.

Skitka, Linda J., Christopher W. Bauman, and Edward G. Sargis. 2005. "Moral Conviction: Another Contributor to Attitude Strength or Something More?" *Journal of Personality and Social Psychology* 88: 895–917.

Skitka, Linda J., and David A. Houston. 2001. "When Due Process Is of No Consequence: Moral Mandates and Presumed Defendant Guilt or Innocence." *Social Justice Research* 14: 305–26.

Skitka, Linda J., and Elizabeth Mullen. 2002. "The Dark Side of Moral Conviction." *Analyses of Social Issues and Public Policy* 2: 35–41.

Skitka, Linda J., Elizabeth Mullen, Thomas Griffin, Susan Hutchinson, and Brian Chamberlin. 2002. "Dispositions, Scripts, or Motivated Correction? Understanding Ideological Differences in Explanations for Social Problems." *Journal of Personality and Social Psychology* 8: 470–87.

Slovic, Paul, Melissa Finucane, Ellen Peters, and Donald G. MacGregor. 2004. "Risk as Analysis and Risk as Feelings: Some Thoughts About Affect, Reason, Risk and Rationality." *Risk Analysis* 24: 311–22.

Smeltz, Dina, Ivo Daalder, Karl Friedhoff, Craig Kafura, and Brendan Helm. 2020. "Divided We Stand: Democrats and Republicans Diverge on U.S. Foreign Policy." *Chicago Council on Global Affairs,* September 17. https://www.thechicagocouncil.org/research/public-opinion-survey/2020-chicago-council-survey.

Sober, Elliott, and David Sloan Wilson. 1998. *Unto Others: The Evolution and Psychology of Unselfish Behavior.* Cambridge, Mass.: Harvard University Press.

Sparkman, David J., Scott Eidelman, and Derrick F. Till. 2019. "Ingroup and Outgroup Interconnectedness Predict and Promote Political Ideology through Empathy." *Group Processes and Intergroup Relations* 22: 1161–80.

Spranca, Mark, Elisa Minsk, and Jonathan Baron. 1991. "Omission and Commission in Judgment and Choice." *Journal of Experimental Social Psychology* 27: 76–105.

Sprong, Stefanie, Jolanda Jetten, Zhechen Wang, Kim Peters, Frank Mols, Maykel Verkuyten, Brock Bastian, et al. 2019. "'Our Country Needs a Strong Leader Right Now': Economic Inequality Enhances the Wish for a Strong Leader." *Psychological Science* 30: 1625–37.

Stack, Steven. 2018. "Why Is Suicide on the Rise in the US—but Falling in Most of Europe?" *Conversation,* June 28. https://theconversation.com /why-is-suicide-on-the-rise-in-the-us-but-falling-in-most-of-europe -98366.

Stanger-Hall, Kathrin F., and David W. Hall. 2011. "Abstinence-Only Education and Teen Pregnancy Rates: Why We Need Comprehensive Sex Education in the U.S." *PloS ONE* 6: e24658.

Statement of Concern. *New America,* June 1, 2021. https://www.newamerica .org/political-reform/statements/statement-of-concern/.

Staub, Ervin. 1989. *The Roots of Evil: The Origins of Genocide and Other Group Violence.* Cambridge: Cambridge University Press.

———. 2015. *The Roots of Goodness and Resistance to Evil: Inclusive Caring, Moral Courage, Altruism Born of Suffering, Active Bystandership, and Heroism.* Oxford: Oxford University Press.

Steinberg, Julia R., Thomas M. Laursen, Nancy E. Adler, Christiane Gasse, Esben Agerbo, and Trine Munk-Olsen. 2018. "Examining the Association of Antidepressant Prescriptions with First Abortion and First Childbirth." *JAMA Psychiatry* 75: 828–34.

Stenner, Karen. 2005. *The Authoritarian Dynamic.* New York: Cambridge University Press.

Stiglitz, Joseph E. 2012. *The Price of Inequality: How Today's Divided Society Endangers Our Future.* New York: W. W. Norton.

Stolberg, Sheryl Gay. 2021a. "11 Years On, the Affordable Care Act Defies Opponents and Keeps Expanding." *New York Times,* March 22.

———. 2021b. "Can New Gun Violence Research Find a Path Around the Political Stalemate?" *New York Times,* March 27. https://www.nytimes .com/2021/03/27/us/politics/gun-violence-research-cdc.html.

Stoppler, Melissa Conrad. 2020. "Embryo vs. Fetus: Differences Between Stages Week by Week." *MedicineNet,* July 14. https://www.medicinenet .com/embryo_vs_fetus_differences_week-by-week/article.htm.

Stotland, Nada L. 1992. "The Myth of the Abortion Trauma Syndrome." *JAMA* 268: 2078–79.

Sullivan, Kathleen M. 1992. "The Supreme Court, 1991 Term—Foreword: The Justices of Rules and Standards." *Harvard Law Review* 106: 22–123.

Suls, Jerry, and Richard L., eds. 1977. *Social Comparison Processes: Theoretical and Empirical Perspectives*. Washington, D.C.: Hemisphere.

Sutton, Steven K., and Richard J. Davidson. 1997. "Prefrontal Brain Asymmetry: A Biological Substrate of the Behavioral Approach and Inhibition Systems." *Psychological Science* 8: 204–10.

Swanson, Ana. 2016. "US Mobility Might Be Even Worse Than You Thought." World Economic Forum, October 10. https://www.weforum.org/agenda/2016/10/us-social-mobility-might-be-even-worse-than-you-thought.

Tangney, June Price, and Ronda L. Dearing. 2002. *Shame and Guilt*. New York: Guilford.

Tangney, June Price, Jeff Stuewig, and Debra Mashek. 2007. "Moral Emotions and Moral Behavior." *Annual Review of Psychology* 58: 345–72.

Taub, Amanda. 2016. "The Rise of American Authoritarianism." *Vox,* March 1. https://www.vox.com/2016/3/1/11127424/trump-authoritarianism.

Telford, Taylor. 2019. "Income Inequality in America Is the Highest It's Been Since Census Bureau Started Tracking It, Data Shows." *Washington Post,* September 26. https://www.washingtonpost.com/business/2019/09/26/income-inequality-america-highest-its-been-since-census-started-tracking-it-data-show/.

Terrizzi, John A., Natalie J. Shook, and W. Larry Ventis. 2010. "Disgust: A Predictor of Social Conservatism and Prejudicial Attitudes Toward Homosexuals." *Personality and Individual Differences* 49: 587–92.

Tetlock, Philip E. 2002. "Social Functionalist Frameworks for Judgment and Choice: Intuitive Politicians, Theologians, and Prosecutors." *Psychological Review* 109: 451–71.

Thomas, Kyle, Peter DeScioli, Omar Sultan Haque, and Steven Pinker. 2014. "The Psychology of Coordination and Common Knowledge." *Journal of Personality and Social Psychology* 107: 657–76.

Tomasello, Michael, and Amrisha Vaish. 2013. "Origins of Human Cooperation and Morality." *Annual Review of Psychology* 64: 231–55.

Trivers, Robert L. 1971. "The Evolution of Reciprocal Altruism." *Quarterly Review of Biology* 46: 35–57.

Trope, Yaacov, and Nira Liberman. 2003. "Temporal Construal." *Psychological Review* 11: 403–21.

Tsai, Alexander C., Michael Lucas, and Ichiro Kawachi. 2015. "Association Between Social Integration and Suicide Among Women in the United States." *JAMA Psychiatry* 72: 987–93.

Tsai, Alexander C., Michael Lucas, Ayesha Sania, Daniel Kim, and Ichiro Kawach. 2014. "Social Integration and Suicide Mortality Among Men: 24-Year Cohort Study of U.S. Health Professionals." *Annals of Internal Medicine* 161: 85–95.

Turner, John C., Michael A. Hogg, Penelope J. Oakes, Stephen D. Reicher, and Margaret S. Wetherell. 1987. *Rediscovering the Social Group: A Self-Categorization Theory.* Oxford: Basil Blackwell.

Tversky, Amos, and Daniel Kahneman. 1992. "Advances in Prospect Theory: Cumulative Representation of Uncertainty." *Journal of Risk and Uncertainty* 5: 297–323.

Twenge, Jean, W. Keith Campbell, and Nathan T. Carter. 2014. "Declines in Trust in Others and Confidence in Institutions Among American Adults and Late Adolescents, 1972–2012." *Psychological Science* 25: 1914–23.

Tyler, Tom R. 2000. "Social Justice: Outcome and Procedure." *International Journal of Psychology* 35: 117–25.

Uberoi, Namrata, Kenneth Finegold, and Emily Gee. 2016. "Health Insurance Coverage and the Affordable Care Act, 2010–2016." *ASPE Issue Brief,* Department of Health and Human Services, March 3, 2016.

Unger, Peter. 1996. *Living High and Letting Die: Our Illusion of Innocence.* New York: Oxford University Press.

U.S. Census Bureau. 2019. "American Community Survey Provides New State and Local Income, Poverty and Health Insurance Statistics." September 26. https://www.census.gov/newsroom/press-releases/2019/acs-1year.html.

Uslaner, Eric. M. 2002. *The Moral Foundations of Trust.* Cambridge: Cambridge University Press.

van der Meer, Tom, and Jochem Tolsma. 2014. "Ethnic Diversity and Its Effects on Social Cohesion." *Annual Review of Sociology* 40: 459–78.

van der Toorn, Jojanneke, Jaime L. Napier, and John F. Dovidio. 2014. "We the People: Intergroup Interdependence Breeds Liberalism." *Social Psychological and Personality Science* 5: 616–22.

van Kleef, Gerben A., Christopher Oveis, Ilmo van der Lowe, Aleksandr LuoKogan, Jennifer Goetz, and Dacher Keltner. 2008. "Power, Distress, and Compassion: Turning a Blind Eye to the Suffering of Others." *Psychological Science* 19: 1315–22.

Van Lange, Paul A. M. 1999. "The Pursuit of Joint Outcomes and Equality in Outcomes: An Integrative Model of Social Value Orientation." *Journal of Personality and Social Psychology* 77: 337–49.

Van Lange, Paul A. M., Jeff Joireman, Craig D. Parks, and Eric Van Dijk. 2013. "The Psychology of Social Dilemmas: A Review." *Organizational Behavior and Human Decision Processes* 120: 125–41.

van Vugt, Mark, Robert Hogan, and Robert B. Kaiser. 2008. "Leadership, Followership, and Evolution: Some Lessons from the Past." *American Psychologist* 63: 182–96.

V-Dem Institute. 2021a. "Autocratization Turns Viral, Democracy Report 2021." V-Dem Institute, University of Gothenburg. https://www.v-dem.net/media/filer_public/74/8c/748c68ad-f224-4cd7-87f9-8794add5c6of/dr_2021_updated.pdf.

———. 2021b. "V-Dem: Varieties of Democracy—Global Standards, Local Knowledge." University of Gothenburg, Sweden. https://www.v-dem.net/en/.

Vigil, Jacob M. 2010. "Political Leanings Vary with Facial Expression Processing and Psychosocial Functioning." *Group Processes and Intergroup Relations* 13: 547–58.

Vohs, Kathleen, Nicole Mead, and Miranda Goode. 2006. "The Psychological Consequences of Money." *Science* 314: 1154–56.

Vollhardt, Johanna Ray. 2015. "Inclusive Victim Consciousness in Advocacy, Social Movements, and Intergroup Relations: Promises and Pitfalls." *Social Issues and Policy Review* 9: 89–120.

Vozzella, Laura. 2020. "This Rural Virginia Community Thought It Could Escape the Pandemic; Now, It Has Among the Highest Number of New Cases in the State." *Washington Post,* September 5. https://www

.washingtonpost.com/local/southwest-virginia-coronavirus-cases-rising
/2020/09/05/b82f6b0a-ec6a-11ea-ab4e-581edb849379_story.html.

Walker, Lawrence J., and Russell C. Pitts. 1998. "Naturalistic Conceptions
of Moral Maturity." *Developmental Psychology* 34: 403–19.

Walker, Mark. 2020. "Scenes from a Biker Rally, Undaunted by the Virus."
New York Times, August 11. https://www.nytimes.com/2020/08/09/us
/sturgis-motorcycle.html.

Walster, Elaine, G. William Walster, and Ellen Berscheid. 1978. *Equity: Theory and Research.* Boston: Allyn and Bacon.

Walzer, Michael. 1983. *Spheres of Justice: A Defense of Pluralism and Equality.*
New York: Basic Books.

Wang, Wendy. 2015. "The Link Between a College Education and a Lasting
Marriage." Pew Research Center, December 4. https://www.pewresearch
.org/fact-tank/2015/12/04/education-and-marriage/.

Warneken, Felix, and Michael Tomasello. 2006. "Altruistic Helping in
Human Infants and Young Chimpanzees." *Science* 311: 1301–3.

Warren, Robert, and Donald Kerwin. 2017. "The 2,000 Mile Wall in Search
of a Purpose: Since 2007 Visa Overstays Have Outnumbered Undocumented Border Crossers by a Half Million." *Journal on Migration and
Human Security* 5: 124–36.

Washington Post. 2019. "Federal Deficit Hits $209 Billion in November, on
Course for $1 Trillion Annual Shortfall." December 11. https://www
.washingtonpost.com/business/economy/federal-deficit-hits-209-bil
lion-in-november-on-course-for-1-trillion-annual-shortfall/2019/12/11
/7b88e9c6-1c2f-11ea-8d58-5ac3600967a1_story.html.

Weber, Elke U. 2006. "Evidence-Based and Description-Based Perceptions
of Long-Term Risk: Why Global Warming Does Not Scare Us (Yet)."
Climatic Change 77: 103–20.

Weeden, Jason, and Robert Kurzban. 2014. *The Hidden Agenda of the Political Mind: How Self-Interest Shapes Our Opinions and Why We Won't
Admit It.* Princeton, N.J.: Princeton University Press.

Wehle, Kimberly. 2021. "Is America Slipping to Autocracy?" *Hill,* May 3.
https://thehill.com/opinion/white-house/551439-is-america-slipping
-to-autocracy.

Weiner, Bernard, Danny Osborne, and Udo Rudolph. 2011. "An Attributional Analysis of Reactions to Poverty: The Political Ideology of the Giver and the Perceived Morality of the Receiver." *Personality and Social Psychology Review* 15: 199–213.

Wenzel, Michael. 2004. "A Social Categorization Approach to Distributive Justice." *European Review of Social Psychology* 15: 219–57.

Whitehead, Andrew L., and Joseph O. Baker. 2012. "Homosexuality, Religion, and Science: Moral Authority and the Persistence of Negative Attitudes." *Sociological Inquiry* 92: 487–509.

Wilkerson, Isabel. 2020. *Caste.* New York: Random House.

Wilkinson, Richard D., and Kate Pickett. 2009. *The Spirit Level: Why More Equal Societies Almost Always Do Better.* New York: Allen Lane.

Wilkinson, Will. 2019. "Executive Summary: The Density Divide: Urbanization, Polarization, and Populist Backlash." Niskanen Center Research Paper. https://www.niskanencenter.org/wp-content/uploads/2019/09/Wilkinson-Density-Divide-Final.pdf.

Will, George. 2008. "Bleeding Hearts but Tight Fists." *Washington Post,* March 27. https://www.washingtonpost.com/wp-dyn/content/article/2008/03/26/AR2008032602916.html.

———. 2020. "The Difference Between Trumpism and Fascism." *Washington Post,* July 10. https://www.washingtonpost.com/opinions/the-difference-between-trumpism-and-fascism/2020/07/09/377ae76e-c208-11ea-9fdd-b7ac6b051dc8_story.html.

Williams, Joan C. 2016. "What So Many People Don't Get About the U.S. Working Class." *Harvard Business Review,* November 10, 2016. https://hbr.org/2016/11/what-so-many-people-dont-get-about-the-u-s-working-class.

———. 2017. *White Working Class: Overcoming Class Cluelessness in America.* Cambridge, Mass.: Harvard Business Review Press.

Wilson, Edward O. 2012. *The Social Conquest of Earth.* New York: W. W. Norton.

Wilson, William Julius. 1996. *When Work Disappears: The World of the New Urban Poor.* New York: Alfred A. Knopf.

Wintemute, Garen J. 2013. "The Epidemiology of Firearm Violence in the

Twenty-First Century United States." *Annual Review of Public Health* 36: 5–19.

Wood, Wendy, and Alice H. Eagly. 2010. "Gender." In *The Handbook of Social Psychology,* vol. 1, 5th ed., edited by Daniel T. Gilbert, Susan T. Fiske, and Gardner Lindzey, 629–67. Hoboken, N.J.: John Wiley.

Woodward, Bob. 2020. *Rage.* New York: Simon and Schuster.

Worthen, Molly. 2018. "Is There Such a Thing as an Authoritarian Voter?" *New York Times,* December 15. https://www.nytimes.com/2018/12/15/opinion/sunday/trump-authoritarian-voters-political-science.html.

Yamagishi, Toshio, and Midori Yamagishi. 1994. "Trust and Commitment in the United States and Japan." *Motivation and Emotion* 18: 129–66.

Young, Isaac F., and Daniel Sullivan. 2016. "Competitive Victimhood: A Review of the Theoretical and Empirical Literature." *Current Opinion in Psychology* 11: 30–34.

Zakaria, Fareed. 2008. "Fareed Zakaria: How Obama Sees the World." *Newsweek,* July 18. https://www.newsweek.com/fareed-zakaria-how-obama-sees-world-92749.

Zaki, Jamil. 2019. *The War for Kindness: Building Empathy in a Fractured World.* New York: Crown.

Zebrowitz, Leslie A., Benjamin White, and Kristin Wieneke. 2008. "Mere Exposure and Racial Prejudice: Exposure to Other-Race Faces Increases Liking for Strangers of That Race." *Social Cognition* 26: 259–75.

Acknowledgments

A book reflects the influence and support of many people over time. I will surely fail to thank all who deserve it, but I welcome the opportunity to openly thank so many for so much.

Writing this book in my retirement, I realize the debt I still owe to people at the very start of my academic career. Philip Brickman, Donald Campbell, and Camille Wortman, my graduate school mentors and giants in social psychology, had an outsized influence on me. Superb researchers and theorists, they were also models of collegiality and student advocacy. Their cross-disciplinary, innovative approach to the study of human behavior has guided me through the years.

I became a college professor at the age of twenty-four, when I joined the Personality and Social Psychology Program at the University of Massachusetts–Amherst. It remained my chosen home for the next four decades. The esteemed faculty in the program at the time included Alice Eagly, who became a role model for her graceful blending of work and family, and Icek Aizen, Jim Averill, Sy Epstein, George Levinger, and Ervin Staub, who remained at UMass until their retirement decades later, a testament to the supportive, intellectually exciting atmosphere they created in the program. I thank my most recent colleagues—Nilanjana (Buju) Dasgupta, Linda Isbell, Bernie Leidner, Brian Lickel, Paula Pietromonaco, and Linda Tropp—for maintaining this nurturing, stimulating environment during my last years at UMass.

Special thanks to the National Science Foundation, which provided generous multiyear funding for my research on morality that served as the groundwork for this book. This support came in my final years as a faculty member, but I have a long history with NSF, which also helped launch my career with an NSF Graduate Research Fellowship.

Over four decades I worked with many excellent graduate students, who kept me on my toes, informed me of the latest statistical techniques, and improved the product of our collaborations. There are far too many to name here, but I am very grateful for the contributions of Cindy Frantz, who got me thinking about moral psychology many years ago, and for my most recent graduate students—Prerana (Ria) Bharadwaj, Nate Carnes, Mindi Rock, and Sana Sheikh—who were partners in my research on morality.

Many thanks to the top-notch people at Yale University Press, especially Bill Frucht. Little did I know at the beginning of this project that I would have the perfect editor. From his meticulous line editing to his big-picture insights, his responses to my questions to the better ones he asked, Bill was a constant source of invaluable guidance and feedback. His faith in this project was more important to me than he can know. Bill is an editor of renown whose extraordinary skills are matched by his dry sense of humor and humility. There are inevitably ups and downs in writing a book, but working with Bill was a pure pleasure and privilege.

My deepest appreciation goes to my family—the anchor and joy of my life. My loving parents were unflagging in their encouragement, and they imbued me with a love of learning that has been a lifelong gift. Always close to my brother, Jeff, I could not have known when young how comforting a kind, caring sibling would be in later life. My amazing children, Jessica and David, inspire me with their brilliant minds and moral compasses. From their caring concern and thoughtfulness to their gentle chapter critiques, they have supported me in ways large and small. With their wonderful spouses, Dave and Cassandra, they are my sounding board. This giving, intellectually fearsome foursome has tolerated my political rants and informed my views with their knowledge and enlightened perspectives. They have also given me late life's incredibly marvelous gift—grandchildren. Sam, Clara, Isaac, and Eli are smart, funny, kind, and curious. I adore them. Their laughter and smiles, affection and pranks, creative ideas and conversations both playful and serious fill me with delight. When I bemoan the state of the nation, I think of my grandchildren and believe there is hope for the future.

With everything I have I thank my husband, Mike. The love of my life for five decades, my wondrous partner has filled my days with love, fun, caring, and humor. Mike read and reread chapter after chapter, and as I sat writing hour after hour, he nurtured me with food, wit, and encouragement. Selfless and self-reliant, creative and playful, spontaneous and reliable, smart and funny, Mike has been my loving partner in parenting and grandparenting and in our shared passions for travel, music, reading, theater, and walks in the woods. How lucky I am to have gone through life with him.

Index

abortion: conservatives and liberals and, 2–3, 70, 110, 115–16, 118, 120, 122, 125, 127, 129, 138–39, 140–41; and contraception, 153–57; fertility clinics and, 159–60; human life and, 145, 273n30; legislation and court cases on, 141–44, 151, 152, 160, 271–72n15; medication, 142–43; misinformation and, 157–59, 274n53, 275n55; "moral values vote" and, 117; protesters and, 124; religious right and, 144–46; statistics of, 139, 271n14; Supreme Court and, 115, 139–40, 143, 271–72n15; targeted regulation of abortion providers (TRAP laws), 142, 272n19; terminology, 271n13; women and, 138, 139, 149–53, 157–61

abstinence-only-until-marriage (AOUM) education, 156, 274n49

Abramowitz, Alan, 94

Adorno, Theodor, 234

Aesop's fable, 27–28

Affordable Care Act (ACA, 2010), 154, 164–69, 274n51, 276nn10, 12, and 13, 277n14

Alexander, Michelle, 177–78, 278n33

Alito, Samuel, 135, 143, 272n23

Allport, Gordon, 101

Altemeyer, Robert, 234, 285n41

altruism and selfishness: empathy and, 33; group selection and, 13, 252n12; moral circles and, 85, 263nn11 and 17; parochial altruism, 86; political liberalism and, 40; reciprocal altruism, 12–13; studies of, 13–14, 255n13

Amabile, Teresa, 210

American Academy of Family Physicians, 135

American Academy of Pediatrics, 135, 216

American College of Obstetricians and Gynecologists, 142, 158

The American Democrat (Cooper), 229

American Medical Association, 135, 142, 158, 216

American National Election Studies survey, 233, 285n38

American Psychiatric Association, 135, 216

American Psychological Association, 135, 158, 216, 283n4

American Rescue Plan, 114, 174

Analects (Confucius), 26

Anti-Drug Abuse Act (1986), 177

Antonio, Robert, 270n24

Hogan, Larry, 261n29
homosexuality and gay rights, 134–36,
  277n19
Hopkins, Daniel, 264n23
Hopkins, David, 269n13
"How America Gives," 81

identity politics, 190–91, 279n11
ideology, 109–10, 268nn3–4
illusory truth effect, 225–26
immigration, 87–92, 264nn23, 25,
  and 26, 266n46
implicit association test, 104–5,
  268n56
Inhofe, James, 182
Intergovernmental Panel on Climate
  Change, 181
intergroup contact, 100–103, 105,
  266n48, 267nn50–51
interpersonal morality, 29, 52, 58, 172
intuitive ethics, 44

JAMA Psychiatry, 158
James, William, 8
Janoff-Bulman, Ronnie, 25, 51, 252n16,
  253n1
Javits, Jacob, 112
Jefferson, Thomas, 95–97
Johnson, Lyndon B., 59
Johnson, Ron, 169
Joseph, Craig, 44
Jost, John, 70, 112, 269n13, 271n27
June Medical Services v. Gee (2019),
  142

Kahan, Dan, 124, 270n23
Kahneman, Daniel, 15
Kakkar, Hemant, 284n35
Kant, Immanuel, 17, 20–21, 255n19

Kellerman, Arthur, 130
Keltner, Dacher, 255n13
Kemp, Brian, 225
Kennedy, Anthony, 134, 136
Kennedy, Duncan, 253n25
Kerry, John, 81–82
King, Martin Luther, Jr., 38, 173,
  255n20
Kinzinger, Adam, 226
Kirk, Russell, 111
Klein, Ezra, 270n20
Knobe, Joshua, 17–19
Kochanska, Grazyna, 11, 251n6
Kohts, Ladygina, 33
Krider, Stephanie Ranade, 152–53
Kristof, Nicholas, 179, 220, 223
Kron, Josh, 98–99
Krueger, Alan, 208
Kyl, Jon, 276n10

labels, political, 109, 124–28, 247
Lakoff, George, 73
Land, Richard, 145
Lawrence v. Texas (2003), 134
Lazzarini, Zita, 274n53
Lee, George W., 238
Levitsky, Steven, 241
liberals and liberalism: and abortion,
  2–3, 70, 110, 115–16, 118, 120, 122,
  125, 127, 129, 138–39, 140–41;
  Covid-19 and masks, 75–76, 78,
  261nn28–29; external causes of
  poverty, 169–72; and global problems, 66–67; and government's
  role, 117–18; and immigration, 89;
  optimism and hope, 59–61; parenting attitudes and heritability of,
  72–74, 247, 286n5; policies of,
  110–12, 117–18, 230, 277n21; policy